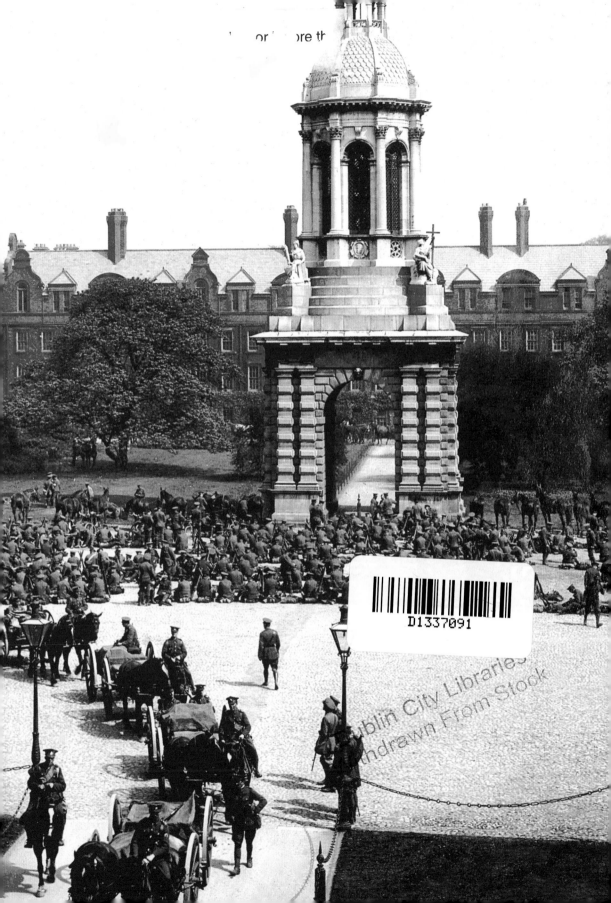

or more th

TRINITY IN WAR
AND REVOLUTION
1912–1923

TRINITY IN WAR AND REVOLUTION 1912–1923

TOMÁS IRISH

Trinity in War and Revolution 1912–1923

First published 2015
Royal Irish Academy, 19 Dawson Street, Dublin 2
www.ria.ie

Text © Tomás Irish and Trinity College Dublin

ISBN 978-1-908996-78-7

Editor: Helena King
Design: Fidelma Slattery
Index: Eileen O'Neill

Printed in Italy by Printer Trento

Opening images: Detail from *Ireland's memorial records 1914–1918* (Dublin, 1923),
vol. vii, illustration by Harry Clarke. Courtesy of the Royal Irish Academy.

'Halt! Who goes there?' Detail from a World War I recruitment poster, 1915.
RIA C 32 2 E, No. 60; courtesy of the Royal Irish Academy.

Opposite: Detail from 'O.T.C. a forecast', illustration from *T.C.D.: a College Miscellany*,
2 March 1910, p. 34. Reproduced by permission of the Board of Trinity College Dublin.

Front endpaper: Troops in Front Square (Parliament Square) during the Easter Rising,
April 1916. TDC, MS Ex-02-057-HI; reproduced by permission of the
Board of Trinity College Dublin.

Back endpaper: 'Parliament Square, T.C.D.', by M.K. Hughes, *c*. 1914. NLI, ET C155;
courtesy of the National Library of Ireland.

MIX
Paper from
responsible sources
FSC
www.fsc.org
FSC® C015829

CONTENTS

Acknowledgements vii • Foreword ix • Prologue xiii

INTRODUCTION

'Behind the Great Wall'

1

CHAPTER 1

Trinity and Ireland 1912—14

41

CHAPTER 2

Trinity and the First World War

77

CHAPTER 3

Trinity and the Easter Rising

125

CHAPTER 4

The Politics of War and Revolution 1914–19

165

CHAPTER 5

The End of Old Certainties 1919–23

201

EPILOGUE

'*Eppur si Muove*'—Towards a New Trinity, 1923–52

233

Picture credits 277 • Bibliography 283 • Index 294

LECTURES

ACKNOWLEDGEMENTS

One of the central arguments of this book is that a university is more than four walls containing lecture halls, laboratories and libraries. It is a community. Throughout the book, I try to show how a unique group identity formed amongst Trinity's students, staff and alumni as the university negotiated the cataclysmic local, national and international events of the first half of the twentieth century. Sharing the same space, living, studying and socialising together created bonds that were strong and durable, and which people carried with them for much of their post-university lives. This wider Trinity community stretched across Dublin, Ireland and the wider world of the time, as it does for the students, staff and alumni of the university today.

This book is a testament to the strength of these ties. At every step my research was aided by Trinity academics and alumni who freely gave their time and expertise to help in my writing of this part of the history of an institution that has played an important part in so many lives. The book is immeasurably richer for their suggestions and recollections. I would like to thank Peter Boyle, Anna Chahoud, Aidan Clarke, Davis Coakley,

Opposite: Members of the Trinity College Dublin Officers Training Corps marching through Front Square, 1910.

Ronald Cox, Eric Finch, Roy Johnston, Mike Jones, John Parnell, Michael Purser, David Simms, Cyril Smyth, Tom Turpin, Denis Weaire and Patrick Wyse Jackson. In the Department of History, I am thankful to John Horne, Anne Dolan, Ciaran O'Neill, Ciaran Wallace, Conor Morrissey and David Ditchburn for their support of the project that led to the publication of this book. I am especially grateful to David Fitzpatrick for reading a full draft of the manuscript. Farther afield, Heather Jones, Roy Foster and Norman Vance shared their expertise and enthusiasm for the project and made many useful suggestions.

The staff of the Trinity library was unfailingly helpful, and I am grateful for the advice and assistance of the departments of Manuscripts and Early Printed Books. In particular, I thank Jane Maxwell for her enthusiasm and efficiency in dealing with queries about the college's vast archival collections. I would also like to thank Dáire Courtney, the Records Secretary of the College Historical Society (2014–15), for making the Hist's collections available to me.

Outside of the walls, but very much part of the college community, I am deeply grateful to the Luce and Woods families for sharing their rich family connections to Trinity with me, as well as for allowing me access to private letters, memorabilia and other papers. I am also thankful to the Trinity Association and Trust for funding a research trip to London in 2013, which facilitated additional work on the book.

This book would not have been written without the incredible support and enthusiasm of Patrick Geoghegan, who mentored the project, provided astute observations on its development, and was instrumental in getting the project up and running in 2012. I would also like to thank Ruth Hegarty, Helena King and Fidelma Slattery at the Royal Irish Academy for their support of the project and assistance in producing this monograph.

It is an immeasurable privilege to contribute to the history of an institution as venerable as Trinity College Dublin, especially as it has already been served by excellent histories from eminent scholars such as J.V. Luce, R.B. McDowell and D.A. Webb. My greatest debt, therefore, is to Patrick Prendergast, the forty-fourth provost of Trinity College Dublin, for both entrusting me with this tremendous responsibility and giving me the opportunity to immerse myself fully and freely in the college's history.

Tomás Irish
DUBLIN, FEBRUARY 2015

FOREWORD

In 1912, it was taken for granted by all but a radical few that Ireland's future lay within the United Kingdom. A bill giving 'home rule' to Ireland was introduced in the Westminster parliament, and it was passed in 1914. But 1914 also witnessed the outbreak of the First World War, a war that shocked and traumatised all of Europe with its ferocity and loss of life. In 1916, a small but determined group, taking advantage of that war and serving (as they put it) neither King nor Kaiser, staged a military rebellion in Ireland. In doing so they set off a chain of events that led eventually to the War of Independence, the Anglo-Irish Treaty, and the creation of an independent Irish state. By 1923 Ireland had become divided politically into the twenty-six county Free State and the six counties of Northern Ireland—an outcome neither desired nor foreseen in 1912. In the course of a decade, Ireland had experienced a rapid and elemental transformation.

When An Taoiseach Enda Kenny, TD, launched the Decade of Centenaries in 2012, he asked that events of 1912 to 1922 be studied and commemorated by communities around the country. In response to that call, Dr Tomás Irish has written this history of how Trinity College Dublin experienced those years.

A native of Crossabeg, Co. Wexford, Dr Irish is a Trinity graduate and gold-medallist in history, and he was awarded a PhD for his research on universities during the Great War. Knowing the college as both an undergraduate and a postgraduate, and then as a postdoctoral researcher, he is especially well placed to write this history. In the process of doing so he has interviewed many people, engaging with students, staff and alumni. He has consulted archives throughout Ireland and the UK, including the private papers of some of the public figures of the time. Most importantly, and with great originality, he has also studied the records of Trinity student clubs and societies of the early decades of the twentieth century, and has uncovered—perhaps for the first time—the authentic voice of the students through their vibrant, energetic and marvellously expressive publications.

In an important sense, therefore, this book is a community history. Many Trinity people will be familiar with the individuals whose names appear, and will be fascinated by their reaction to tumultuous events in Irish history. So too will our neighbours in the locality of Dublin city centre: the St Andrew's National School on Great Brunswick Street (now the St Andrew's Resource Centre on Pearse Street) was closed during the week of fighting in Easter 1916. In the school's roll book, the headmaster wrote simply but effectively across the blank pages: 'Poets' Rebellion'. But this book is also an institutional history in a wider sense—the story of a university being forced to adapt to circumstances.

And adapt it did. Slowly, but with deliberation, Trinity transitioned from its role as an integral part of the education system of the British empire to become the Irish institution with a global reputation that we know today. All this change, however, didn't come without some stresses and tensions. There were disappointments, mistakes, some failed careers, and perhaps some shattered notions of privilege and superiority. But Trinity succeeded.

There is much to be gained from reading about an institution whose history intersects both the events of the First World War and the dramatic changes of Ireland's revolutionary period. We learn, for instance, that in 1916 British soldiers were billeted in the college—some on furlough from the front, and others who had been destined for France but were routed to Ireland instead. The Trinity Centre for Health Sciences at St James's Hospital (then the site of the South Dublin Union) is where Éamonn Ceannt, one of the signatories of the 1916 Proclamation, commanded a garrison of rebel forces; one of his key lieutenants was W.T. Cosgrave, a future leader of the Free State government.

And rather than see the First World War and the events of the Irish revolution as separate or in isolation, this book affirms the value of studying them together. In so doing it is possible to discern complex forces—local and global, intellectual and emotional, political and personal—in action. In this book, we see how such forces shaped the modern university, and something of that kind must also have shaped the modern country.

In the Trinity of the 1920s we see a university internally traumatised from the Great War, financially destitute, and out of touch politically and emotionally with the newly independent Ireland. It was in this context that two of Trinity's greatest alumni—E.T.S. Walton and Samuel Beckett, both Nobel Prize winners—entered the university, and came of age intellectually. These men, along with a host of other men and women, helped to shape Trinity's image as a place of academic innovation and scholarly genius.

Trinity's story forms a significant part of the broader narrative of the emergence and growth of modern Ireland. What changes were necessary for Trinity College to survive, and how were those changes brought about? This book does not give definitive answers to such questions; the past is not simple, and deep study of it does not make it any simpler. What the book does provide is an opportunity to engage again with the events of that decade from the perspective of a Dublin institution that was not aligned with the nationalist or republican politics of the time.

I recommend Dr Tomás Irish's *Trinity in War and Revolution* to you, not so much for the inward look at Trinity that it offers (though that is interesting as well), but because it shows just how heavily inter-related were the national and international events of 1912 to 1923. This is, no doubt, obvious to historians but it has never been made so clearly obvious to me as it is through this book. For many who were caught up in the tumultuous events of 100 years ago, their lives were lives of sacrifice and idealism. It befits us to understand their motivations better, so that we may better understand ourselves. Their lives contributed collectively to the distinctive historical narrative that has shaped our republic, and, we may say, more often than not shaped it for the better.

Patrick Prendergast
Provost
14 April 2015

PROLOGUE: JULY 1892

We are aware of the lustre you have reflected on our city and our country. Abstruse and remote from the common thoughts of men as are the problems with which you have to grapple, and the sciences which you have so amply enlarged, we can all appreciate the splendour and rarity of the mental gifts which have qualified you for these achievements, and the importance of the labours to which your life has been devoted. We know that a great scholar and thinker is as well worthy of public honour as a great soldier, or statesman, or poet, or a great mechanical inventor. In each and all of these classes of men practical and speculative Ireland has been rich; and as long as she produces such men, Irishmen will be proud of their country, and claim for her a high intellectual place among the nations of the earth.

Joseph Meade, Lord Mayor of Dublin, July 1892[1]

For a week in July of 1892, Trinity College Dublin was at the centre of the international community of scholars. The college's tercentenary was the occasion for a lavish celebration of its history, its contribution to learning and its place amongst the great universities of the world. On the morning of Monday, 4 July, the first day of the tercentenary festival, the old campus was adorned with flags; they ran from the Examination Hall to the Campanile and from there to the College Chapel. In front of the chapel, a military band played music from around the world, with the

Opposite: The Long Room, Trinity College Dublin, 1892.
Following pages: View of Front (Parliament) Square and the Campanile, c. 1900, with the Chapel and Public Theatre (Examination Hall) to the left and right of the frame, respectively.

guests recognising 'the national airs of their various countries'.[2] The delegates came from all over the globe. The 'sister universities' of Oxford and Cambridge provided the bulk of those in attendance. From Ireland, the Queen's Colleges and Catholic University sent delegates, as did the Royal College of Physicians; from Britain, the Royal Society and the ancient universities of Scotland were well represented; while delegates also came from the universities of the British empire in Canada, India, Australia and South Africa. The Trinity tercentenary was more than an imperial affair, however. Respects were paid by the powerhouse universities of Germany, while the scholars of France, Austria-Hungary, Belgium, Holland, Italy, Russia and beyond likewise had delegations in attendance. The cumulative effect was to place Trinity at the heart of the old Republic of Letters. More than this, the celebrations acknowledged the rise of a new power: American universities, such as Columbia, Harvard, Cornell and Yale were represented, as were its learned societies.

On that July morning a procession of 1,200 distinguished delegates made their way from Trinity, up Grafton Street, across York Street and Bishop Street to a service at St Patrick's Cathedral.[3] The *Irish Times* noted that 'Dublin has been the arena of many striking spectacles at different times, but even the Irish metropolis has rarely witnessed a more remarkable sight than this.'[4] Thousands of spectators watched the spectacle and 'gazed with wonder at the quaint and various robes of those whom the four corners of the world had sent to do honour to the University'.[5] In London, *The Times* called it 'a spectacle of unique interest'.[6]

The week that followed was marked by receptions, balls, the bestowing of honorary degrees, ceremonial cricket matches, speeches and banquets. Each night a toast was proposed to a selection of the nations represented. On the Wednesday, the delegates presented their congratulatory addresses to the chancellor of the university, the Earl of Rosse.

As each delegate advanced to the platform, the band of the Sussex Regiment played the national air of the country to which he belonged. Thus the 'Marseillaise' was played when the address from the University of Paris was presented; 'Auld Lang Syne' when the delegates from Scotland advanced; Monsignor Molloy, representing the Catholic University was saluted with 'St. Patrick's Day'; and the Johns Hopkins deputation was welcomed with 'Yankee Doodle' amid applause and merriment. Nothing could have been more lively or effective, nothing could have brought more vividly before the minds of the audience the world-wide character of the congratulations which the university was receiving than this feature of the ceremony.[7]

The tercentenary celebrations expressed a clear but complex vision of where the university felt it owed allegiance. It paid its respects to the city of Dublin by bestowing an honorary degree on the Catholic lord mayor, Joseph Meade. The procession to St Patrick's Cathedral emphasised Trinity's close connection to the Church of Ireland. The delegations present reflected Trinity's sense of belonging to a number of distinct and overlapping groupings: of ancient universities whose traditions of scholarship dated back centuries;[8] of Irish institutions of learning; of imperial universities; and, last but not least, of the international community of scholarship.[9] These different groupings mirrored the various traditions and functions of the university in an age of rapid changes in communications, technology and scholarship.[10]

During the tercentenary, Trinity's position as one of the leading lights of both the Republic of Letters and the British empire was secure. The college could look back on 300 years of tradition, privilege and pomp with pride. It enjoyed 'a position of monolithic security', typical of the politically tranquil decade following the death of Parnell.[11] The tercentenary festival was the act of a confident and secure institution. In the words of J.V. Luce, who wrote a history of the college 100 years later, Trinity's 'scholarly achievement was then at its zenith'.[12] After 1892, however, the college's position would become increasingly insecure.

The decades following the tercentenary, marked by a violent polarisation of Irish politics and punctuated by an unprecedentedly brutal global war, shattered this sense of assurance. Trinity men and women would be witnesses to and participants in all of this upheaval, and on all sides. Even within weeks of the tercentenary, a number of events took place that presaged the undoing of Trinity's calm and confident place in Dublin, Ireland and the world.

Less than a week after the conclusion of the festival, a barrister and graduate of the college was elected as the junior member of parliament for Dublin University, pledging to do all in his power to uphold the union between Britain and Ireland.[13] His name was Edward Carson, and his 26 years in parliament, elected by the fellows, scholars and masters of Dublin University, left a lasting and contentious legacy for Ireland and Britain. At the same general election, a Catholic Trinity alumnus was busy trying to consolidate support for his party. John Redmond had the unenviable task of leading the minority faction of the Irish Parliamentary Party after the acrimonious split it had endured in late 1890— following the controversy created by the relationship of its founder Charles Stewart Parnell with Katherine O'Shea—and Parnell's death in October 1891. The Parnellite wing was routed in the 1892 election, but Redmond was, like Carson, only beginning his political journey. Redmond's association with his alma mater was less pronounced than that of Carson, but his influence on Irish history was every bit as significant in the following two-and-a-half decades. As Carson and Redmond were embarking on their respective journeys towards parliamentary influence and personal confrontation, another Trinity alumnus was on the cusp of inaugurating a deeply influential but non-parliamentary movement. In November 1892, an Irish-language scholar from Roscommon lectured to the National Literary Society on 'The necessity of de-Anglicising Ireland'. In this lecture, he argued that Irish political nationalism needed reinforcement by a cultural nationalism built upon a revival of the Irish language. To make this goal a reality, the speaker, Douglas Hyde, founded the Gaelic League the following year.

Carson, Redmond and Hyde all had complex histories in and relationships with their alma mater. None could be said to embody a particularly Trinity political ethos. Even Carson, elected in the name of the university, found his views were unpalatable to many of his constituents by 1912. These three men were the products of a conservative institution with a propensity for producing radical figures. They were solidly middle class and in the enviable position of being able to benefit from the professional advantages available only at Trinity College Dublin in the decades before the establishment of the National University. All three would go on to have a profound influence on Irish political and cultural life in the ensuing decades. Hyde's advocacy of the Irish language was a motor for the cultural revival, which both reinforced the Home Rule movement and lent weight to more radical visions of Irish nationalism. Carson became the union's staunchest defender and the leader of the Ulster Unionist party. Meanwhile, Redmond came within an ace of achieving his dream of Home Rule. Thus, 1892 affords the historian a moment to look forward and back simulta-

The Rt. Hon. SIR E. CARSON, K.C., M.P.

Ready to give the Word of Command.

"A FIGHT TO A FINISH."

"Come what may, or happen what will, so long as God gives me strength, I will see this fight through to a finish. When the moment comes, whatever may be the consequences, I shall not hesitate to give the Word of Command."

neously, offering an opportunity for understanding where Trinity College Dublin came from, and where it then stood, while casting an eye forward towards a traumatic decade that would change Ireland and the world.

This book details the story of an institution that saw much of its political and cultural influence dismantled as a result of the revolutionary events of 1912–23. Undertaking the telling of such a story may seem counter-intuitive; after all, Trinity was on the 'wrong side' in the national story, instinctively and emotionally suspicious of—if not outright hostile to—the nationalist project and new state. The story that will be told here, however, seeks to move beyond this view; it will describe the university more broadly, as a divided community of students, staff and alumni; as an educational institution; and as a witness to historic events. This community was disparate, and its men and women experienced the revolutionary years of 1912–23 in a multitude of ways, often with radically conflicting attitudes concerning the events unfolding. Some of the names that form part of this story, such as Carson, Hyde and Redmond, are famous. Some are not. The way in which Trinity and emergent nationalist Ireland viewed one another changed slowly, but significantly, over the decade considered in this book, and how this change unfolded tells us much about the emergence of the modern Irish state and about the capacity of one of the most iconic of Irish institutions to adapt and survive in the changed circumstances in which it found itself.

NOTES:

[1] Speech of Lord Mayor Joseph Meade, July 1892, while bestowing the provost of Trinity College Dublin, George Salmon, with the Honorary Freedom of the city of Dublin. *Records of the tercentenary festival of the University of Dublin held 5th to 8th July, 1892* (Dublin, 1894), 70–1.

[2] *Records of the tercentenary festival*, 74.

[3] *Records of the tercentenary festival*, 75–9.

[4] 'Dublin University: Tercentenary', *Weekly Irish Times*, 9 July 1892, 4.

[5] *Records of the Tercentenary Festival*, 79.

[6] Editorial, *The Times*, 7 July 1892, 9.

[7] *Records of the Tercentenary Festival*, 157.

[8] The term 'ancient universities' is used to refer to the medieval and early modern universities of Britain and Ireland: Oxford, Cambridge, St Andrews, Glasgow, Aberdeen, Edinburgh and Dublin.

[9] The similarity of the Trinity tercentenary celebrations to the tercentenary festival of Edinburgh University that took place in 1884 is notable, and underscores the shared assumptions of ancient universities when performing public ceremonials of this sort. See R. Sydney Marsden, *A short account of the tercentenary festival of the University of Edinburgh* (Edinburgh, 1884).

[10] Emily Rosenberg (ed.), *A world connecting: 1870–1945* (Cambridge, MA, 2012).

[11] R.F. Foster, *Modern Ireland: 1600–1972* (London, 1988), 434.

[12] J.V. Luce, *Trinity College Dublin: the first 400 years* (Dublin, 1992), 110.

[13] 'Dublin University election: Declaration of the poll', *Irish Times*, 11 July 1892, 6.

Opposite: 'A fight to the finish', political postcard, *c.* 1912, featuring Sir Edward Carson, who represented Dublin University as an MP in Westminster from 1892 to 1918.

INTRODUCTION

'Behind the Great Wall'

Trinity and Ireland before 1912

Trinity College Dublin is a famous Irish institution. It was founded by Queen Elizabeth I in 1592, following the donation of lands from Dublin Corporation, to provide 'education, training and instruction of youths and students in the arts and faculties'.[1] In the centuries that followed, the university established itself as a leading institution in Ireland's cultural and intellectual development, distinguishing itself as the alma mater of literary figures such as Jonathan Swift and Oliver Goldsmith, the political philosopher Edmund Burke, the natural scientists William Rowan Hamilton and George Francis Fitzgerald, and the nationalist icons Robert Emmet and Theobald Wolfe Tone. Throughout its history, Trinity's intellectual influence has, through its distinguished alumni, been felt across Ireland, Europe and the world.

At the same time, Trinity has had a complex relationship with modern Ireland. In the centuries following its foundation by the ruling elite it developed into a bastion of Protestant Ascendency; an establishment institution that supported the government of the day and catered to the middle and upper classes. This position of traditional privilege came into

Opposite: Royal visit of 1903: King Edward VII and Queen Alexandra exiting the Public Theatre.

particularly sharp focus in the late nineteenth century, against the backdrop of growing political and cultural nationalism in Ireland. The discourse that emerged around the college was built upon a binary distinction between Trinity—as Protestant, unionist, anti-Irish and closed to the wider world—and emerging nationalist Ireland, which was Catholic, desirous of greater autonomy from Britain and energised by a revival of interest in its native language and indigenous culture. The historian F.S.L. Lyons famously spoke of a battle of 'two civilisations' in Ireland: between the ancient Gaelic tradition (which cultural nationalists sought to revive) and the 'Anglo-Irish' tradition born of the seventeenth-century plantations.[2] While more recent accounts of Irish history have nuanced this binary distinction, it held much weight in late-nineteenth-century Ireland and in subsequent historiography. In both perspectives, Trinity came to act as a symbol of this 'battle of civilisations' in the decades of national cultural awakening and political intensification leading to 1912.[3] That symbolic role forms the subject of this chapter, which will examine the polarising power of Trinity College Dublin in public discourse in the early twentieth century. Subsequent chapters will explore what the institution was and how it was changed by the cataclysmic and revolutionary events that unfolded between 1912 and 1923. This wider context is vital to understanding how the university operated, how it saw itself and its place in the world and how it was viewed from the outside. Public representations of the university were important points of mobilisation for nationalists and unionists alike in this period.

Trinity's symbolic role was important in the early 1900s, in that it served to reinforce the respective identities of not only the conservative Protestant elites who Trinity traditionally represented, but also Catholic nationalists. The university was 'intensely conscious of its position as a bastion of the Ascendancy'.[4] It gave focus to different nationalist gripes while at the same time polemical assaults from outside were emphatically rebuked by fellows and students of the college, reinforcing their sense of difference. *The Leader*, an especially vituperative nationalist newspaper, frequently referred to Trinity as 'the Parochial University', 'England's Faithful Garrison' and 'the Souper University of the mud-throwing cads'.[5] Most famously, Trinity was unflatteringly compared to Oxford and Cambridge as 'the silent sister'. William Macneile Dixon, a Trinity graduate and historian, wrote in 1904 that Trinity was 'a loved and hated institution, as only institutions which are held to have a political complexion can be loved and hated'. It was loved 'as few English colleges are loved' and hated 'as none are hated'.[6] It was cited, in less colourful terms, in parliament, in the press and in other publications as an example of what nationalists and Catholics railed against but aspired towards, as religious, educational, cultural and political privilege all converged there. The symbolism was important.

Of course, simple black-and-white distinctions rarely tell the whole story. In response to frequent claims of its being anti-national, one could cite, as future provost John Pentland Mahaffy did in 1904, the college's unusual history of producing iconic figures in the nationalist movement, such as Tone, Emmet and Thomas Davis.[7] Similarly, while many depicted it as hostile to the Irish language, Trinity had a proud tradition of Irish scholarship, and graduates such as Standish O'Grady, T.W. Rolleston and Douglas Hyde were crucial in spurring the revival of interest in both the language and Irish folklore.[8]

The college's location in the centre of the city, standing behind imposing walls and wrought iron railings, gave an aura of impenetrability and conquest and strengthened the garrison metaphor. Trinity's disconnectedness from Dublin, and Ireland more generally, was frequently cited as a criticism; a physical expression of its supposed emotional detachment from the surrounding country and its accumulated tradition. A good example comes from Arthur Griffith's *United Irishman* newspaper in 1901, which mockingly described the nationalist poet, Thomas Davis, as having been born and educated 'behind the Great Wall', before he 'escaped beyond it and openly allied himself with the natives'.[9] In the early twentieth century, however, radicals and radical ideas often entered and were heard in Trinity; the metaphorical walls were porous.

The opening decades of the twentieth century were turbulent and transformative ones for universities across Europe, and Trinity College Dublin was no different in this respect as its traditional emphasis on classical and clerical education was augmented by the slow emergence of modern professional and research agendas. What made it different was the unique place it occupied in Ireland, situated at the heart of a capital city in-waiting but simultaneously disconnected from many of the values and ideas that informed the national revival. The remainder of this chapter considers how, in the decade before 1912, Trinity was central to debates about the future direction of Ireland. Some definitions are required first. In what follows, a description of what the university was at the turn of the twentieth century is provided, and this is followed by a discussion of Trinity's involvement with the language revival movement and its relationship with the Roman Catholic Church; the chapter concludes by demonstrating how its symbolic value was invoked at key junctures in the decade before 1912.

What is a university?

Writing in 1902, William Macneile Dixon argued that a description of the life of Trinity College Dublin was 'difficult, if not impossible', because it was 'a microcosm of the great world, the sphere of so many and varied interests, so much intellectual and physical activity'.[10] Historically, universities have been diverse institutions, performing many functions, and they remain difficult to describe neatly.[11] The vexed historical question of what a university is takes on greater difficulty in the case of Trinity, which is, unusually, the sole constituent college of the University of Dublin. Strictly speaking, the university was the degree granting body, while the college was the residential teaching institution. This has been a source of confusion to present-day policymakers as well as to historic actors. Indeed, the Act of Union of 1800, the document central to the debates and conflicts of the early twentieth century in Ireland, itself referred vaguely to 'the university of Trinity College'.[12] Most contemporaries referred to Trinity College Dublin (or TCD) when referring to both the degree-granting body and the teaching institution; the invocation of Dublin University was rarer.[13] Throughout this book, the terms 'university' and 'college' are used synonymously with Trinity College Dublin as a whole. The distinction between the two is, in most cases, not always pertinent to the narrative, save for certain specific instances that will be noted in the text.

Trinity, like any university of its age, does not want for institutional histories. The unparalleled work of McDowell and Webb is the definitive account of Trinity's history from its foundation in the late sixteenth century. What many of the existing histories have in common is that they have treated the institution's history as a whole, covering four centuries in a couple of hundred pages.[14] Understandably, the development of university administration, curricula and 'big names' have tended to dominate, while relatively little has been written about students, alumni, or wider political, cultural and social developments.[15] The present volume takes a different approach, building on the work of previous institutional historians but viewing the university in a broader sense, as a community of students, staff and alumni, and examining how this community experienced and informed Ireland's decade of war and revolution. At the same time, it places the university in a broader context of international universities, showing where its experiences differed in a period that was a crucial moment in the development of higher education internationally.

In the period dealt with in this book, Trinity was most obviously an educational institution, or, as John Henry Newman famously described universities of the mid-nineteenth century, 'a place of teaching universal knowledge'.[16] It furnished students with qualifications leading to careers in medicine, law, engineering and the Church of Ireland, among other professions. Newman's definition spoke of university function, but the life of the institution encompassed much more than this; it constituted a community of students, academic and non-academic (support) staff, and alumni. The Trinity community of the early twentieth century numbered around 1,300 students and staff and around 5,000 registered electors. In addition, around 200 new alumni came into being each year on graduation, with the award of degree of bachelor of arts (BA).[17] Thus, the college community spoken of in this book can be said to number around 7,000–8,000 people, dispersed across Dublin, throughout Ireland and further afield.

At the turn of the twentieth century, the college's structures and titles had lasted, more or less intact, from the late sixteenth century. The Chancellor was the head of the university and was responsible, in the main, for the conferring of degrees. The Provost was head of the college, responsible for overseeing the running of the institution. He was supported in this by the board, comprising, until 1911, seven senior fellows (those who had been fellows of the college longest). Fellowship was for life and entitled holders to membership of the body corporate of the college. Those fellows who were not amongst the seven longest serving were known as junior fellows, of whom there were 28 in 1912, and who performed much of the teaching work in the college. Fellowship was attainable through examination and allowed holders to earn additional income through work as college tutors. There were 70 scholars in 1912; these were undergraduates who had passed an examination that entitled them to be part of the corporation of the college. The vast majority of other students were 'pensioners', officially defined as 'ordinary students in the arts'. While other categories of students existed historically, most had fallen into disuse by the turn of the twentieth century. An exception were the 'sizars', students of limited means who, on successfully passing a special examination, had their annual fee waived and were allowed to dine on Commons (partake in the daily formal meal in the Dining Hall) for free.[18] All other undergraduates entered the college by successfully taking one of five matriculation examinations scheduled throughout the year.[19]

The majority of students took a BA degree, which was the cornerstone of a Trinity education at the time. While these degrees were popular in their own right, they were also required if students wished to proceed either to higher degrees in divinity, law, science and literature, or as part of professional qualifications such as medicine, engineering, surgery and dental science.[20] The degree was divided into two freshman years (junior and senior) and two sophister years (junior and senior). During the two freshman years, students were required to study mathematics, languages (ancient and modern) and English composition, before pursuing (optional) study in their sophister years in education, history, experimental science, or languages, alongside compulsory modules in logic, mathematical physics, English composition, and astronomy.[21]

One-quarter of all students—around 250—lived in rooms in college.[22] Indeed, in his 1902 history Dixon argued that those who did not live on campus were not truly part of the college. Residence was an important part of the collegiate ethos.[23] The result was an immediate college community that was small and relatively self-contained, and somewhat insulated from the wider city. In the intimate college setting students, staff and fellows knew one another and lived a life that was regulated by rites and observances that did not exist outside of Trinity's walls. A.A. Luce, who became a fellow in 1912, claimed that everybody in Trinity knew everybody else.[24] Front Square was far from the thoroughfare it is today— a city-centre shortcut linking College Green and Nassau Street where students, tourists and city-centre workers cross paths. Instead, it was a relatively quiet and empty space; people generally only entered the Trinity campus if they had business there, not simply to pass through. While the college grounds were seen as the preserve only of Trinity students, that did not mean that they spent all their time within the walls: the bars and entertainment venues around the college, such as the Royal, the Empire and the Tivoli theatres, were all popular with students and staff alike, who would also eat and drink at venues such as the Bailey Restaurant and Fanning's Pub at Lincoln Place.[25]

Sociological scholarship has shown the importance of shared spaces, routines, rites and experiences for the fostering of a community identity.[26] Indeed, this scholarship even suggests that the university experience can create bonds that are pseudo-familial in nature, and this was certainly the case in some Oxford and Cambridge colleges. While it is perhaps not as applicable at Trinity, where only a proportion of students were resident,[27] these ideas are nevertheless important in understanding the larger group mentality. Simply put, members of the college community saw themselves as part of a wider network; it meant something to be of Trinity, not only professionally, but socially and emotionally too. This sense of mutual identification was not premised upon friendship; people could be antagonists but still form a bond through sharing the same experiences, spaces, language and rituals in their time at university. Of course, professional considerations also informed this phenomenon: to be a 'Trinity man' opened professional doors in the worlds of law, medicine and beyond. The term 'Trinity man' is used here to describe anyone who spent time studying at TCD; the use of the term does not presuppose a shared political or philosophical outlook, but a connection that linked an Irish and increasingly global network together. It is also worth emphasising that the female equivalent of this term did not have the same currency; Trinity at the turn of the twentieth century was, as we shall see, a highly gendered community.

Trinity's non-academic staff existed on the periphery of the main community. The porters manned the entrances to the college and its buildings but were poorly paid by comparison with academic staff. While the resident community of students and staff was firmly middle class, these men lived off-campus, in working-class suburbs of the city, in some instances sharing their small dwellings with up to ten family members.[28] They had little in common with the wider body of students and academic staff but were integral to the full functioning of the university.[29] So, while the sense of community and shared institutional identity was an important unifying factor at Trinity, it did not embrace all, nor was it applied equally.

Student life

Writing in 1899, Provost George Salmon remarked that the majority of students attended Trinity

> not to be taught advanced mathematics or very high classical scholarship but to get qualifications for learned professions and just the moderate amount of knowledge which is necessary for the purpose.[30]

Almost one-third of the student body was enrolled in one of Trinity's professional schools of Law, Engineering, Divinity and Medicine. At the turn of the century, a professional qualification was a licence to travel, as employment opportunities were plentiful within the British empire; the college, especially the Engineering School, was proud to play its part in the imperial project.[31] Trinity also trained students for the Indian Civil Service examinations, although the numbers following this option were fewer than those enrolled in medicine or engineering.[32] Indeed, the potential for careers outside of Ireland offered by a professional Trinity education meant that many graduates left the country, resulting in an alumni network scattered around Dublin, Ireland and the world.[33] In turn, this meant that for many students, their time at the college represented a transitional space on the road to a career elsewhere, and this could be argued to have heightened the sense of disconnect between 'town and gown'.

The college community needs to be understood qualitatively as well as quantitatively. What did it mean to be part of this community, how did students and staff relate to the university and one another, and what customs—specific to Trinity—bound community members closer together? Aside from the residential distinction, much also depended upon one's hobbies, interests and natural proclivities; Dixon described this well in 1902.

> The newly-fledged undergraduate drifts into the companionship of men with similar tastes and sympathies, and to none is it given to share in all the emotions or gather the fruit of all the proferred experiences of the university world. The rowing man learns the stern joys of the river and its racing crews, but not the green carpet of the park with the wicket and the nets in June; the budding orator is claimed by the competition for office, the honours of the 'Historical' or the 'Phil', and the high politics of their 'Private Business'; the honour man eschews the seductive company ... the wilder spirits, who give their days to contemplative idleness and their nights to revelry; the musician frequents the rooms of the 'Choral'; the classical man consorts with his fellows; the poet, it may be, dreams his dreams with the makers of the past. Though they may meet in Hall, and though the inexorable days of examination claim all as victims, yet each man moves in a circle of his own within the wider society.[34]

This account betrays many of the hallmarks still typical of the modern university, save for the male-only composition of the student body in 1902. Broadly speaking, the college in the early twentieth century was, like most residential institutions, a vibrant place with much to offer its undergraduates. Contemporaries were keenly aware of the sense of difference that was sometimes affected by those in residence in the college, reinforcing the larger collective identity. One undergraduate in the years before the outbreak of the First World War, Walter Starkie, claimed that Trinity at the time housed so many eccentrics that 'all the undergraduates collectively created around them a mass of legends which were transmitted to the later generations'.[35] Names of charismatic dons such as Mahaffy, Henry Stewart Macran and Robert Yelverton Tyrrell—all classical scholars—became legendary both inside and outside the college, and were frequently satirised in the pages of *T.C.D.: a College Miscellany*, the student newspaper.

'The inter-varsity debate', illustration from *T.C.D.: a College Miscellany*, 9 February 1910, p. 5.
Note the motion for the debate: 'That compulsory military service is necessary for the safety of the empire'.

Idiosyncrasy was further entrenched by the college's position as, in Starkie's words, a 'walled fortress of the spirit in the midst of the Irish maelstrom'.[36]

History was omnipresent at Trinity. The university had ostentatiously celebrated its tercentenary in 1892, invoking its place as one of Europe's ancient universities. Customs inherited from a bygone age created a sense of tradition and informed how students acted and understood their wider group identity. Many elements of college life were antiquated, and these remnants of previous times became part of what Dixon called the 'circle of life':

> Morning chapel, lectures, rowing or football or cricket, the debates in the societies, Hall and night roll, and 'corrections' with the Dean on Saturday mornings for delinquents. The college gates are closed at nine o'clock, after which hour entry or exit is only possible through the wicket, guarded by the sleepless college watch in the lodge.[37]

Walter Starkie made caricatured observations of his fellow undergraduates in this period, which in turn provide a fascinating window into the perceptions of one undergraduate towards his fellow students. He claimed that there were two different types of student: the extrovert and the introvert. The extroverts, also known as 'solid men', were the sort who were 'bluff, hearty and cocksure'.[38] These tended to play sports: cricket, tennis, hockey, rowing and rugby. In Starkie's words, 'the exaggerated display of interest in things of the mind was contrary to the ethic of the "Solid Men".'[39] The introverts were plenty in number, although, by Starkie's reckoning, in a minority. These men 'pursued their own individual course through life without allowing themselves to be deflected either to left or right'.[40]

Politics are often taken to be a key element of the collective Trinity identity. The college was a conservative and historically unionist institution. It was politically influential, electing two representatives to the Westminster parliament, as it had done for much of its history, like many universities in Britain and elsewhere in the empire.[41] Fellows, scholars, masters of the college and those with higher degrees were entitled to vote in elections.[42] Graduates with a BA degree could, in exchange for payment of a bi-annual fee, register as masters three years after graduation, thus joining the list of electors.[43] In 1910, the year in which the last pre-1912 elections were held, there were 5,036 registered electors.[44] The provost and board of the college tended to be politically engaged, but political consensus was less obvious amongst the students. Trinity liked to bill itself as a space 'where men of all creeds and political opinions can meet in free and friendly intercourse'.[45]

Politics were curiously absent in contemporary accounts of student life. Kevin O'Shiel, who graduated in 1913, recalled that

> the students, neither Protestant nor Catholic, unionist nor [nationalist], seemed to take any particular interest in politics—Irish, imperial or world. Indeed, they seemed to avoid, to fight shy of the subject.[46]

Starkie's account of life emphasised the same tendency among his contemporaries, with the bulk of students being more interested in sports or student politics. This attitude is entirely understandable when one considers the vast number of distractions and interests available to undergraduates in Dublin. While they were the beneficiaries of the privileged position of a political class, they were not all concerned with the intricacies of high politics.

T.C.D., the student newspaper, deliberately and explicitly dealt with non-political issues, only commenting on national or international politics reluctantly and at times of great stress. In 1907, an editorial noted that 'the ordinary undergraduate is a person usually not keenly interested in politics', but it added that 'there are times when the movements of the outer world affect us so closely that even the most light-hearted must pause and think'.[47] The avowedly non-political stance professed by the student newspaper became harder to maintain from 1912, however, and the freedom of expression of the newspaper, like that of the student societies, was closely monitored by the college's governing board, lest they say something controversial.[48] The board's desire to keep both *T.C.D.* and the student societies in check would lead to some contentious incidents.

There were times when the Trinity community did voice its political views. The masters, fellows and scholars of the university returned unionist members of parliament to Westminster with regularity. The university had a strong affinity with the British empire, whether born of deep-rooted political convictions or professional aspirations. This imperial identity emerged at different times, such as during the South-African War of 1899–1902 or during King George V's visit to Ireland in 1911. Such events provided an opportunity for the expression of collective political identity, but at the same time, the disparate nature of the college community should not be understated.

More regular rituals reinforced the college's sense of difference. Trinity Week, usually held in May, was simultaneously a microcosm and an exaggeration of the college's collective set of identifiers. It both reflected and contributed to the college's sense of otherness. Trinity Week was important for a number of connected reasons. It saw the announcement of new scholars and fellows by the provost, amidst much ceremonial pomp from the steps of the Examination Hall in Front Square. In this way, an important academic ritual, steeped in tradition, was performed and reinforced. It was also the backdrop for student 'rags'. Starkie described these as occasions 'when the students momentarily overflowed the College grounds and invaded the streets, claiming with all the arrogance of youth the right to paralyse the traffic in the centre of the capital'.[49] Rags usually involved a degree of self-parody; students would frequently dress up as the board and mimic their announcement of new fellows and scholars. They often became bawdy and riotous affairs, however, and arrests were common. An *Irish Times* report of the 1914 rag carried the tongue-in-cheek headline: 'Students create excitement: Ten arrests.'[50] Trinity Week also saw the staging of the College Races in the College Park; in the years before 1914 these were a highlight of Dublin's social calendar. The College Races were more notable for their social prestige than for their sporting prowess.[51] They attracted significant crowds throughout the late nineteenth century, and although they had lost some of their prestige in the years before the First World War, they still presented an opportunity for Dublin's social elites to be seen.[52] The band of the Dublin Metropolitan Police usually played, and the races were frequently attended by the lord lieutenant. The College Races placed Trinity at the centre of Dublin's social life and reinforced both its sense of its own place in the world and its own internal hierarchy.[53]

A changing institution

The decade and a half before the outbreak of the First World War was a period of reform and modernisation for many universities, and Trinity College Dublin was part of this trend. While great political turmoil would be unleashed from 1912, Trinity had already been involved in much administrative and academic change in the preceding decade. Throughout this period the provost of the college was Anthony Traill, who had been appointed to the post in 1904 on account of his political connections rather than his scholarly accomplishment. While he is better remembered for his committed unionism rather than for his achievements as provost, his period in charge was one of significant reform for the university.

In 1904 Trinity admitted women to take full degrees; this was fifteen years before Oxford did so, and almost half a century before Cambridge. Although this was a progressive move, it was limited. Women did not suddenly become equal members of the college community. Their movements were closely monitored and regulated. They had to be out of Trinity by 6pm every evening, wear cap and gown at all times and be chaperoned if they wished to enter any chambers in the college.[54] Female students were not entitled to membership of the historic societies such as the Historical or the Philosophical, and instead had to form their own society, the Elizabethan.[55] Women students were expected to live at home with their parents, or in halls of residence, and it was for the latter reason that Trinity Hall opened in Dartry, several miles south of the city, in 1908.[56] Nor could they become fellows or part of the college administration. So, while Trinity was making an important provision for the higher education of women, this came with strict caveats. Women were allowed to take full degrees but would remain peripheral figures within the college community. In contrast, when the National University opened in 1908, it immediately gave women full equality. Suddenly female students had options, and consequently, Trinity began to value its female students more. Never-theless, the admission of women to take full degrees at Trinity in 1904 was a significant change for a college that, although founded by a woman, had been dominated by men for over 300 years.

Academically, too, the institution was gradually changing. The college's traditional scholarly preoccupation with divinity and the classics was, as at universities elsewhere, being challenged to meet the demands of modern society. The natural sciences began to emerge in their modern form in the late nineteenth century and were slowly establishing themselves at the older universities. This meant that research was becoming a priority for the first time; traditionally, universities were seen as teaching institutions, as Newman had described in 1852.[57] The movement to ensure a greater role for science in society and government took on a great momentum towards the end of the nineteenth century in both Britain and France, and in both countries this movement looked to Germany for inspiration. At Trinity, this movement had its own specific inflection. The physicist, George Francis Fitzgerald, led a campaign to furnish the sciences with laboratories and apparatus befitting the university. This culminated in the construction, after his death, of the Botany and Physics school buildings, as well as in the refurbishment of the Geology laboratories, the result of donations from the Guinness family.[58]

Trinity's scholarly successes in this period were modest at best, but it was significant that the changes in wider scholarship manifested themselves physically at the university. And although research in the sciences remained underfunded in this period, meaning that each scientific school was often made up of just one professor and his assistant, Trinity nevertheless

boasted a number of brilliant scientific minds. Perhaps the greatest of all was the theoretical physicist Fitzgerald, described by the great Cambridge mathematician Joseph Larmor as 'the idol of the undergraduates and the hope of the older men'.[59] Fitzgerald was held in the highest esteem in the international scientific community, and Trinity's Physics School struggled to recover from his untimely demise in 1901. Fitzgerald's legacy lived on through his advocacy of educational reforms in favour of the sciences and through his ideas, which influenced the development of quantum physics.[60] His legacy was also secured through his brilliant students.[61] One of these was John Joly, professor of Geology and Mineralogy and a scientific polymath with an international reputation. Joly's collaborator Henry Dixon, the Professor of Botany, and Sydney Young, the Professor of Chemistry, were similarly accomplished. All were fellows of the Royal Society in London, recognition of their contributions to science, and all, in turn, produced research students who themselves would have distinguished careers.

The university was also slowly modernising in the humanities. In 1903 compulsory Greek was abolished in the arts course at Trinity—again ahead of Oxford and Cambridge—and the study of the modern languages of French and German was permitted in its stead.[62] In the cases of Trinity's two more accomplished sister universities in Britain, it required the upheaval of the First World War to bring about the removal of Greek from its lofty position and, as already noted, the full admission of women.[63]

This slow diversification of study did, however, have repercussions for the governance of Trinity. The board of the college had essentially held the same form since its foundation, comprising the provost and seven senior fellows. This began to present a major problem by the late nineteenth century; fellowship was seen as a comfortable job for life. Oliver St. John Gogarty saw the advantages as purely social. 'It must be wonderful to be a fellow and to be able to order port with such assurance and to have such a dependable butler.'[64] Fellowship provided significant financial rewards. Critics both inside and outside of Trinity noted the excessive proportion of college resources that were diverted into the salaries of the senior fellows.[65]

Furthermore, fellowship was only attainable by success in an examination, described by Gogarty as simultaneously 'inhuman and superhuman', which was dominated by the classics and mathematics and geared towards the production of generalists rather than specialists.[66] In an era of increasing specialisation, this presented a real problem. Professors of modern languages or sciences, and others holding chairs of a more recent vintage,

Opposite: Visit of King George V and Queen Mary, 1911. Group assembled in front of the Dining Hall. George V is at the centre; to his right is John Pentland Mahaffy, to his left Provost Anthony Traill. In the foreground, the guns of the Officers Training Corps can be identified.

found it difficult, if not impossible, to attain fellowship with its greater financial rewards and stake in the governance of the college. In this regard the distinction between college and university is crucial; these non-fellow professors were appointed by the university rather than the college, as there were no regulations allowing for their incorporation into traditional college structures. Thus, they constituted a marginalised academic underclass in the university and were paid significantly less than the fellows and denied the additional financial rewards that came through that system. This situation came to a head in the first decade of the twentieth century, with the mounting agitation peaking in the establishment in 1906 of a Royal Commission to investigate Trinity's functions and its provisions for Catholic attendance, and a resolution finally being found by 1911.[67] The resolution widened the composition of the board to include two junior fellows and two professors who were not fellows alongside the seven senior fellows and provost.[68] It also allowed for fellows to be nominated rather than having to pass the examination, thus opening the door to scientists for the first time. John Joly was the first appointed fellow, 'elected' in 1919. While all of this may seem like an academic footnote, the fact that a change had been effected to the structure underlying the governance a 320-year old institution was significant.

Mahaffy

One figure recurs in accounts of Trinity in this period: John Pentland Mahaffy. His name appears not only in histories of the college from the early years of the twentieth century, but in many standard works of wider Irish history too.[69] His personality, which combined gregariousness, conversational flourishes and outright snobbery, has also lived on in the work of writers such as Oliver St. John Gogarty. Mahaffy's name has resounded over the past century undoubtedly as a result of his ability to offend and cause controversy, but also because of an international reputation that saw him fraternising with kings, queens and emperors, and being awarded honorary degrees at British and European universities.[70] Mahaffy was a polymath. A classical scholar of Ancient Greece by vocation, he also published on ancient history, papyrology and the history of music, and he was an ordained clergyman and doctor of Divinity. *The Athenaeum* described him as 'the most popular Hellenist of his generation'.[71] His friend, the politician J.G. Swift MacNeill, described him in 1912 as the college's 'most distinguished living ornament'.[72]

Mahaffy's opinions influenced wider popular opinion; his interventions were taken seriously and garnered many column inches in both English and Irish newspapers and periodicals; at different times he wrote with regularity for *Nineteenth Century* and *Blackwood's Magazine*. His public comments were frequently provocative, and, as we will see, Irish nationalists were simultaneously outraged and energised by his pronouncements. He was a controversialist who boasted a talent for awakening 'hitherto dormant public opinion through his intemperate language' and for 'presenting his enemies with ammunition'.[73] A contemporary account noted that he enjoyed being 'witty and wounding and rather welcomed the unpopularity which his outbursts so often provoked'.[74]

Provost Anthony Traill, John Pentland Mahaffy is behind, to the right of the photograph, with (?) J.W. Barlow on the left.

The classical heritage was central to Mahaffy's understanding of the world and to his intellectual and political identity. He saw the rise of science, specialisation and secularisation, and the revival of previously dormant languages, as a threat to his cosmopolitan world. He firmly believed that civilisation and cultivation derived from the Greeks. Writing in 1909, he claimed that, for men brought up as he had been, the supremacy of Greek studies was 'a fact that no man could contest'. Moreover, he asserted, the cultural achievements of the nineteenth century owed their greatness to the classical Greek world.[75] While he is often considered to be the quintessential Trinity figure, in fact he was unlike most of his colleagues; his international reputation, his influence and his moderate political views made him a suspect figure in the eyes of the college's more committed unionists. Mahaffy's personality, too, was inherently contradictory; despite his snobbery and occasional pugnaciousness he was a deeply generous man for whom the students had a profound affection—which they did not for many other fellows of the college. And despite Mahaffy's propensity to say the wrong thing in public, privately he was well liked by the intellectual elites of Dublin.[76]

Even his friends called Mahaffy a snob.[77] In 1887 he took it upon himself to write a guide to conversation, but he had no qualms about breaking the rules that he established in this text—such as the necessity for modesty and tact—on a regular basis and in spectacular fashion. Mahaffy, a fellow of the college since 1864, was seen as part of the furniture in Trinity, a figure who had been there forever and would continue to be. In the words of his godson Walter Starkie, he 'towered over the College', and became a legendary figure in his lifetime. A panoply of apocryphal stories and quotes were attributed to him.[78] For all this, however, Mahaffy was very much an individualist; he rarely saw himself as representative of any larger body, always taking care to express idiosyncratic opinions.

In 1904, Mahaffy, widely understood to be the best-qualified candidate, had been passed over for the provostship as a result of the agitation of unionists who wanted one of their own in the post. Traill was duly appointed.[79] *The Leader* alleged acerbically that 'Dr. Traill is a long-established bigot, an anti-Irishman, and an anti-Irish Irelander. Traill, therefore, suits Trinity, and Trinity Traill, and the two should get on well together.'[80] Mahaffy had damaged his standing amongst unionists by supporting Lord Dunraven's scheme to devolve legislative power to Ireland on purely Irish affairs. The scheme was rejected by most unionists, who saw it as too akin to Home Rule.[81] Unionism encompassed diverse views and traditions before 1912 and was sometimes a divided movement, as this incident demonstrated.[82] Mahaffy and Traill were opposites in every way;

Traill was truculent and dour, while Mahaffy was flamboyant and brilliant. Much might be inferred from the handwriting of the two men. Traill's is fastidiously executed, neat to a fault, perfectly formed, and the product of time and care; Mahaffy's diagonal scrawls are frequently illegible and suggestive of great haste and much flourish. Mahaffy, in life and death, looms large over the period explored in this book; his career and personality were illustrative of many of the preconceptions, contradictions and changes taking place in Trinity and Ireland in the early twentieth century.

Trinity and the Irish language

The changes taking place in Irish society around the turn of the twentieth century made Trinity a target for cultural nationalists. For many Irish-Irelanders who would come to prominence in this period, the Irish nation should be Irish speaking and Catholic. Consequently, English-speaking Irish Protestants simply could never fit this conception of the nation. In this context, Trinity College Dublin was, almost by definition, regarded as being opposed to the cultural nationalist project. The Gaelic League had experienced significant growth by the start of the century, with its desire to make Irish a working language again acquiring many followers. The increasing support for the movement served to bolster the arguments of many political nationalists, especially separatist republicans.[83] Within this movement, much vitriol was directed against Trinity for its attitude towards the study and teaching of the Irish language. Eoin MacNeill, one of the leading members of the Gaelic League and later founder of the Irish Volunteers, stated that Trinity 'is inspired by a firm tradition of hostility to whatever stands for an Irish nation—a primitive spirit of racial antagonism kept alive in a modern seat of learning'.[84] This attitude was not uncommon in the period; but from where did it spring?

Trinity had a complex attitude towards the study of Irish and its place in contemporary society. A chair of Irish was established in 1838, not for the purposes of language revival, but to expand the influence of the Church of Ireland in Irish-speaking communities. For that reason, the chair itself was attached to the Divinity school.[85] John Millington Synge wrote disparagingly of the situation in 1889:

> If an odd undergraduate of Trinity...wished to learn a little
> of the Irish language and went to the professor appointed
> to teach it in Trinity College, he found an amiable old
> clergyman who made him read a crabbed version of the

New Testament, and seemed to know nothing, or at least care nothing, about the old literature of Ireland.[86]

Trinity's official disconnectedness from contemporary Irish scholarship was confirmed by the passing over of Douglas Hyde for the chair of Irish in 1896; instead, the Church of Ireland clergyman James Murphy was appointed to the post.[87] Scholars such as Hyde, the previously mentioned Rolleston and E.J. Gwynn had, however, emerged from Trinity to make significant contributions to contemporary Irish scholarship. Indeed, the latter's brother, Stephen Gwynn, claimed that it could be argued that

> the modern Irish revolution came out of the Divinity School of Trinity College; for a theological student Hyde was, though he never passed into orders: and the Gaelic League came from Hyde, and from the Gaelic League came the movement that was called Sinn Féin.[88]

Gwynn's argument was too neat in this instance. Hyde's relationship with his alma mater was famously contentious, as we shall see. That said, Trinity's indirect influence on the language revival was important to subsequent events.

Language revivalists became increasingly antagonistic towards the college on account of an incident that took place in 1899, when a commission on intermediate education sat to consider whether Irish should be part of the secondary school curriculum. Trinity was asked to provide two expert witnesses to the commission: it sent the polymath Mahaffy and the Professor of Sanskrit, Robert Atkinson. The selection of both men was curious; Mahaffy knew nothing of the Irish language and had been railing against language revivals across Europe since at least 1896.[89] Atkinson was a gifted linguist but had little knowledge of Irish. Their comments, especially those of Mahaffy, became infamous for their dismissiveness, reinforcing the notion that Trinity was disconnected from and hostile to Irish-Ireland. In the words of Eoin MacNeill, their attitude was proof of Trinity's 'frigid and unsympathetic attitude towards everything distinctively Irish in the field of education'.[90]

Mahaffy argued that the textbooks used in Irish schools were either silly or indecent, and that the language was of no educational value for schoolchildren. His one contemptuous concession was that Irish was 'sometimes useful to a man fishing for salmon or shooting grouse in the West'.[91] Atkinson was no more conciliatory. The opinions of these 'experts' were taken as representative of the university as a whole and

'Trinity Week in prehistoric times', cartoon illustration from *T.C.D.: a College Miscellany*, 23 June 1910, p. 126.

were sharply rebuked. Douglas Hyde led the charge against the representatives of his alma mater, and in a famous article entitled *A university scandal*, he described Mahaffy's evidence to the education commission as a 'long drawn scoff', accusing him of having used his position, rather than his knowledge, 'to damage a movement which he feared and hated.' This was, Hyde argued, typical of Trinity College Dublin.[92] Hyde became a fierce—albeit somewhat reluctant—critic of Trinity's policy on the teaching of Irish in the decades that followed.[93]

Mahaffy's opposition to the Irish language in 1899 drew on his cosmopolitan anxieties; he reasoned that the widespread study of Irish would be parochial and would tend to isolate Ireland from the great Republic of Letters that utilised German, French and English. For example, in his presidential address to the Modern Language Association in London in December 1901, he argued that people should learn two of English, German and French, in order to 'enter into the atmosphere of our great civilization'.[94] At the same time, he dismissed the 'band of cranks' who were trying to revive Flemish, while also criticising the Czech, Erse and Irish language revivals.[95] Mahaffy's utterances were considered to be important and were frequently repeated; to Irish cultural nationalists they demonstrated the ignorance, snobbishness and failings of existing educational institutions in Ireland and were 'not to be easily forgotten or forgiven'.[96]

Although the offensive and flippant remarks of 1899 would long resonate, attitudes towards the teaching of the Irish language did begin to change at Trinity. On the back of criticisms levelled at the college by language revivalists in the Royal Commission of 1906, a chair of Celtic Languages was introduced in 1907, and E.J. Gwynn was appointed the first chair holder.[97] Gwynn was an accomplished scholar of Old Irish and an important figure in the scholarly network that revolved around the Royal Irish Academy (RIA). He was general editor of the RIA's catalogue of Irish Manuscripts. What distinguished Gwynn from many of his fellow Irish scholars, however, was that he viewed the language purely in scholarly terms and saw no utility in its revival as a spoken language.

Nevertheless, attitudes to the Irish language were slowly changing within Trinity. While Irish was not designated an 'honours subject'—on a level with other modern languages such as French and German—until 1927, it grew in popularity amongst students, and attitudes towards it also changed amongst the fellows, showing how the wider cultural context informed college life. The College Gaelic Society was founded in 1907. At its inaugural meeting in May that year, E.J. Gwynn, the first president, argued that it was founded specifically to counter the false notion that Trinity was aloof from Ireland.[98] The society's records show that many fellows of the college lent their support by taking on honorary roles in the society, including E.P. Culverwell (professor of education), R.M. Gwynn (the college chaplain), and E.H. Alton (fellow in classics and later provost).[99] In 1909, Hyde was invited to attend the annual inaugural meeting and by then his criticisms of Trinity's attitude to Irish had become noticeably gentler.[100] Mahaffy, too, was frequently invited to speak at the society's public meetings and participated enthusiastically. By 1908 he announced that his position had changed. Speaking at such a meeting alongside W.B. Yeats and Eoin MacNeill, Mahaffy acknowledged that his public attitude in 1899 towards the language revival had been wrong. The *Irish Independent* noted that 'Dr Mahaffy said that, looking back at the time the movement began, he confessed he was wrong—he was at fault— he did not judge the state of it, nor the permanence of it'.[101]

By 1911, the annual inaugural meeting of the Gaelic Society had become quite an important event, and it attracted a distinguished list of guests from inside and outside of Trinity, including the truculent provost, Anthony Traill, the influential civil servant T.P. Gill, the former unionist MP Sir Horace Plunkett, UCD historian Mary Hayden, Douglas Hyde, journalist and emerging nationalist politician Arthur Griffith, nationalist journalist The O'Rahilly, and the Irish scholars (and members of the RIA) F.J. Bigger and R.I. Best.[102] By 1914, Culverwell noted the change of attitude within Trinity in relation to Irish, claiming that even Mahaffy was wiser and 'inclined to think Irish ideas ought to be encouraged'.[103] However, these limited changes did little to counter the broadly held view that Trinity was hostile to the study of Irish. Mahaffy's public renunciation of his 1899 position went virtually unremarked upon in the nationalist press, and he continued to be seen as the *bête noire* for language revivalists. Mahaffy was more useful as an oppositional figure, and thus his older comments were often repeated. In order to understand the full context for the controversy about the teaching of the Irish language, however, the other components of emergent Irish nationalism need to be considered.

The Roman Catholic Church and the university question

For much of its history, Trinity College Dublin had been closely associated with the perpetuation of Protestant Ascendancy; Catholics were barred from entering the university until 1793. In that year religious tests were removed as entry requirements, meaning that Catholics could enter the college freely. In the early nineteenth century, many middle-class Catholics did so, including Daniel O'Connell's son, Maurice.[104] In 1873, Fawcett's Act removed religious requirements for the holding of a fellowship or scholarship, meaning that Catholics could become full members of the college, while at the same time the traditional requirement that students must attend chapel was relaxed.[105] Fawcett's Act was of great symbolic importance, but in reality the religious composition of the college community remained strongly Anglican. In the early years of the twentieth century, there was only one Catholic fellow of the college, Stephen Barnabas Kelleher, elected in 1904.[106]

The Catholic Church was not well disposed towards Trinity. From the mid-nineteenth century, Catholic bishops began campaigning for explicitly Catholic university education for Catholics, a consequence of the foundation in 1845 in Belfast, Cork and Galway of the secular Queen's Colleges, which were seen as unsuitable. Increasingly, Catholic attendance at Trinity was condemned and, ironically, in the wake of Fawcett's Act, formally proscribed.[107] It was not good enough that Trinity was becoming non-denominational in the wake of the disestablishment of the Church of Ireland and the more general trend towards secularisation in European universities: the Catholic bishops wanted an exclusively Catholic education for Catholic students. Thus, Trinity became a symbol of frustrated Catholic desires for an institution of their own. This was well articulated in 1886 by William Walsh, the Catholic archbishop of Dublin, who claimed that 'so long as that central fortress of the education that is not Catholic is allowed to stand, as it has now so long stood, in the very foremost position, and to occupy the most glorious site in our Catholic city of Dublin' it would be impossible to achieve 'full and absolute equality for the Catholics of Ireland'.[108]

By the turn of the twentieth century, the 'university question' had become a major political issue. It centred on the desire of middle-class Catholic Ireland and the Catholic Church to secure a system of higher education acceptable to them, which would in turn provide them with the professional opportunities enjoyed by Protestants. (The 'Catholic University', established in 1854 with John Henry Newman as rector, had no charter or endowment and was never formally recognised as a university. It had struggled to attract students.) The 1911 census showed how Protestants, comprising just over thirteen per cent of the population, were disproportionately represented in professions such as law, medicine and engineering.[109] At the start of the twentieth century, this issue of Catholic access to higher education had become 'saturated by the wider issues of nationalism and nationality', and so it overlapped with the language revival and the wider constitutional nationalist movements.[110] The issue implicitly and necessarily engaged Trinity, because the demands that Catholics made for a university of their own were frequently defined in opposition to what it was claimed that Trinity stood for: elitism and Protestant Ascendancy. More importantly, Trinity was taken as the starting point or template for any settlement of the issue of providing Catholic-oriented university education; all potential solutions to the matter were derived from or contrasted to the existing situation at Dublin University.[111]

Within Trinity, there were many who hoped that the college, or, to be more accurate, the university, could be the solution, not the problem. They pointed to the incremental increase in Catholic admissions since 1873 and the non-denominational spirit of the institution. Figures presented to the Royal Commission of 1906 show how Catholics made up ten percent of the student population at that point. Far from being seen as evidence of the college becoming more accessible, however, Catholics attending Trinity were often dismissed as 'Castle Catholics'—those who surrendered their national and religious identity for professional advancement.[112] The college community was, and remained, an Anglican one, although the admission of women in 1904 had led to many female English students, known as 'Steamboat ladies', coming to Trinity to take degrees. Consequently, there was an increase in the number of Church of England and students of other denominations on the books.[113]

In 1907 E.J. Gwynn wrote of the tolerance Trinity aspired towards. The university, he argued,

> should be the meeting ground of all sections of the community; that it should be, as it has always been, a place of religion and learning; that the direction of its affairs, and the teaching of secular knowledge, should be free from partisan spirit and religious bias.[114]

The former junior dean, Thomas Gray, made a similar argument, claiming that Protestants and Catholics should be educated together so they could 'form lasting friendships, and in after life regard one another as allies [and] not as natural enemies'.[115] Similarly, Harold Lawson Murphy, a precocious young graduate who had written a history of the college while still an undergraduate, argued that Trinity was

> probably the one spot in Ireland where a non-sectarian atmosphere might be said to prevail, the one spot where every man was at liberty to work out his own career and his own future, unfettered by questions of class and creed.[116]

This line was regularly promulgated in the decades following 1873.[117]

STUDENTS ENTERING TCD
FOR EACH OF THE SIX YEARS 1900-6
(PERCENTAGES IN PARENTHESES)

YEAR	ANGLICAN	ROMAN CATHOLIC	PRESBYTERIAN	METHODIST	OTHER	TOTAL
1900-1	177 (77.2)	19 (8.2)	20 (8.7)	8 (3.4)	5 (2.1)	229
1901-2	172 (79.2)	23 (10.5)	11 (5)	6 (2.7)	5 (2.3)	217
1902-3	160 (75.8)	24 (11.3)	15 (7.1)	4 (1.8)	8 (3.7)	211
1903-4	215 (77.0)	29 (10.3)	14 (5.0)	7 (2.5)	14 (5.0)	279
1904-5	205 (64.0)	34 (10.6)	33 (10.3)	9 (2.8)	39 (12.1)	320
1905-6	164 (61.5)	35 (13.1)	18 (6.7)	9 (3.3)	40 (15.0)	266

SOURCE: TCD MS2388/253.

AVERAGE NUMBER OF STUDENTS ENTERING TCD
BETWEEN 1860 AND 1900, BY RELIGIOUS DENOMINATION
(AVERAGES OVER TEN-YEAR PERIODS; PERCENTAGES IN PARENTHESES)

DECADE	ANGLICAN	ROMAN CATHOLIC	PRESBYTERIAN	METHODIST	OTHER	TOTAL AVERAGE
1860-70	262.8 (86.2)	21.0 (6.9)	6.9 (2.2)	0.8 (0.2)	12.6 (4.1)	304.1
1870-80	245.0 (79.7)	28.0 (9.1)	16.5 (5.3)	1.7 (0.5)	16.0 (5.2)	307.2
1880-90	232.6 (78.6)	25.8 (8.7)	17.5 (5.9)	8.0 (2.7)	12.0 (4)	295.9
1890-1900	208.2 (80.1)	18.8 (7.2)	15.0 (5.7)	8.6 (3.3)	9.1 (3.5)	259.7

SOURCE: TCD MS 2388/253.

The 'university question' became a major political issue and its resolution in 1908 had far-reaching consequences.[118] In 1906 the Royal Commission called expert witnesses from other institutions and provided another occasion for Trinity's foes to criticise its workings. For example, William Magennis and Thomas Kettle, both academics working at University College, Dublin, the institution that had emerged from Newman's Catholic University, argued:

> The university is hopelessly out of touch with the national life of the country. It was founded originally for the purposes of political proselytism and denationalisation, and has persistently and constantly carried on its mission. It has been opposed to every national movement. It is the custom of the great bulk of its professors and students, either to neglect Ireland, its history, its language, its antiquities, its problems altogether, or else to treat them from a bitterly partisan and hostile point of view. This attitude is, of course, abhorrent to the great majority of Irish Catholics; it undoubtedly creates a gulf between the work of the University and the life of the nation.[119]

In 1903 the Trinity board had approached Catholic leaders, offering to make provisions for the construction of a Catholic chapel on campus, but the offer was immediately declined by Cardinal Logue.[120] A similar approach was made to Presbyterian leaders. The board, and especially Provost Traill, maintained this policy of pragmatic conciliation in 1906, indicating a willingness to make further provision within the college for Catholics. Specifically, Traill proposed to ensure that no denominational spirit would prevail at Trinity, with the exception of the Divinity School, which had a special function in training Anglican clergymen.[121] Traill's proposals would never be acceptable to the Catholic bishops, however; they sought not greater access to a non-denominational college, but a college of a distinctly Catholic flavour. They wanted a Catholic Trinity.

The commissioners ultimately recommended a scheme to create a second, Catholic, college within the University of Dublin. This was to exist alongside the old Queen's Colleges, which would be reorganised into a new National University.[122] This scheme, known as the Bryce Plan (after James Bryce, the chief secretary who proposed it), received the assent of the Catholic hierarchy and many nationalists. The *Freeman's Journal*, the organ of the Irish Parliamentary Party, celebrated 'the nationalisation of Dublin University'.[123] However, the scheme was steadfastly resisted at Trinity. A Dublin University

Defence Committee was set up; its slogan was 'Hands off Trinity', and its members lobbied and published energetically to highlight their cause.

Trinity opposition to the Bryce Plan had two major axes. The DU Defence Committee argued that Catholic doctrine was incompatible with disinterested scholarly research and intellectual liberty, especially in the sciences. 'It is contrary to our best traditions that the boundaries of science should be fixed, directly or indirectly, by ecclesiastical authority, or the impulse of speculation arrested by clerical intervention.'[124] John Joly argued that 'the history of the conflict between science and religion shows that again and again the Church—and the remark applies to all Churches in varying degree—has exerted her influence against the views of the pioneer'.[125] In short, the DU Defence Committee held that the university's scholarly freedom and academic integrity would be compromised by the Bryce Plan.

Trinity's representatives also claimed that the institution of a college of a Catholic character within Dublin University would necessarily cause sectarian antagonism because, even though Trinity College remained non-denominational, the binary distinction between the two colleges would cause friction. E.J. Gwynn summed up this line of thinking:

> I am afraid it is only too easy to see that the tone of feeling between the colleges will resemble that which tinges not only public but private life in Ireland; that is to say it will be nor-mally a tone of reserve and suspicion, ready to blaze out on occasion into open animosity.[126]

Gwynn also reiterated Traill's point of view. 'So long as you mix individuals, not classing them according to fixed religious or social categories, differences of belief and opinion need not create obstacles to free intercourse.'[127] One name that was notably absent from the Trinity lobbying was Mahaffy's; he was sympathetic to the Bryce scheme, was a friend of Archbishop Walsh and, despite his snobbery, generally viewed the widening of access to Trinity as a good thing. This was another instance whereby Mahaffy's moderation marked him out to many others in the college hierarchy as different and suspect, and the college's critics, such as *The Leader*, exposed this gleefully.

> The name of the great Mahaffy is eminent by its absence—and has been all through. How be this? Is the pass sold? Is John Pentland going to leave alma mater to her doom? Looks like it.[128]

The Roman Catholic Hierarchy are not satisfied,

and

The Government proposes to meet their demands

by

(*a*) **Abolishing the Royal University.**

(*b*) **Enlarging the University of Dublin,** by incorporating with Trinity College several other Institutions, in at least two of which the Roman Catholic Hierarchy will inevitably be masters. **In these new Colleges all the appointments, books, and courses of study must have the approval of the Roman Catholic Bishops,** who are deemed to be the sole judges of everything appertaining to Faith and Morals.

RESULTS:

The Enlarged University will be controlled by a Governing Body nominated by (*a*) **The Crown**—that is by the Politicians, dominated by the United Irish League. These men will not be nominated as scholars but rather on account of Religion and Politics. (*b*) **The Representatives of the Incorporated Colleges.** Here, the Liberal, Cultured and Progressive element, represented by Trinity College, will be completely overborne by the Reactionary and Ultramontane element from the Clerical Colleges. The progress and development of independence of thought and intellectual freedom in Ireland will be retarded for generations.

The Religious and Political Asperities

Which are

The Heritage of an Unhappy Past

Will be

Perpetuated and Intensified.

The Rising Generation will be fed and nourished on Racial and Religious hatred by being subjected, during their Collegiate course, to Clerical Control, and separated into rival Colleges, with utterly different ideals. Thus the last state of Ireland will be worse than the first.

This

Return to Mediævalism is the Government's idea of Irish University Education.

ARE the Electors of Great Britain prepared to tax themselves in order to satisfy the imperious demands of the Roman Catholic Bishops which are now being repudiated by every other civilized nation? This question transcends all Party considerations, and appeals to the elementary principles of Freedom and Progress which are dear to the people of this country.

Printed and Published by McCorquodale & Co. Ltd., "The Armoury," London, S.E.

Leaflet produced by the Dublin University Defence Committee criticising the proposal under the Bryce Plan of 1906 to create a Catholic college within the university.

In Westminster, the Trinity unionist MP Edward Carson, who would become Mahaffy's great rival, argued that

> for years and years Trinity College had been emerging from denominationalism. From the moment they set up this college of Catholics, Trinity College would become nothing more than a Protestant College, and would be going back to absolute denominationalism.[129]

The DU Defence Committee was successful in mobilising academic colleagues in Britain to oppose the Bryce Plan, and such was the storm generated that it was dropped. Consequently, in 1908 Augustine Birrell, the new chief secretary, established the National University of Ireland, which encompassed the Queen's Colleges in Galway and Cork and a transformed University College, Dublin. Trinity College survived as the only constituent college of Dublin University, but the success of the DU Defence Committee in opposing the Bryce Plan only served to reinforce the idea that it was anti-Catholic and anti-Irish.[130]

The establishment of the National University was a landmark in modern Irish educational history. It resolved the interconnected political, cultural, professional and religious issues surrounding the university question. It was a triumph for nationalist MP John Redmond, who hailed the first meeting of the senate of the National University as 'the first instalment of Home Rule'.[131] But whereas the creation of the new university lessened nationalist gripes aimed at Trinity College, it did not arrest them completely. Redmond bemoaned the fact that University College Dublin was not a residential college. More pertinently, Trinity's financial resources and its antiquated administrative structure and curricula continued to draw the ire of *The Leader* and, from 1911, the vitriolic *Catholic Bulletin*. One commentator, Daniel Coghlan, a conservative Catholic theologian working at St Patrick's College in Maynooth, cited the evidence presented to the Royal Commission to claim that Trinity should use its financial resources to promote national causes. He concluded that 'the development of character in Trinity College has been un-Irish, if not anti-Irish, from the absolute neglect of national studies in the College'.[132]

Much was also made of Traill's comment to the Royal Commission that

> what people in England and elsewhere ought to realise is, that there are two nations in Ireland; the sooner they realise that the better; there is not one nation in Ireland.[133]

This statement resounded in nationalist circles; Coghlan, Patrick Pearse and Eoin MacNeill all cited and criticised it.[134] Traill's view neatly underlined the difficulty presented to the Trinity community by the rise of cultural and political nationalism. The Trinity community was, for the most part, Protestant, unionist and frequently unsympathetic to the claims of moderate or more advanced nationalists. While those who were part of the Trinity community generally considered themselves Irish, theirs was a different form of Irishness, incompatible with the idealised vision of the national community as Gaelic, Catholic and no better off for English influence.[135] This conception of Irishness was also forcefully expressed by Trinity graduate and former *Times* correspondent W.F. Monypenny in a 1913 book called *The two Irish nations*. He argued that two nations existed in Ireland in opposition to each other, framed by religious difference but given added venom by the Union of 1801.[136] Identity, however, rarely remains fixed, and the collective identity of the Trinity community would, as we shall see, change and fragment with the tumultuous events of the decades to come.

While many nationalists argued that Trinity epitomised all that was wrong with the status quo, within the college there was much grappling with the wider questions of what it meant to be Irish at a moment when identity politics had taken on a new urgency.[137] In November 1910, the auditor of the Historical Society, Arthur P.I. Samuels, whose father was a prominent unionist politician, gave his inaugural address on the topic of 'Irish possibilities'. He argued that Trinity and its constituent community were Irish; they had, however, important professional, cultural and political connections to Britain and the empire, and this explained why, following graduation, large numbers of Trinity students left Ireland to pursue careers elsewhere. While Samuels acknowledged the criticisms of Trinity as anti-Irish, he argued that 'all through the past this College, no matter what opponents have said, has been Irish', and reiterated that 'her first duty as a great Irish institution is to Ireland'.[138] Samuels's viewpoint may not have been reconcilable with an Irish-Ireland outlook, but it was more-or-less typical of the majority attitude at Trinity at the time.

Most members of the Trinity community would have strongly disagreed with claims that they were not really Irish at all. For advanced nationalists who were gaining much support by 1912, however, there was increasingly a single, exclusivist version of the Irish nation, premised upon language, common history, habits and religion. This increasingly narrow definition of the Irish nation simultaneously and explicitly defined what was un-Irish.[139] Arguments about the existence of any Irish nation beyond the ancient Gaelic one were further proof to advanced nationalists that the mostly Anglican community of Trinity was not really 'Irish' at all.

Typically, John Pentland Mahaffy's view differed from mainstream understandings of the nation. While he labelled himself an 'Anglo-Irishman', this was a limited concept; he rejected the idea of an Irish or an 'Anglo-Irish' nation, preferring to throw in his lot with ancient notions of the Republic of Letters, where no national boundaries or national languages inhibited the free flow of ideas and scholars.[140] Mahaffy's cosmopolitan viewpoint was as incompatible with the idealised vision of the national community as Gaelic and Catholic as it was with the orthodox view of Southern unionists.[141] On this point, he stood alone.

Conclusion

Bernard Lascelles, the protagonist of Eimar O'Duffy's 1919 novel *The wasted island*, is the English-educated son of an Irish Protestant physician. Having finished school in the years following the resolution of the university question, Lascelles considers his university options. His father, reasoning that Oxford was too expensive, suggests that he attend Trinity instead.

> Bernard, bitterly disappointed, said it would have to do. It was a hard blow to him. It meant losing all his hopes and projects, all the grand talks and theorisings he had promised himself, all his plans for galvanising the academic heart of the Empire with revolutionary ideas.[142]

Later, a friend makes the argument that instead of Trinity, he should attend the National University.

> 'It's something new in Universities,' said Manders. 'No traditions about it at all. Trinity's just a second rate Oxford. Quite as musty and not half so magnificent. You'd only stifle there. It's a mere Rathmines university, if you know what I mean. The National's new. It may be a bit shoddy, but we might make something of it.'[143]

Lascelles follows his friend Manders to the National University where his eyes are opened to the claims of Irish nationalism. Thereafter O'Duffy's protagonist joins the Volunteers and becomes involved in gun running, but is later disillusioned with the nationalist movement following the Easter Rising. O'Duffy's novel is important for the trope it uses:

Trinity is portrayed as intellectually stagnant, elitist and snobbish; moreover, not only are nationalists not welcome there, nationalist viewpoints could not organically emerge there. Hence, O'Duffy's protagonist—loosely based on the author herself—has to go to the National University for both his intellectual and political awakening.

In reality, the situation was rather more complicated. From 1912, when the Home Rule crisis peaked, through the outbreak of the First World War and the Easter Rising, to the War of Independence and Civil War, both Trinity College and Ireland experienced unprecedented convulsions. The strict binary construction that posited that Trinity was anti-national, anti-Irish and the epitome of everything that nationalists claimed to stand against, would be challenged by the course of events. Students and staff would have cause to reflect at length on their collective and institutional identity, as well as on their political allegiances. Moreover, the period would demonstrate that the notion that Trinity was isolated from ideas emerging outside its walls was not strictly accurate either. The remaining chapters of this book will explore the experiences of an institution that was a key participant—sometimes rhetorically, sometimes as an observer, and sometimes on the 'wrong' side—in the years during which the Irish state was founded and Europe descended into conflict. They will consider the consequences of these changes until 1952, when a 'palace revolution' began a new period in Trinity's history, whereby it rapidly modernised and ultimately thereafter came to play a full part in Irish national life.

NOTES:

[1] R.B. McDowell and D.A. Webb, *Trinity College Dublin: an academic history: 1592–1952* (Cambridge, 1982), 3.

[2] F.S.L. Lyons, *Ireland since the famine* (London, 1971), 241.

[3] Senia Pašeta, 'Trinity College Dublin and the education of Irish Catholics, 1873–1908', *Studia Hibernica* 30 (1998–99), 7–20: 20.

[4] Lyons, *Ireland since the famine*, 81.

[5] *The Leader*, 26 March 1904, 69; 31 March 1906, 83; 17 December 1904, 274.

[6] William MacNeile Dixon, 'Trinity College, Dublin', *Times Literary Supplement*, 29 January 1904, 29.

[7] 'Irish University Question', *Irish Times*, 17 December 1904, 9.

[8] F.S.L. Lyons, *Culture and anarchy in Ireland 1890–1939* (Oxford, 1979), 37–45.

[9] 'Meeting of the Royal Trinity College Academy', *United Irishman*, 23 February 1901.

[10] William Macneile Dixon, *Trinity College Dublin* (London, 1902), 264.

[11] Stefan Collini, *What are universities for?* (London, 2012).

[12] 'An act for the union with Ireland', in Charles Grant Robertson (ed.), *Select statutes cases and documents to illustrate English constitutional history, 1660–1832* (9th edn, London, 1949), 283–92: 286.

[13] McDowell and Webb, *Trinity College Dublin*, 4.

[14] J.V. Luce, *Trinity College Dublin: the first 400 years* (Dublin, 1992); Constantia Maxwell,

A history of Trinity College Dublin, 1591–1892 (Dublin, 1946); Kenneth Bailey, *A history of Trinity College, Dublin, 1892–1945* (Dublin, 1947); Macneile Dixon, *Trinity College, Dublin*. Maxwell and Bailey's books were written in conjunction with one another, to survey the college's entire history.

[15] The pioneering work of Susan Parkes on female students is an exception to this trend. See Parkes (ed.), *A danger to the men: a history of women in Trinity College Dublin* (Dublin, 2004).

[16] John Henry Newman, *The idea of a university* (6th edn, London, 1966), xxxvii.

[17] The figure for alumni is based on those who chose to become masters of the college, in the process earning the right to vote in the university election. Data are taken from the *Dublin University Calendar*, pt II, 1902–14.

[18] *Dublin University Calendar for the year 1912–13*, pt I (Dublin, 1912), 19.

[19] *Dublin University Calendar 1912–13*, pt I, 30.

[20] *Dublin University Calendar 1912–13*, pt I, 6–16.

[21] *Dublin University Calendar 1912–13*, pt I, 47–55.

[22] *Royal commission on Trinity College, Dublin and the University of Dublin: appendix to the final report* (Dublin, 1907), 8; Bailey, *Trinity College Dublin*, 159.

[23] Dixon, *Trinity College Dublin*, 268.

[24] A.A. Luce, Interview, *Sunday Press*, 21 November 1971, 21.

[25] Bureau of Military History (BMH), Witness Statement (WS) 1170, Section 2, 175, Kevin O'Shiel, 181; J.B. Lyons, *Oliver St John Gogarty: the man of many talents, a biography* (Dublin, 1980), 82.

[26] D.H.J. Morgan, 'The social definition of the family', in Michael Anderson (ed.), *Sociology of the family: selected readings* (Harmondsworth, 1980), 325–49: 325–8.

[27] Tomás Irish, 'Fractured families: educated elites in Britain and France and the challenge of the Great War', *Historical Journal* 57 (2) (June 2014), 509–30.

[28] Trinity College Dublin, Department of Manuscripts (hereafter TCD, MS), 2388/70–90.

[29] Dixon, *Trinity College Dublin*, 137.

[30] British Library (hereafter BL), Add MS 49709, ff. 102–3, George Salmon to Edward Carson, 22 February 1899.

[31] Ronald Cox, *Engineering at Trinity, incorporating a record of the school of engineering* (Dublin, 1993), 81.

[32] By 1920, Trinity had, since the mid-nineteenth century, produced a total of 180 Indian civil servants. Christopher Shepard, 'Cramming, instrumentality and the education of Irish imperial elites', in Justyna Pyz *et al.*, *Irish classrooms and the British empire: imperial contexts in the origins of modern education* (Dublin, 2012), 172–83.

[33] David Dickson, '1857 and 1908: two moments in the transformation of Irish universities', in Pyz *et al.*, *Irish classrooms and the British empire*, 184–205: 198–9.

[34] Dixon, *Trinity College Dublin*, 264–5.

[35] Walter Starkie, *Scholars and gypsies: an autobiography* (London, 1963), 95.

[36] Starkie, *Scholars and gypsies*, 111.

[37] Dixon, *Trinity College Dublin*, 265.

[38] Starkie, *Scholars and gypsies*, 107–8.

[39] Starkie, *Scholars and gypsies*, 108.

[40] Starkie, *Scholars and gypsies*,110–11.

[41] Joseph S. Meisel, *Knowledge and power: the parliamentary representation of universities in Britain and the empire* (Oxford, 2011).

[42] *Dublin University Calendar 1912–13*, pt I, 16.

[43] *Dublin University Calendar 1912–13*, pt I, 6, 22–3.

[44] *Dublin University Calendar 1909–10*, pt II, 359.

[45] 'Editorial', *T.C.D.*, 3 June 1908, 99.

[46] BMH, WS 1770, Section 2, 170–1; Eda Sagarra, *Kevin O'Shiel, Tyrone nationalist and Irish state-builder* (Dublin, 2013), 53–8.

[47] 'Editorial', *T.C.D.*, 16 February 1907, 13.

[48] Trinity College Dublin Muniments (hereafter TCD, MUN), V/5/20, 41, Minutes of board meeting, 28 May 1910.

[49] Starkie, *Scholars and Gypsies*, 107.

[50] 'Scenes in Dublin: Students create excitement: ten arrests', *Irish Times*, 9 June 1914, 7.

[51] TCD, MUN, CLUBS/ATHLETICS/4, 5.

[52] Trevor West, *The bold collegians: the development of sport in Trinity College, Dublin* (Dublin, 1991), 37–46.

[53] The skips and porters were to receive the fewest free tickets for the event. See West, *The bold collegians*, 40.

[54] McDowell and Webb, *Trinity College Dublin*, 349–51.

[55] Susan M. Parkes, 'The first decade, 1904–14: a quiet revolution', in Parkes (ed.), *A danger to the men*, 55–86: 59.

[56] Parkes, 'The first decade', 75.

[57] Newman, *The idea of a university*, xxxvii.

[58] McDowell and Webb, *Trinity College Dublin*, 406–11, and Denis Weaire, 'Social conscience', in Weaire (ed.), *George Francis Fitzgerald* (Vienna, 2009), 120–3.

[59] Joseph Larmor, quoted in Denis Weaire and J.M.D Coey, 'Mentor and constant friend: the life of George Francis Fitzgerald (1851–1901)', in Weaire (ed.), *George Francis Fitzgerald*, 11–19: 14.

[60] Walter Isaacson, *Einstein: his life and universe* (London, 2007), 113–16.

[61] Weaire and Coey, 'Mentor and constant friend', 14–15.

[62] Bailey, *Trinity College Dublin*, 28.

[63] Tomás Irish, '"The aims of science are the antitheses to those of war": the debate about academic science in Britain and France during the First World War', in Alisa Miller, Laura Rowe and James Kitchen (eds), *Other combatants, other fronts: competing histories of the First World War* (Newcastle, 2011), 29–54.

[64] Oliver St John Gogarty, *Tumbling in the hay* (Dublin, 1939), 71.

[65] Daniel Coghlan, *Trinity College: Its income and its value to the nation* (Dublin, 1911).

[66] Gogarty, *Tumbling in the hay*, 69; McDowell and Webb, *Trinity College Dublin*, 396.

[67] McDowell and Webb, *Trinity College Dublin*, 402–5.

[68] Bailey, *History of Trinity College Dublin*, 26–9.

[69] Diarmaid Ferriter, *The transformation of Ireland* (New York, 2005), 98–9; Terence Brown, *Ireland: a social and cultural history, 1922–2002* (London, 2004), 103; Lyons, *Culture and anarchy*, 45–6; Roy Foster, *Modern Ireland* (London, 1988), 167; Declan Kiberd, *Inventing Ireland* (London, 1995), 145. Aside from general histories, Mahaffy's name frequently appears in more focused studies of the period, such as Ruth Dudley Edwards, *Patrick Pearse: the triumph of failure* (Dublin, 2006; originally published1977), 38–41, 226–7; Murray Pittock, *Celtic identity and the British image* (Manchester, 1999), 67, 71; Boyce, *Nationalism in Ireland*, 229.

[70] Patrick Maume, 'Mahaffy, Sir John Pentland', in James McGuire and James Quinn (eds), *Dictionary of Irish Biography* (Cambridge, 2009).

[71] 'What have the Greeks done for modern civilization?' *The Athenaeum*, 11 December 1909, 726–7: 726.

[72] 'Trinity College and Home Rule', *Irish Times*, 24 October 1912, 12.

[73] Dudley Edwards, *Patrick Pearse*, 39, 226.

[74] 'A notable Provost,' *Freeman's Journal*, 2 May 1919, 3.

[75] Mahaffy, *What have the Greeks done for modern civilisation?* (New York, 1909), 20–1.

[76] He counted William Walsh, Horace Plunkett and Douglas Hyde amongst his friends.

[77] Walter Starkie, 'John Pentland Mahaffy', in D.A. Webb (ed.), *Of one company: biographical studies of famous Trinity men* (Dublin, 1951), 89–100: 96.

[78] Starkie, 'John Pentland Mahaffy', 95.

[79] McDowell and Webb, *Trinity College Dublin*, 358–9; 'Castle friction,' *Irish Independent*, 16 February 1905, 6.

[80] 'The prestige of Trinity College', *The Leader*, 2 April 1904, 91.

[81] Earl of Dunraven, *Past times and pastimes*, (2 vols, London, 1922), vol. 2, 25–31.

[82] Alvin Jackson, *The two unions: Ireland, Scotland, and the survival of the United Kingdom 1707–2007* (Oxford, 2012), 283, 304–10.

[83] Foster, *Modern Ireland*, 456.

[84] Eoin MacNeill, quoted in Patrick Pearse, 'Trinity and the Gael', in Séamas O'Buachalla (ed.), *A significant Irish educationalist: the educational writings of P.H. Pearse* (Dublin, 1980), 120.

[85] Máirtín Ó Murchú, 'Irish language studies in Trinity College Dublin', *Hermathena: a Trinity College Dublin Review, Quatercentenary Papers 1992*, 43–68: 60–1.

[86] Ó Murchú, 'Irish Language studies', 62.

[87] Mary Robinson, 'Douglas Hyde (1860–1949). The Trinity Connection. Quatercentenary Discourse, 11 May 1992', in *Hermathena, Quatercentenary Papers*, 17–26.

[88] Stephen Gwynn, *Experiences of a literary man* (London, 1926), 68.

[89] John Pentland Mahaffy, 'The modern Babel', in *Nineteenth Century* 40 (228) (November 1896), 782–97.

[90] *Royal Commission, appendix*, 307.

[91] R.B. McDowell and W.B. Stanford, *Mahaffy: a biography of an Anglo-Irishman* (London, 1971), 104–5; David Greene, 'Robert Atkinson and Irish studies', *Hermathena: a Trinity College Dublin Review*, 102 (1966), 6–15.

[92] Douglas Hyde, *A university scandal* (Dublin, c.1900), 3.

[93] In 1907 and 1908 he spoke of his reluctance in rebuking Murphy in a spat played out in the pages of the *Church of Ireland Gazette*. 'The Gaelic League and Professor Murphy', *Church of Ireland Gazette*, 15 November 1907, 1012, and 'The Church of Ireland and the Gaelic League', *Church of Ireland Gazette*, 3 April 1908, 274.

[94] 'Modern Languages Association', *Manchester Guardian*, 21 December 1901, 9.

[95] 'Scheme to revive Flemish', *New York Times*, 22 December 1901, 4.

[96] Brown, *Ireland: a social and cultural history,* 103.

[97] McDowell and Webb, *Trinity College Dublin*, 414–15.

[98] 'Dublin University Gaelic Society', *Irish Times*, 22 May 1907, 7.

[99] TCD, MUN/SOC/GAELIC /1, Gaelic Society Minutebook.

[100] 'Dublin University Gaelic Society', *Irish Times*, 24 November 1909, 5.

[101] 'Trinity and Gaelic: Dr. Mahaffy's change,' *Irish Independent*, 17 November 1908, 5.

[102] 'Dublin University Gaelic Society', *Irish Times*, 22 November 1911, 9.

[103] TCD, MS 6830/15, Culverwell to John Dillon, 1 February 1914.

[104] James Lydon, 'The silent sister: Trinity College and Catholic Ireland', in C.H. Holland (ed.), *Trinity College Dublin and the idea of a university* (Dublin, 1991), 33–9.

[105] McDowell and Webb, *Trinity College Dublin*, 255–8, 387.

[106] 'Death of Mr. S.B. Kelleher', *Irish Times*, 20 August 1917, 3.

[107] Luce, *Trinity College Dublin*, 93–8.

[108] Archbishop William Walsh, 'Speech at Thurles', 14 January 1886, in Walsh, *The Irish university question: the Catholic case* (Dublin, 1897), 88.

[109] R.B. McDowell, *The Church of Ireland, 1869–1969* (London, 1975), 121.

[110] Senia Pašeta, *Before the revolution: nationalism, social change and Ireland's Catholic elite, 1879–1922* (Cork, 1999) 5–16.

[111] Thomas J. Morrissey, *Towards a national university: William S. Delany SJ (1835–1924)* (Dublin, 1983), 117.

[112] Pašeta, 'Trinity College, Dublin, and the education of Irish Catholics, 1873–1908', 11.

[113] Parkes, '"The Steamboat ladies", the First World War, and after', in Parkes (ed.), *A danger to the men?*, 87–112: 87–90.

[114] E.J. Gwynn, *Trinity College, Dublin and Roman Catholic education* (Dublin and London, 1907), 4.

[115] TCD, MS 8408, letter of T.T. Gray to the *Daily Express*, 19 January 1904.

[116] H.L. Murphy, quoted in John Joly, 'An epitome of the Irish university question, by John Joly', in *Dublin University Defence: pamphlets bearing on Mr Bryce's proposed university legislation for Ireland, 1907* (Dublin, 1909), 14.

[117] McDowell and Webb, *Trinity College Dublin*, 257.

[118] Lyons, *Ireland since the famine*, 85.

[119] Cited in Coghlan, *Trinity College*, 87.

[120] McDowell and Webb, *Trinity College Dublin*, 367.

[121] *Royal commission, appendix*, 101.

[122] Pašeta, *Before the revolution*, 18.

[123] Dermot Meleady, *John Redmond: the national leader* (Dublin, 2014), 140.

[124] Dublin University Defence Committee, *Dublin University Defence*, 5.

[125] Joly, 'Epitome of the Irish university question', 58.

[126] Gwynn, *Trinity College, Dublin and Roman Catholic Education*, 13.

[127] Gwynn, *Trinity College, Dublin and Roman Catholic Education*, 15.

[128] 'Trinity on Tour', *The Leader*, 23 February 1907, 11.

[129] House of Commons debate, vol. 177, col. 917 (4 July 1907).

[130] Pašeta, *Before the revolution*, 20–1.

[131] Meleady, *Redmond: the national leader*, 141.

[132] Coghlan, *Trinity College*, 90.

[133] *Royal commission, appendix*, 107.

[134] Coghlan, *Trinity College*, 51–2; Pearse, 'Trinity and the Gael', in O'Buachalla (ed.), *A significant Irish educationalist*, 119–21.

[135] Lyons, *Ireland since the famine*, 237–41.

[136] W.F. Monypenny, *The two Irish nations: an essay on Home Rule* (London, 1913), 10–17.

[137] D.G. Boyce, *Irish nationalism 1798–1922* (London, 1998), 228.

[138] A.P.I. Samuels, *'Irish possibilities': an address delivered in the Dining Hall of Trinity College at the opening meeting of the 141st session* (Dublin, 1910), 9–30.

[139] Richard English, *Irish Freedom: the history of nationalism in Ireland* (Basingstoke, 2006), 238–9.

[140] McDowell and Stanford, *Mahaffy*, 122.

[141] Lyons, *Ireland since the famine*, 237–41.

[142] Eimar O'Duffy, *The wasted island* (New York, 1920), 120.

[143] O'Duffy, *The wasted island*, 121.

CHAPTER ONE

To 'stand and fall with the fortunes of the country'?
Trinity and Ireland, 1912–14

SOME FAMILIAR FACES WE HOPE TO SEE

LECTURES

Introduction

Twenty years to the day after the tercentenary celebrations of June 1892, Trinity once more conjured up a spectacle full of symbolism. In this instance, the occasion was the bicentenary of the medical school. The college looked back to 1892 and utilised many of the same ceremonials; distinguished guests were invited from 'almost every known university in the two hemispheres'.[1] Observers remarked upon the effect of the many different coloured gowns worn by the eminent visitors. 'The silk of the many-coloured gowns caught the sunlight, and the effect was kaleidoscopic as the brightly attired throng moved about the [Fellows'] garden.'[2] The celebration was marked by receptions, addresses, the awarding of honorary degrees and, as in 1892, a procession.

In 1912, the procession of distinguished guests and college staff took a different route from that followed for the tercentenary. Beginning at the medical school in the east end of college, it passed the College Park, came through Front Square, exited the campus and turned left onto Nassau Street before finishing at the Royal College of Physicians on Kildare

Opposite: 'O.T.C. a forecast', illustration from *T.C.D.: a College Miscellany*, 2 March 1910, p. 34, depicting the university's Officers Training Corps.

Street.[3] This procession also had a new element, however, that had been missing in 1892. Leading the procession and the distinguished guests was a large body of Trinity students from the university's Officers Training Corps (OTC), armed and dressed in military uniform.

The contrast between the processions of 1892 and 1912 was stark. The latter spoke to the anxiety that had crept into the life not only of Trinity, but of universities and colleges across Britain and Ireland, where military drill had become an accepted part of campus life. International incidents proliferated and nations armed; war was spoken of with regularity and universities readied themselves for such an eventuality. In addition, in the summer of 1912 strong opposition was growing amongst unionists to the Home Rule bill that had been making its way through parliament since April. The Medical School procession hinted at the emergence of new anxieties in the life of the college, which were the product of external developments but which would have severe repercussions for the institution and for Ireland as a whole.

From 1912 to 1914 the rapidly radicalising political and social situation in Ireland was both experienced at and shaped by Trinity and its community. These years saw Irish politics and life transformed. They mark the end of late-Victorian and Edwardian assuredness and the beginning of a period of upheaval and anxiety, peaking with the outbreak of the First World War in August 1914. The radicalisation of political life in Ireland was due largely to the re-emergence of Home Rule as a major issue. Following the general elections of 1910, John Redmond's Irish Parliamentary Party held the balance of power in Westminster. It could make or break the Liberal government, and its MPs made the implementation of Home Rule the price for their support. The Parliament Act, passed in 1911, removed the power to veto legislation from the House of Lords, which had impeded the passing of Home Rule in 1893. Suddenly, there were no impediments to the introduction of a Dublin parliament; consequently the years 1912 to 1914 marked the pinnacle of the Home Rule movement.[4] The removal of the Lords' veto posed an 'urgent and formidable' threat to the status and security of Irish unionists.[5] At Trinity, it would show just how disparate political allegiances were.

The slow passage of the Home Rule bill through parliament from April 1912 polarised political groupings. The mass signing of the Ulster 'Solemn League and Covenant' on 28 September 1912, with Sir Edward Carson—Dublin University's senior member of parliament—the first signatory, was a dramatic manifestation of the potential for serious opposition to the bill and to the consequent inclusion of Ulster in a self-governed Ireland. The formation of the Ulster Volunteer Force in January 1913, the reciprocal formation of the Irish Volunteers in November of that year, and the gun-running perpetrated by both sides in 1914 meant that within two years Ireland had drifted to the brink of civil war, with two private armies—representing two different traditions and political desires—facing one another.[6] In the midst of this, a new class-consciousness emerged in Dublin, where the working classes were energised by the dynamic leadership of Jim Larkin. In August 1913, regular life in Dublin was interrupted by a mass strike of transport workers, followed by their being locked out by the employers. Thus, the transformations of this period were social as well as political; Dublin and its inhabitants were animated by myriad new ideas, personalities, expectations and anxieties.

The previous chapter described the commonly used metaphor that presented Trinity College as a 'garrison university', an island in the centre of Dublin, cut off from the wider life of the city and the surrounding country. The events of 1912–14 demonstrate conclusively that this metaphor, however appealing it may have been to editors of nationalist newspapers and periodicals, did not hold up. The walls of the institution proved far from impermeable to outside happenings.

Students entering Trinity College Dublin in 1912 would live through historic events for the institution, for Ireland and for the world, but who were they? In the academic year 1912–13 there were 1,285 students on the books, comprising 1,074 men and 211 women. The new cohort of junior freshmen who came onto the books in that year provides a snapshot of the wider community.[7] Of the 214 for whom statistical data are available, 24 were women and 190 were men. Sixty per cent of these students were members of the Church of Ireland, thirteen per cent were Roman Catholics, seven per cent were members of the Church of England, seven per cent were Presbyterians and five per cent were Methodists.

Place of birth can be traced for 204 of these students. Eighty-two per cent were born in Ireland, with sixteen per cent born in the nine Ulster counties and sixty-six per cent born elsewhere in Ireland. Ten per cent were born in Britain and six per cent were born overseas (Canada, India, Russia and the United States). Details of educational background are available for 201 of the 1912–13 junior freshmen. Sixty-nine per cent were educated at schools in Ireland; twenty per cent were educated in Britain; seven per cent were home-educated; and three per cent were educated at schools overseas. While Trinity students came from a variety of educational backgrounds, a number of schools were especially prominent in sending pupils to the university, namely the High School, Mountjoy School, St Andrew's College and St Columba's College in Dublin; Campbell College in Belfast; and Clongowes Wood College, a Jesuit school, in Kildare. Alexandra

'We won't have Home Rule', unionist postcard *c*.1912, from the ephemera collection of
A.W. Samuels, lawyer and MP for Dublin University from 1917 to 1919.

College in Dublin was the secondary school attended by most of the women entering Trinity. Students who came to Trinity in this period were drawn mainly from middle-class backgrounds; their fathers were employed as accountants, bankers, businessmen, medical doctors, farmers, lawyers and teachers. Many were the sons and daughters of Church of Ireland clergymen. These were the students who would live through the Home Rule crisis and the outbreak of the First World War.

The Home Rule crisis

In the summer of 1912, the Home Rule bill was, as already mentioned, making slow progress through the House of Commons, and Ulster unionists were beginning to plan firm opposition to the inclusion of their province in the scheme for a separate parliament for Ireland. Central to this was Sir Edward Carson, 'a lawyer whom the Irish question made into a politician'.[8] The connections that Carson made at Trinity lasted a lifetime: as a member of the College Historical Society in the early 1870s he had first met James Campbell, who was later his fellow member of parliament for the university. He also encountered Oscar Wilde, whom he would meet again in 1895 when acting for the defence of the Marquess of Queensbury in a trial that sent Wilde to Reading gaol.[9] He may also have come across John Redmond in his time at Trinity. Redmond entered in October 1874, an unusual move for a Catholic at the time. He did not complete his studies, however, leaving in 1875, and thereafter had little to do with his alma mater.[10] Carson represented Dublin University in Westminster from 1892 until 1918. His political trajectory was unusual; he was a Dubliner who began his political life as a liberal-unionist but who came to prominence as the champion of the Ulster unionists. His close association with the Ulster position on Home Rule would bring him into conflict with many senior figures at Trinity, none more so than John Pentland Mahaffy.

Carson emerged as the unswerving leader of the Ulster party in 1910, and in a defiant speech at a dramatic open-air meeting attended by 100,000 people at Craigavon, Co. Armagh, on 23 September 1911, he positioned himself as the 'strong man' of the unionist movement. The following year, he continued to make dramatic appearances at mass rallies where he emphasised Ulster's growing opposition to Home Rule. He was supported in this by the new leader of the Conservative Party, Andrew Bonar Law. The symbolic peak of opposition to Home Rule was Ulster

Day, 28 September 1912, when Carson signed the Ulster Covenant. In total, 470,000 people signed either the covenant or its female equivalent, the Women's Declaration.[11] Throughout this period, Carson used explicitly militaristic language and warned the British government of Ulster's readiness to use force to oppose its inclusion under a Home Rule parliament. Carson stated that his support for the Union was 'the only alternative to financial ruin and exterminating civil dissensions'.[12] He did all of this as the elected representative of Dublin University.

The looming passage of the Home Rule bill led to much debate in Trinity. It was traditionally a unionist institution with a strong Ulster population. Carson's political prominence added to Trinity interest in the Home Rule debate; nevertheless, not all agreed with his position. Both the provost, Anthony Traill, and James Campbell signed the Ulster Covenant. Other senior members of the college community did not. John Henry Bernard, former Archbishop King's Lecturer in Divinity and then Bishop of Ossory, pointedly wrote to a friend that 'I have just returned from a short holiday in Ulster, which—I hasten to say—I visited in the interests of pleasure and not of the Covenant'.[13] Mahaffy wrote of his fear that Home Rule would lead to a Catholic dominated Irish legislature; he urged that the position of Protestants in the south be safeguarded but, in a somewhat idiosyncratic turn, and possibly with an eye to the on-going culture wars in France, claimed that a Catholic state would be preferable to a secular one.[14] Mahaffy's and Bernard's position was orthodox for many unionists in the south; they feared that Home Rule would leave them an isolated Protestant minority, removing their previous professional and social advantages and undermining their cultural heritage.

As no obstacles lay in the way of the Home Rule legislation, Ulster unionists under Carson's leadership dealt with it as a *fait accompli*. Rather than trying to obstruct the passage of the bill, they sought to ensure that the nine counties of Ulster would not be subject to a new Dublin-based parliament. This presented a dilemma for Trinity. The Ulster unionist position, as articulated by Carson, accepted the application of Home Rule to the rest of Ireland, therefore it assumed that Trinity would be subject to the new Irish legislature. Under this scenario, the fears expressed by Mahaffy would be magnified. In an Ireland ruled by a Home Rule parliament with Ulster excluded, the Protestant community, and by association the majority of those who called Trinity their home or alma mater, would be in an even smaller minority. A cleavage was forming between southern and northern unionists.

In May 1912 Provost Traill had written to Carson asking him and Campbell, as the university's two parliamentary representatives, to sound out support for an amendment to the Home Rule bill that would make Trinity exempt from legislation emanating from an Irish parliament.[15] In other words, it would make Trinity an island in the centre of Dublin and Ireland, answering to Westminster rather than the new Dublin parliament across the road in College Green. Edward Parnall Culverwell, the College Registrar and Professor of Education, immediately identified the potential ruin that exclusion from governance by the new Home Rule parliament would bring to Trinity. He wrote to *The Times* in London to voice his concern that Trinity would secure 'special treatment as would in effect make it a British Colony in Ireland'.[16] This marked the beginning of a tussle that pitted the board of the college against many junior staff and students, all against the backdrop of a deepening crisis about the future of Ireland.

On 21 October 1912 Traill got his way. Campbell moved an amendment to the Home Rule bill to exempt Trinity from its provisions. If it were approved, the college would be playing out the role ascribed to it in scurrilous nationalist periodicals over the previous decade—standing apart from Ireland and expressing its preference for Britain and union. The practical implications of this scarcely seem to have been considered and were clearly not in the college's best interests. Theoretically, partition would encompass a pocket of College Green alongside a yet to be determined number of Ulster counties. In moving the amendment, Campbell was acting out Traill's desires; crucially, neither the board, nor the wider college population, were consulted. Compounding this, John Redmond backed the amendment as a gesture of goodwill towards would-be minorities, reasoning that safeguards requested by Protestants should be granted.[17] Of course, it quickly and publicly became apparent that the amendment was not the desire of the wider college community. The decision to allow the amendment caused uproar, both for the manner in which it was moved as well as for its impractical substance. Mahaffy was first to act, writing to *The Times* on 24 October that Campbell's unilateral action not only contravened convention but posed 'a great danger to the future of Trinity College'.[18] Hoping to address the first of these arguments, Traill arranged for the college board to vote on the issue on 26 October; Campbell's proposed amendment was passed, by nine votes to two. Mahaffy and T.T. Gray, the latter a firm unionist, voted against it.[19] However, the college's governing body had now approved the amendment. This set the stage for strong opposition from students and staff.

J.G. Swift MacNeill, an MP and friend of Mahaffy who had studied at Trinity in the 1860s, also wrote to *The Times*. He argued that his and Mahaffy's opposition to the amendment was premised upon the idea that 'Trinity College under Home Rule should be an Irish institution whose

Photograph of Edward Carson inspecting Ulster Volunteers *c.* 1921.

sons would regard Ireland as their own'. The Campbell amendment would make 'an institution of which the majority of Irishmen are justly proud no longer Irish'.[20] The amendment struck right at the heart of Trinity's complex identity. The college was often accused of West-Britonism, of having a greater affinity for Britain than for Ireland. Opposition to the amendment demonstrated that this was not the case. Moreover, it demonstrated that the issue was not an explicitly political one; both unionists and nationalists opposed the amendment. Trinity invocations of 'Irishness' were not nationalist per se, but rather were emblematic of a current in southern unionist thought that was proud to call itself Irish but did not reject English influence on Irish cultural or political life.[21]

Culverwell took it upon himself to organise a campaign against the Campbell amendment. Ironically, he had been a leading figure in organising opposition to the Home Rule bill of 1893 but had become disillusioned with the anti-Home Rule movement since Carson had begun using militant language.[22] In 1912, his public intervention on the Campbell amendment was an act of great courage, which likely gained him much notoriety amongst senior college figures while simultaneously winning him favour in nationalist circles. Public opposition to the amendment could potentially stall an academic career. Culverwell's campaign took three forms. First, he quietly organised petitions of the junior fellows and professors in Trinity, co-ordinating the efforts of the disaffected. Second, he wrote open letters to all the major newspapers, expressing not only his own distaste for Campbell's measure, but communicating the sentiment of the college community to a wider audience. Finally, he wrote letters to leading political and religious figures, explaining to them the mood within Trinity and soliciting their support.

Rumblings of widespread discontent emerged on 27 October, the day after the board approved the Campbell amendment. On that same day, eight junior fellows, led by Culverwell, published a petition in the *Irish Times* condemning the amendment. To them, it was not a political issue.

> Without expressing any opinion on the merits of the Government of Ireland bill as a whole, [we] desire to repudiate the proposal of Mr Campbell to exclude Trinity College from the control of an Irish parliament.[23]

Among the eight were two future provosts—Alton and Gwynn—as well as a number of other moderates.[24] Privately, Culverwell wrote that 'this does not nearly represent the feeling among the Junior Fellows'; the problem was that many were afraid to express discontent publicly.[25]

Following this first expression of discontent opposition grew within the college. By 2 November the protest had gained the names of two more junior fellows, including the Public Orator, Louis Purser. An undergraduate protest also emerged, in the form of a petition bearing the signatures of 184 students. The undergraduates acted as representatives of different political and religious backgrounds, and in defence of Trinity's oft-invoked tradition of inclusiveness; and the document bore the names of Catholics and Protestants, unionists and nationalists, drawn from across Ireland. They circulated their document to leading nationalist and unionist politicians, as well as to the chief secretary, Augustine Birrell. Unsurprisingly, the petition received most coverage in the nationalist press, with the *Freeman's Journal* describing it as a 'remarkable manifesto'. The petition claimed that:

> Trinity College is an Irish Institution, which has given prominent men to every Irish movement, and it should not be used as a pawn in the political party game ... almost every Trinity man, whatever his politics may be, will claim that Trinity is an Irish University, and should stand and fall with the fortunes of the country.[26]

It spoke in the name of a wide body of students and did not attempt to categorise them according to political beliefs. Indeed, it intentionally eschewed making a political declaration, respecting the institution's pluralist tradition and instead placing the emphasis on Trinity's Irishness. Irishness, of course, meant different things to different groups, but its general invocation served as a unifying point for most unionists and nationalists in this instance. Moreover, the undergraduates' manifesto was testimony to a sense of institutional loyalty and pragmatism; signatories sensibly understood that any attempt to turn Trinity into an island, cut off from the new Irish legislature in College Green yet facing it, was far from being in the university's best interests.

Meanwhile, Culverwell's letter-writing campaign saw him write to William Walsh, the Catholic archbishop of Dublin and chancellor of the National University. Culverwell argued that Campbell 'does not voice the feeling of Trinity College'.[27] Knowing that the question was due to be discussed in the House of Commons in Westminster, Culverwell also sent a number of forthright telegrams to John Redmond in London. In one sent on 28 October he asked Redmond to repudiate his support for the amendment on the grounds that he had mistakenly believed that it was the wish of Trinity as a whole at the time he had initially voiced support for it.[28]

Another telegram on the same day clearly set out Culverwell's reading of the mood of the Trinity community:

> unbiased opinion of fellows distinctly opposed...great body of student opinion opposed...general feeling among university graduates in Dublin strongly opposed...those who oppose are far more emphatic than those who accept [.] all this means that amendment should be dropped.[29]

Culverwell also wrote to the nationalist MP John Dillon to explain the feelings of the college community and condemned the intransigence of Campbell and Carson on the issue.[30] While he quietly lobbied influential figures, he also threw himself into the public arena as the main opponent of the Campbell position, citing correspondence with these influential figures. In a letter to the *Irish Times* of 11 November he claimed that Redmond had supported the amendment because he was misinformed as to the level of support for it in Trinity, the position that he had privately suggested Redmond adopt. In the same letter, he threatened that a public meeting of disaffected Trinity men would be held if the amendment were not withdrawn. The consequences of the amendment passing would be disastrous, he argued, and would serve to intensify attacks on the college as 'non-national'. Culverwell claimed that the amendment was 'worse than useless', as it incited opponents to attack the college while affording 'no effective means of defence'.[31]

At the height of the standoff, with Campbell—Carson and Traill steadfast in their position and the controversy garnering column inches in the nationalist and unionist press alike—Culverwell took the unusual decision to address the Literary and Historical Society of University College Dublin as part of its inaugural meeting on 8 November. The auditor, Arthur Cox, gave an address in which he argued that universities had a duty to the nation. Referring specifically to the vehemence of Trinity's opposition to the Campbell amendment, he expressed the hope that Dublin University would join the National University in performing this duty in the future, hence developing national literature and industry. Culverwell was afforded a 'most enthusiastic reception', and his speech was punctuated by applause and enthusiastic laughter, where appropriate. Culverwell described those who had supported the amendment as 'covenanters who were bound in principle to oppose whatever is in the Home Rule bill', adding wryly that 'sometimes a doubt comes into my mind as to whether these gentlemen are actuated by logic alone'. He continued,

I feel sure that [Trinity] will take her part, and a worthy part, in the work of Irish education (applause). If, in her great past, she has been predominantly of one party, it is also true that she has been of all parties (applause). If the older men among her and her rulers have been unsympathetic to a large part of Irish life, the younger men have been bounded by no lines of party—they have taken all parts in Irish life (applause). Now, at present, it is largely a question of party politics; but remember that Trinity College, even in her official position, no longer stands apart from Celtic language, Celtic thought and Celtic culture (applause). Whether the amendment is withdrawn or not, the trend of thought and feeling in Trinity College will go on in the direction in which it has been going on, and you have had, I think, no more striking evidence of the trend of things than the support which has been given, under very difficult circumstances, to the protest of which your Auditor spoke (loud applause).[32]

The provost's hand was forced by the growing dissent, and a meeting of fellows and professors was held on 11 November at which it was resolved 'that in the event of an Irish Parliament being established by law we do not desire that Trinity College and the University of Dublin shall be excluded from its jurisdiction'.[33] Traill had called the meeting on the assumption—according to Culverwell—that the Campbell amendment would pass unchallenged. He was defeated in the two votes taken at the meeting. The first, condemning the action of the board in backing the Campbell amendment, passed by twenty-three votes to thirteen. The second, endorsing the resolution that Trinity not be excluded from the jurisdiction of an Irish parliament, was passed by twenty-one votes to thirteen, 'a complete surprise to the Provost'.[34] The text of the resolution was published in the media. Ultimately, the Campbell amendment was dropped; the voice of the wider community of staff and students drowned out that of the college board.

The debate over the Campbell amendment shaped wider discussions beyond Trinity. Patrick Pearse, then a language activist and educator, argued in a letter to the *Freeman's Journal* that education was a vital component of Irish self-government and that the exclusion of a university from the jurisdiction of an Irish parliament would undermine the project.[35] Ultimately, a new resolution was brought, which ensured that safeguards were put in place within the Home Rule legislation to protect Trinity's statutes from being changed by the Irish parliament without consent.[36] This addressed the fears of senior figures in the college that a nationalist Home Rule parliament would be hostile to Trinity. The means to achieve such a safeguard, however, were pursued in different ways. A declaration that Trinity was not subject to a new Irish parliament would have fed into the old accusations that the college was not an Irish institution; this was clearly a point of contention for those who opposed the Campbell amendment. Culverwell concluded that having come through the controversy 'we have earned some good will in Ireland'; clearly, the public image of the university mattered to him and others in this instance.[37] Whether he earned goodwill within the upper echelons of Trinity itself is another question.

Opposition to the Campbell amendment within Trinity was, in many instances, non-political. The warring camps did not divide along nationalist–unionist lines; it was significant that no nationalist supported the amendment while significant numbers of unionists opposed it. Among those opposed were the ardent unionist Gray, the idiosyncratic Mahaffy, Culverwell, who had developed moderate Home Rule sympathies, and pragmatic unionists such as E.J. Gwynn and Alton. Among the students opposed to the amendment a more diverse set of sympathies and trajectories appear. There were nationalists such as language enthusiasts J.W. Bigger and Charles Wyse Power (son of radical nationalist and suffragette, Jennie), as well as E.M. Stephens (a future associate of Michael Collins) and the Home Rulers Bolton Waller and Robert Hannay. Rejection of the amendment was premised upon the idea that Trinity was a non-political space where Irishmen (and women) of all backgrounds and political persuasions could come together in a spirit of openness and tolerance. What was being rejected was the politicisation of the university and its life.

The affair was notable for other reasons too. It was to be one of Traill's last major acts as provost of the college. Illness would render him unable to perform his duties or even attend board meetings for much of 1913 and 1914, and he died in November 1914. It was also one of the few occasions when the university's parliamentary representatives acted on a national issue that related directly to the university; this was especially true of Carson, who supported Campbell's decision to move the amendment. The incident demonstrated, however, that the priorities of the professional politicians representing the university, and the graduates who elected them, diverged greatly from those of the student body and the staff. Furthermore, senior figures, speaking anonymously, used the controversy about the amendment to criticise the college's restrictive and unrepresentative electoral process.[38]

The issue proved divisive amongst the student body. At the Historical Society, the Campbell amendment led to heated debate. Two members put forward the motion that 'this society disapproves of any legislation which would tend to separate Trinity College from the rest of Ireland, believing such legislation opposed to the best interest of their University and of this Society.' The members in question—Charles Wyse Power and E.M. Stephens—were, as already noted, nationalists, and members of the Gaelic Society. The motion was ruled out of order by the society's Pro-Auditor, and his ruling was in turn challenged. Meetings of the society descended into acrimony, which was exacerbated when details of their proceedings were leaked to the press.[39]

The pages of *T.C.D.: a College Miscellany*, became politicised. The newspaper traditionally claimed interest only in the 'literary, social and athletic' side of college life and was expressly non-political. The amendment debate was so contentious and important, however, that the newspaper felt it had no choice but to comment upon it, but it was clearly uncomfortable in so doing. (Commentary upon political events and their relation to college would become a frequent element of *T.C.D.*'s life over the coming decade.) Essentially backed into a corner on the matter, the editors decided to publish one article in favour of the amendment and one against. Both were written anonymously.

The anti-amendment article claimed that support for the amendment was based upon an assumption that nationalists hated Trinity. There was no evidence for this, the author claimed. Furthermore, he argued that Trinity was an Irish institution:

> There are those who ask what injury can it do to Ireland
> or to Trinity College if the College asks to stand in with
> England instead of with Ireland. I am an Irishman, and I
> can hardly understand the state of mind of him who puts
> the question. Why should a man stand in with his country?
> It is enough for most of us to answer that it is his country.[40]

Ireland's main problems, to the author, were based on misunderstanding between different communities. In this context, Trinity, as a space where students of different political, social and religious backgrounds met, could be a centre for conciliation and understanding. Removing the college from the remit of the new Irish parliament would remove this potential. The article argued that while mutual suspicion informed how unionists and nationalists viewed one another, those who shared a common alma mater learned to respect each other, aye, and to love each other, in spite of all their differences of creed and politics; these men carry into every rank of life and every sphere of activity a degree of mutual respect, of mutual toleration, and of mutual good will, the value of which it is beyond our power to estimate.

The following week, *T.C.D.* published the counter-point to this piece. The author, a 'well known Junior Fellow', made much the same argument as the previous correspondent, but in favour of the amendment. To him, Trinity's exemption from the purview of the Irish parliament would guarantee it freedom to persist in its historic role as a space where those from different backgrounds could meet and engage in friendly debate:

I want the university to be outside and beyond politics; ...I want it to be open to all, a place where all may meet and learn, as they now do, freedom of thought and respect for the views and opinions of others; ...I want learning and the search for knowledge alone to be there the desire of all and distractions like the present un-thought-of abomination.[41]

Having tested the waters of political debate, *T.C.D.* did not comment further upon the crisis. The views it printed were significant, however, as they revealed the nuances of student opinion about the amendment, and, by association, how parties in Trinity formed opinions about Home Rule, the union and the university. The majority of the Trinity community were proud of their role in Irish society historically and eager for this to continue, irrespective of whether they were nationalist or unionist. However, they differed in how this should best be achieved, and the Campbell amendment clearly demonstrated this.

After the amendment

Just after the immediate crisis of the Campbell amendment had passed, a spoof article appeared in *T.C.D.*, which imagined an attack on the college by a German military force. In this colourful but worrying account, 20,000 German soldiers easily fought off the 'motley horde' garrisoning the college. This throwaway account reflected two parallel anxieties: the

'Michaelmas Term', drawing from *T.C.D.: a College Miscellany*, 11 December 1912, p.191.

18, Woburn Buildings,

Upper Woburn Place,

W.C.

May 14

Dear Professor Mahaffy,

I see from the papers that there is a proposal to found a chair of Poetry, in T C D. Should this be done I would gladly be a candidate. On the other hand if the Board decide against this but for a chair of literature I would be greatly obliged if I could be told the conditions as I would like to look into the matter before deciding, to offer myself for such a chair.

Yours

WB Yeats

rise of international tensions and the threat of war, and the political isolation of Trinity and fear that it could be targeted by nationalists in the future. Both would become realities—in rather different forms—in the years that followed. Nevertheless, the article demonstrated that both the domestic and international moods were becoming increasingly tense. In 1913, anxieties born of political polarisation grew; some members of the college community reacted by joining the Ulster Volunteers when they were founded in January, others, with nationalist leanings, joined the Irish Volunteers when they were founded later in the year, while still others were politicised by the rise of the labour movement and the lockout of autumn and winter 1913.

Nineteen-thirteen saw Trinity flirt with nationalist Ireland, as if to show its credentials after the amendment controversy. Edward Dowden, the professor of English Literature and Erasmus Smiths' Professor of Oratory, died in April. Dowden was an internationally respected scholar and had occupied that chair for 45 years. He was an outspoken unionist, a former president of the Irish Unionist Alliance and a friend and ally of Sir Edward Carson.[42] Academically, Dowden, a specialist in sixteenth-century English literature, was a cosmopolitan who dismissed the Irish literary revival as parochial.[43] He had been involved in a number of public spats with William Butler Yeats on this topic over the fifteen years prior to his death.[44]

In 1910 Dowden had suffered a nervous breakdown and consequently was afflicted with intense insomnia.[45] He ceased teaching as his health deteriorated. His temporary replacement was Olive Purser, the first female student to attain a scholarship at Trinity, and later the college's Lady Registrar.[46] Meanwhile, Trinity began considering who might succeed Dowden to the chair of English literature. The classicist Robert Tyrrell and Mahaffy began cultivating Yeats for the position, with the bulk of the senior fellows supportive. For his part, the nationalist Yeats had softened in his attitude towards Trinity. Dowden's sudden resurgence later in 1910 postponed Yeats' potential accession to one of the university's most esteemed positions; however, in April 1913, the possibility arose again.[47]

At this point, an unusual third party intervened to suggest that Trinity appoint Yeats to the position. On 28 April the *Irish Times*, the mouthpiece of conservative southern unionism, offered 'a suggestion to TCD'. The chair of English literature had such a great reputation that it required a great scholar to fill it, and there was no better choice than Yeats. Such an appointment would 'bring kudos alike to the man and the institution'.

Opposite: Letter from W.B. Yeats to John Pentland Mahaffy, 14 May 1913, expressing an interest in the Chair of Poetry being proposed at Trinity.

Aside from Yeats's eminence, his nationalism would be a boon to the university. While noting that there was already a distinct diversity of political opinion in the institution, the *Irish Times* declared that 'if Mr Yeats is a nationalist, Trinity College is a University'.[48] As Ireland was inching towards self-government, Yeats' appointment would be an important show of goodwill on the part of the college. The following day, a Trinity graduate wrote to the paper in support of this initiative, arguing that 'Trinity College has now an opportunity of showing itself an institution intellectually liberal and broad-minded'.[49] The potential public relations benefits of Yeats's appointment were significant.

Yeats was not the only nationalist to put his name forward. Thomas MacDonagh, a young poet and lecturer at UCD, also applied. He had recently published his masters thesis on the seventeenth-century poet, Thomas Campion. MacDonagh had yet to move to the belief in physical force nationalism which would make him famous in 1916; he was, however, at this time a committed cultural nationalist.[50] His application was accompanied by six diverse testimonials. They were from Coffey, the president of UCD; Robert Donovan, the professor of English at UCD; Douglas Hyde; W.B. Yeats himself; Patrick Pearse; and Stephen Gwynn, nationalist MP and one of the famous Gwynn siblings.[51] There is no record of what the board made of this panoply of cultural and political nationalists supporting the application; in any event, MacDonagh did not get the job.

And neither did Yeats. While senior college figures mooted the possibility of creating a chair of poetry especially for Yeats, with minimal teaching responsibilities, the board ultimately opted to appoint Wilbraham Fitzjohn Trench, a well-connected Trinity graduate who had been lecturing at Galway, to the chair of literature. Trench was on good terms with both Dowden and Traill, which surely helped his candidacy, and he was seen as a safe and conservative appointment. Yeats did not hold him in high esteem.[52] It was perhaps unsurprising that the board opted for the safe candidate, but it was also indicative of the changing political environment—both inside and outside the walls—that Yeats was given what appeared to be serious consideration.

In terms of national politics, the remainder of 1913 was a quiet year at Trinity, save for one remarkable publication. In October, with politics rapidly polarising and physical force being invoked by nationalists and unionists alike, a young fellow called Joseph Johnston published a book called *Civil war in Ulster*.[53] Johnston was a precocious scholar from a Presbyterian background in Tyrone. He took his degree at Trinity in 1910; took a second degree at Oxford in 1912; and successfully sat for the fellowship exam at Trinity in 1913. By then he was still only 23 years old.[54]

Johnston was an all-Ireland Home Ruler, who saw the country's interests being best served through self-governance within the empire. His book was written to oppose the idea that 'if the project of granting Home Rule to Ireland is persisted in, the result will be Civil War in Ulster'. In short, Johnston reasoned that armed resistance to Home Rule in Ulster would 'do more harm to herself than the Home Rule Bill could possibly do'.[55] What is perhaps most remarkable about Johnston's book was that his primary intellectual influences were liberals at Trinity and Oxford; he was not especially well connected to the world of nationalist politics in Dublin, for example, and had little interest in the cultural manifestations of Irish nationalism.[56] His outlook was rooted in economic and political pragmatism. Nevertheless, that an Ulster-born fellow of Trinity would so strongly oppose Ulster's armed resistance to Home Rule surprised many. Johnston's publication caused 'quite a stir', according to his contemporary and fellow Tyrone nationalist, Kevin O'Shiel. The expression of such a contrary political stance could have grave consequences for one's professional standing and required great conviction. Indeed, Johnston suffered; many northern Protestant schools, to which he would ordinarily have turned in his capacity as college tutor, shunned him. Consequently, he was deprived of the accompanying tutorial fees he might have earned.[57]

The Lockout

Nineteen-thirteen was not only remarkable for the simmering tensions over Home Rule and the drift towards armed confrontation; it was also a year of social upheaval and labour turbulence in Dublin. The events of 1913 occurred during an odd lull in the history of Trinity. The high political events of 1912 and 1914—which seem to lead one to the other—tend to dominate narratives of the college's history of the period, as well as political histories of the period more generally. The Ulster Covenant, the formation of the Volunteers, and the Home Rule crisis were all events within which Trinity had a significant part; the drift from here to the First World War seems an obvious narrative, but it is one that leaves numerous gaps.[58]

Superficially, there would seem be no Trinity connection to the labour unrest of 1913; the college was, after all, somewhat insulated from the wider social problems of the city of Dublin. Moreover, it was a transitional space, where students took their professional qualifications in law, medicine, engineering, or for the Indian Civil Service, before moving on to take up a job elsewhere, often within the wide reach of the empire. The student body did not always have a close connection to its environs. Trinity was not, however, cut off from the outside world, and the events of late 1913 and reaction to them again highlight the multiplicity of interests and opinions that existed within the college community.

The labour agitation of 1913 posed acute questions regarding working conditions within the university, especially for the porters, labourers, printing house employees and others employed by the college in a support role. In October 1913 a representative of the college's porters presented a petition to the provost, seeking better remuneration. Traill, who was politically conservative but socially progressive, instituted an inquiry into the working conditions and living arrangements of non-academic staff. He instructed the chief steward to interview all of the porters, not only to ascertain their salaries, but also in order to know more of their general situation: what sort of accommodation they inhabited and where; how many children they had; how many days holidays they were entitled to; and so on.[59]

The results of this inquiry make for fascinating reading and show another side to college life. Porters varied from 32 to 62 years of age. Of the twelve surveyed in 1913, ten were Anglican with one each Presbyterian and Catholic. A number of these men had difficult existences. George Marsh, a 32-year-old ground porter, was recorded as having '3 children alive [and] 5 buried since being in College'.[60] Richard Halpin, aged 46, was married with five children, who between them had '[one] bedroom use of sitting room [and] use of kitchen'.[61] Another porter, John Sheppard, 51, supported the orphans of his late brother and had opened a newspaper shop 'to try and make ends meet'.[62] The lives of these men were far removed from the ostentatious ceremonials and lavish dinners enjoyed by the senior fellows.

There are two points of comparison for living standards of the non-academic staff in Trinity. Their salaries were a fraction of those of the academic staff. Porters' salaries averaged just over £64. A survey of April 1914 revealed that teaching staff were paid considerably more. At the top end, the senior fellows made between £1,734 (the provost) to £1,189, averaging £1,436, or 22 times the average salary of the porters.[63] Junior fellows and professors made between £100 and £1,000, although most were closer to the latter figure. Senior staff members (senior fellows, professors and longer established junior fellows) generally lived in Dublin's salubrious suburbs of Rathgar, Rathmines, Howth, Clontarf and Sutton and had two to three domestic servants to help run their households.

While within Trinity there was a great disparity in the relative salaries received by academic and non-academic staffs, the case of the porters looks much better when compared to that of their fellow unskilled workers elsewhere in the city. The historian Mary E. Daly has put the salary scale for porters working elsewhere in Dublin in 1905 at between £46 and £52.[64] The 1913 figure for the Trinity porters, which varied from £60 to £80, compares favourably. Trinity's non-academic staff were not slum-dwellers either. They lived in areas such as Drumcondra, Harold's Cross, the Quays, Ringsend and Inchicore, generally with Protestant skilled labourers and professionals for neighbours.[65] The non-teaching staff at Trinity were relatively well looked after, and their claims were taken seriously, on this and other occasions.

Labour trouble began in Dublin in late August 1913 when tram drivers who were members of the Irish Transport and General Workers Union (ITGWU) went on strike. The employers at the Dublin United Transport Company locked out these workers; Jim Larkin, the founder of the ITGWU, called over 20,000 union members out on strike; they in turn were locked out, and the city ground to a halt. While disruption to life outside of the walls did not pose an immediate problem to Trinity staff, many were deeply concerned for the plight of Dublin's underprivileged. This was most pronounced amongst those in holy orders, for whom charity was an important part of their vocation, and their activities during the lockout continued a recent missionary tradition.

The decades following the disestablishment of the Church of Ireland in 1869 witnessed the 'high tide of missionary interest' amongst Irish Protestants, and Trinity, either institutionally or through its graduates in divinities, played a leading role.[66] The university had a number of charitable missions, in Chota Nagpur in India (1891), Fukien in China (1885) and Belfast (1912).[67] The Belfast mission, led by A.W. Barton, was established specifically to address the social problems that had become increasingly prevalent in modern cities, and the college was proud of the role its missions were playing.[68] The missions had an altruistic and a religious function: they sought both to provide practical assistance and to minister to deprived communities. Trinity clergymen were also involved in Church of Ireland missions that focused on schools in deprived parts of Dublin. The Catholic Church in Dublin was hostile towards this initiative, seeing it as a battle for influence, or a 'fight for souls'. Archbishop William Walsh kept detailed files on individual schools and families who had fallen under the influence of the Anglican proselytisers, often trying to 'win' them back. In the colourful words of one report:

> the wily manner in which the proselytisers dangle their wretched bait before the eyes of poor slum-dwellers makes it almost impossible for the necessitous poor to remain in ignorance of the fact that candidates for apostasy need never starve.[69]

The Trinity figures involved in this initiative were R.M. Gwynn, who was the college chaplain, and John Henry Bernard. Both involved themselves with the Fishamble Street mission. R.M. Gwynn—the son of Professor John Gwynn and brother of Edward and Stephen—was deeply concerned for the plight of locked-out workers during the labour unrest of late 1913; this can be seen as an extension of his missionary work. Professing to take no sides, he claimed in a letter to the *Irish Times* that 'a fight to the finish in the present trade war would be disastrous to all the inhabitants of Dublin, and to our common Christianity'. Gwynn also publicised an appeal, organised by Tom Kettle's Industrial Peace Committee, which called for an end to the conflict; a manifesto was left at the Mansion House for interested parties to sign.[70] A few weeks later, Gwynn argued in another letter to the *Irish Times* that the employers had a vested interest in eradicating the slums, as this would lead to their employees becoming more productive. He also called for the establishment of an inquiry into the conditions of slum dwellers, with the hope of improving their situation.[71] On 13 November he again wrote to the *Irish Times* to condemn the attitude of the employers, earning himself a stern rebuke from the newspaper's editors in the process.[72]

Gwynn's role in the Peace Committee had consequences that stretched far beyond the immediate context. Other members of the Peace Committee included the writers George Russell (*AE*) and Padraic Colum, and Captain J.R. White, an eccentric Antrim-born veteran of the Boer War, Home Ruler and trade union sympathiser. White was elected chair of this body and the innocuous sounding Dublin Civic League came into being. A meeting of the League took place in Gwynn's rooms in Trinity in November 1913; this resulted in the passing of a resolution calling for the workers to adopt greater military discipline: the Irish Citizen Army was born.[73] Gwynn later recalled that 'the title Army was then not intended to suggest military action, but merely drill on military lines to keep unemployed men fit and self-respecting'.[74] In the early 1920s, with Ireland a changed place, the nationalist journalist Darrell Figgis wrote that

> it is strange to remember now (though there seems to have been almost a conspiracy to forget it) that the actual decision to enrol this army was taken in a fellow's chambers in Trinity College, unlikeliest of all places for the quaintest of all ironies.[75]

Few would remember this in 1916.

Gwynn was not the only fellow of the college to play a prominent role during the lockout. In late September 1913 Culverwell started a fund to provide meals for women and children who were suffering because of the lockout. He was quick to assert his non-partisanship; he was not 'taking sides with the Transport Union, and against the employers'. He asserted that in the ongoing dispute, women and children should be viewed as non-combatants.[76] This suggestion was soon formally embodied in the Relief Fund for Women and Children, to which Culverwell was one of the largest donors.[77] Unlike Gwynn, Culverwell was not a clergyman. He was a social progressive with strong moral convictions. He had much in common with Tom Kettle, the UCD professor of economics who was the chairman of the Industrial Peace Committee. Both were moderate reformers in national, electoral and social politics. Culverwell felt that he could mediate between the workers and the employers to resolve the impasse. In October 1913 he challenged William Martin Murphy, obstinate leader of the employers, to fund a scheme 'directed towards those wider interests in which the citizens generally, as well as the employers and employees, are concerned', promising to pledge £1,000 over five years to the scheme if Murphy backed it.[78]

Culverwell's educational interests also informed his political interventions. He was, after all, the college's first professor of education and a strong advocate of the Montessori method, which, although limited to children under the age of seven, he felt would have an important impact upon university education and national life generally. His views on university education, which he saw as too far removed from the realities of everyday life, may have added to his unpopularity amongst the Trinity governing elites.[79] In the context of the lockout, he made the claim that the incomprehension between employers and employees was proof that the education system was 'lamentably in fault'.[80]

In addition to Culverwell and Gwynn, there were other Trinity figures who sought an end to the lockout crisis. Professors Mahaffy and Bastable, the professor of Political Economy, were enlisted in a symbolic capacity to lend weight to the activities of the Citizens' Peace Committee, another body with wide membership set up to facilitate an end to the conflict.[81] Bastable had eminence due to his position as a well-known economist, whilst Mahaffy's name carried more influence than any other Trinity figure. Otherwise, the college hierarchy was quiet, and one can assume, generally ambivalent—at best—towards what was happening elsewhere in the city in late 1913.

Students too were inspired by events taking place around Dublin. In his memoir, Walter Starkie recalled a number of his student friends being

NOTICE TO STUDENTS.

Any Resident Student who attends Captain White's Home Rule Meeting this evening will be deprived of his rooms.

ANTHONY TRAILL,

Provost.

19th November, 1913.

Notice warning resident students planning to attend a meeting organised by Captain J.R. White on 19 November 1913, to call for an enquiry into the behaviour of the police during the arrest of Jim Larkin, that they would lose their rooms in college.

arrested for participating in scuffles on Sackville Street, where they were baton charged by the police. The Chief Steward, a former member of the Dublin Metropolitan Police, had to negotiate their release from Store Street police station, a task he was accustomed to performing when the annual college rags got out of hand.[82]

Unsurprisingly, it was the college Gaelic Society that became the hub for lockout-related agitation. The society was founded by students primarily as a Trinity outpost for the Gaelic Revival, and as such it stood out in comparison to its more conservative fellow societies. It tended to attract radicals of all persuasions, be they advanced nationalists or those sympathetic to the cause of labour. On 18 November 1913, the previously mentioned Captain J.R. White was invited to attend the opening meeting of the society, along with the lawyer Henry Hanna and nationalist journalist Arthur Griffith. Protocol dictated that White should propose the motion that the society was worthy of the support of the students of the university. This he did, but he followed with an impromptu speech, calling for an inquiry into the behaviour of the police during the recent arrest of Jim Larkin, and calling on students to support this 'even if … they had to tell their professors that they must close the College'.[83] White called on the students of the college to attend a meeting the following night to develop this idea, and it proved popular. Provost Traill, not being one for political radicalism, intervened, but only made the situation worse. Fearing that White's invitation to subversion would resonate with the student body, Traill forbade students from attending the meeting, issuing the warning that 'any resident student who attends Captain White's Home Rule Meeting this evening will be deprived of his rooms'.[84] Traill conflated labour agitation with Home Rule agitation; to his mind, all political subversion was nationalist in origin.

The provost's threat served as an incentive for Trinity students, whether they had any deep political motivations or not. When the follow-up meeting was held the next evening in the Antient Concert Rooms, between 80 and 100 Trinity students attended, mockingly singing 'Oh, Oh, Antonio' of the provost as they made their way down Great Brunswick Street (now Pearse Street) to the event.[85] The students presented a note to the chair of the gathering, the nationalist politician Pierce O'Mahony, 'condemning the unwarrantable attempt to prevent us attending this meeting made by the authorities of the College'. White, James Connolly and R.M. Gwynn spoke at the event, and the latter surely upset some on the college board in so doing. The Trinity students present were only rebellious to a point, however; a representative of theirs called Armstrong announced that they could not stay late, as those resident in college rooms had to return to Trinity for 9pm roll call. He nevertheless assured all present that 'the majority of the students in Trinity were entirely on the side of the workers'.[86] McDowell and Webb note caustically that once the students had let off steam in this way, 'they returned contentedly to bourgeois life in College'.[87] The irony of the students' desire to agitate the provost but not miss roll call is clear; these students were not radical revolutionaries.

Labour unrest was a conduit through which the students could express a more general dissatisfaction with the college board. Traill's overzealous prohibition of student participation at White's meeting showed how fearful he was of its potential to radicalise the student body, as well as his misunderstanding of what was at stake. The incident brought the Gaelic Society to the forefront of college life for the first time; its meetings were given extensive press coverage and the board began trying to control its activities. The result was that a year later, when a similar situation unfolded, the society would, in the eyes of the board, get no second chance.

The real lesson of the lockout was that the college was not an island and it was not insulated from unrest taking place outside its gates. Traill's response to White's call for Trinity's students to support an enquiry into the actions of the police in arresting Jim Larkin showed just how vulnerable the board felt at that moment, and how disconnected it was from the realities of the labour unrest sweeping the city. Any agitation or subversion was only intelligible to the provost in terms of the larger national question. Within less than a year, Ireland had three private armies, the Ulster Volunteers, the Irish Volunteers and the Citizen Army; and Trinity—wittingly or otherwise—had played a role in the development of each.

Towards war

The historian Paul Bew has written that 'all the key events of 1914 seemed to presage further confrontation'.[88] There was a drift towards conflict, and contemporaries were acutely aware of this. It was a time of much anxiety. In February 1914, Culverwell wrote that 'the future seems so pregnant with danger whatever course is adopted'.[89] The membership of the Ulster and Irish Volunteers alike expanded greatly and the potential for armed conflict was underscored by gun-running on both sides; through Larne for the Ulster Volunteers in April, and at Howth and Kilcoole in July for the Irish Volunteers. In between these events, the Buckingham Palace conference tried—and failed—to resolve the issue of Ulster's inclusion in the new Home Rule legislation. In the battle of old Trinity men, Carson was forcing the issue and undermining the credibility of Redmond, who found himself discussing the potential temporary exclusion of Ulster from the provisions of the Home Rule bill, while the Howth gun-running suggested that he was losing authority amongst nationalists.[90]

The events of late 1912 had demonstrated that the university's parliamentary representatives did not embody the desires of the student and staff populations on the issue of Home Rule beyond the board. In the spring of 1914, a group of junior fellows began planning collective action in the name of moderation. They desired to give a voice to conciliatory opinion, to show that 'Carson does not represent us all'.[91] The two main organisers came from different sides of the political divide. They were Joseph Johnston and Wilbraham Trench. They began organising professors and fellows of the college to see if the Government of Ireland bill, to give the Home Rule bill its official title, could be modified and improved in such a way as to mollify all parties and avoid conflict. They planned to call a conference on the matter and gained the support of the former under-secretary for Ireland, Baron MacDonnell of Swinford (formerly Sir Antony MacDonnell), and the Dominion Home Ruler, Sir Horace Plunkett, for their plans. All of this was decided in secret meetings, as Trench and Johnston were aware that the Trinity board would have viewed their actions in a negative light. Johnston wrote that the exclusion of Ulster from Home Rule legislation would perpetuate 'the worst evils from which this country suffers'.[92] Their plan, circulated privately in April 1914, called for the establishment of a bicameral parliament sitting in Dublin, with meetings in Belfast every three years; a degree of autonomy reserved for Ulster on certain issues; and a strong senate comprised of appointed and elected members.[93] The archival trail runs cold here, although it seems that the proposed conference never took place. Realistically, these modest proposals were not likely to placate more extreme factions who were arming at that very moment.

Armed conflict became a frequent topic of debate at Trinity. Among the motions debated by the Historical Society were 'that this society would welcome a holiday in Armaments' (not carried), and 'that this house approves of compulsory military service' (decided in the affirmative).[94] Speakers in the latter debate showed how omnipresent the idea of armed conflict now was in everyday thinking, and how the events of the previous two years had conditioned thought. They discussed the viability of a large invading force—presumably German—conquering Ireland and the best measures to guard against it. One speaker, probably influenced by the events of 1913, predicted that the next great war would be a social one, whilst another confidently asserted that war was economically unsound and thus impossible.[95]

While the college's budding orators debated the rights, wrongs and forms of conflict, others made more practical provision for a militarised future. The Officers Training Corps, led by Robert Tate, flourished, and accounts of its activities took up regular space in *T.C.D.* Others took an even more active role in shaping the future by participating in gun-running activities. Perhaps surprisingly, the most prominent of these were on the nationalist side. Sir Thomas Myles, a Trinity-trained surgeon and nationalist, made his yacht the *Chotah* available to Erskine Childers when planning the gun-running of July 1914, with a quantity of guns eventually being landed at Kilcoole on 1 August.[96] James Creed Meredith, who took a philosophy degree at Trinity in 1898, was part of Myles's crew. Conor O'Brien, a fellow Trinity graduate and Irish language enthusiast, also landed guns at Kilcoole that day in his yacht the *Kelpie*.[97] O'Brien, in turn, enlisted the help of Diarmid Coffey, formerly a leading light in the Gaelic Society who had since joined the Volunteers.[98]

In his inaugural address as president of the University Philosophical Society in November 1914, Bolton Waller argued that 'Trinity College has seen a great change in recent years. There was never less ground for the taunt of being an anti-Irish institution.'[99] Trinity had, with the defeat of the Campbell amendment in late 1912, managed to surmount what seemed the trickiest hurdle, and hoped that it had earned the goodwill of the ascendant nationalist body of opinion. When the amendment was defeated, Culverwell wrote to John Dillon that 'when it comes to a plain issue, Trinity College will stand in with Ireland'.[100] Such a 'plain issue' as Culverwell envisaged never came to pass, however, as subsequent events would demonstrate. By the time Waller addressed the Philosophical Society, the immediate concerns had been superseded by the outbreak of a general European war in August 1914, in which over 200,000 Irishmen would fight and more than 30,000 would die. Thus, the generally held anxiety pervading Trinity during the early summer of 1914 was replaced with a new one. The war changed everything; it further muddied an already complex picture.

NOTES:

[1] 'Medical School, Trinity College', *Irish Times*, 15 June 1912, 7.

[2] 'Trinity College Medical School', *Irish Times*, 13 July 1912, 5.

[3] Letter of A.F. Dixon, *T.C.D: a College Miscellany*, 3 July 1912, 135.

[4] Alvin Jackson, *Home Rule and Irish history 1800–2000* (London, 2003), 123.

[5] F.S.L. Lyons, *Ireland since the famine* (London, 1973), 287.

[6] Paul Bew, *Ireland: the politics of enmity, 1789–2006* (Oxford, 2007), 370.

[7] There were 239 in total listed in the *Dublin University Calendar, pt. II 1912–23*, but full entries for 25 of these students do not appear in the Entrance Books (TCD, MUN V/26/9). All of the statistical analysis that follows is derived from the latter source.

[8] H. Montgomery Hyde, *Carson: the life of Sir Edward Carson, Lord Carson of Duncairn* (London, 1987; originally published 1953), xiii.

[9] Montgomery Hyde, *Carson*, 11–15; John Hostettler, *Sir Edward Carson: a dream too far* (Chichester, 2000), 13–15; Alvin Jackson, 'Carson, Edward Henry Baron Carson of Duncairn', in James McGuire and James Quinn (eds), *Dictionary of Irish Biography* (Cambridge, United Kingdom, 2010); hereafter cited as *DIB*.

[10] James McConnel, 'John Redmond and Irish Catholic loyalism', *English Historical Review*, cxxv (2010), 83–111: 96.

[11] Hotstettler, *Sir Edward Carson*, 165, 174–80.

[12] Edward Carson, 'Introduction', in S. Rosenbaum (ed.), *Against Home Rule: the case for the Union* (London, 1912), 17–38: 17.

[13] Representative Church Body Library (RCBL), MS 38/3/9. Bernard to Lawlor, 10 October 1912.

[14] J.P. Mahaffy, 'Will Home Rule be Rome Rule?', *Blackwood's Magazine*, cxcii (August, 1912), 156–9.

[15] Public Records Office of Northern Ireland (PRONI), D1507/A/3/15. Traill to Carson, 15 May 1912.

[16] 'Education under Home Rule', *The Times*, 28 May 1912, 7.

[17] Dermot Meleady, *John Redmond: the national leader* (Dublin, 2014), 222–3.

[18] 'Trinity College and Home Rule', *The Times*, 23 October 1912, 8.

[19] TCD, MUN, V/5/20, Meeting of 26 October 1912, 264.

[20] 'Trinity College and Home Rule', *The Times*, 24 October 1912, 12.

[21] D.G. Boyce, *Nationalism in Ireland* (London, 1995), 228–30, Lyons, *Culture and anarchy*, 57–61.

[22] 'Loyalists, act!', *Irish Times*, 3 March 1893, 6.

[23] 'Dublin University and Home Rule', *The Times*, 28 October 1912, 8.

[24] The list in full was: Culverwell, E.J. Gwynn, R.M. Gwynn, E.H. Alton, S.B. Kelleher, G.R. Webb, R. Russell and John Fraser.

[25] National Library of Ireland (NLI), MS15254, Culverwell to Redmond, 26 October 1912.

[26] 'Student's protest', *Freeman's Journal*, 28 October 1912, 4.

[27] Dublin Diocesan Archives (DDA), Walsh papers, laity correspondence (WPLC), 377/1, Culverwell to Walsh, 12 November 1912.

[28] NLI, MS15254, Culverwell to Redmond, 28 October 1912.

[29] NLI, MS15254, Culverwell to Redmond, 28 October 1912.

[30] TCD, MS 6830/10, Culverwell to Dillon, 2 November 1912.

[31] 'The Trinity College Amendment', *Irish Times*, 11 November 1912, 7.

[32] 'The University: its functions to the nation', *Freeman's Journal*, 8 November 1912, 6.

[33] NLI, MS15254, Copy of resolution of Fellows and Professors, 11 November 1912.

[34] TCD, MS 6830/11, Culverwell to Dillon, 11 November 1912.

[35] 'The exclusion of Trinity College and Belfast University', *Freeman's Journal*, 23 October 1912, 10.

[36] 'Dublin University and Home Rule', *The Times*, 12 November 1912, 12.

[37] TCD, MS 6830/11, Culverwell to Dillon, 11 November 1912.

[38] 'Trinity Men: College and Home Rule', *Irish Independent*, 25 October 1912, 6.

[39] T.S.C. Dagg, *College Historical Society, a history (1770–1920)* (Cork, 1969), 348.

[40] 'Against the amendment', *T.C.D.*, 20 November 1912, 161.

[41] 'For the amendment', *T.C.D.*, 27 November 1912, 172.

[42] TCD, MS 3154/1178, R.G. Carden to Dowden, 21 January 1911.

[43] Linde Lunney and Pauric J. Dempsey, 'Dowden, Edward Travers-Smith', in *DIB*; Norman Vance, *Irish Literature: a social history. Tradition, identity, and difference* (Oxford, 1990), 167–9.

[44] Terence Brown, *The life of W.B. Yeats* (Oxford, 1999), 89–90; R.F. Foster, *W.B. Yeats, a Life*.vol. I, *The apprentice mage, 1865–1914* (Oxford, 1998), 145–6.

[45] TCD, MS 3154/1173, Dowden to Rudmose-Brown, 21 January 1910.

[46] Susan M. Parkes, 'The 'Steamboat Ladies', the First World War and after', in Parkes (ed.), *A danger to the men*, 87–112: 105–7.

[47] Foster, *W.B. Yeats*, vol. 1, 429–31.

[48] 'A suggestion to T.C.D.', *Irish Times*, 28 April 1913, 4.

[49] 'A suggestion to T.C.D.', *Irish Times*, 29 April 1913, 9.

[50] Johann A. Norstedt, *Thomas MacDonagh: a critical biography* (Charlottesville, 1980), 120–1.

[51] NLI, MS10855.

[52] Foster, *W.B. Yeats*, vol. I, 484.

[53] Johnston, *Civil war in Ulster: its objects and probable results* (Dublin, 1913).

[54] Roy H.W. Johnston, *Century of endeavour: a biographical and autobiographical view of the twentieth century in Ireland* (Dublin, 2006), 11–25.

[55] Johnston, *Civil War in Ulster*, 1–5.

[56] Johnston, 'Introduction', *Civil war in Ulster*, xi–xxiv: xiii.

[57] Bureau of Military History (BMH), Witness Statement (WS) 1170, Section 2, 175, Kevin O'Shiel.

[58] McDowell and Webb, *Trinity College Dublin*, 418–9.

[59] TCD, MS 2388/70, Petition of porters to the provost, 23 October 1913.

[60] TCD, MS 2388/77.

[61] TCD, MS 2388/74.

[62] TCD, MS 2388/71.

[63] TCD, MS 2388/90.

[64] Mary E. Daly, *Dublin: the deposed capital, a social and economic history 1860–1914* (Cork, 1984), 69; Pádraig Yeates, *Lockout: Dublin 1913* (Dublin, 2000), xxi–xxii.

[65] TCD, MS 2388 and the 1911 Census (the data from the 1911 Census can be accessed online at: http://www.census.nationalarchives.ie/search/ (9 March 2015)).

[66] Alan Acheson, *A history of the Church of Ireland 1691–2001* (Dublin, 2002), 221–3.

[67] R.M. Gwynn, E.M. Norton, B.W. Simpson, *T.C.D. in China: a history of the Dublin University Fukien Mission 1885–1935* (Dublin, 1936; 2nd edn 1986); RCBL, MS 196295.

[68] 'A T.C.D. mission in Belfast', *Church of Ireland Gazette*, 1 March 1912, 173.

[69] DDA, LC 1913, 337/3, 'Proselytising schools and institutions', 4 July 1913, 8.

[70] 'To the Editor of the Irish Times', *Irish Times*, 11 October 1913, 9.

[71] 'The labour crisis: an appeal', *Irish Times*, 31 October 1913, 8.

[72] 'The Peace Committee's report', *Irish Times*, 13 November 1913, 8.

[73] R.M. Fox, *The history of the Irish Citizen Army* (Dublin, 1944), 44; Captain J.R. White, *Misfit: an autobiography* (Dublin, 2005), 145–6; Donal Nevin, *James Connolly, 'a full life'* (Dublin, 2005), 468.

[74] Fox, *The history of the Irish Citizen Army*, 45.

[75] Darrell Figgis, *Recollections of the Irish war* (New York, 1927), 9.

[76] 'Providing meals', *Freeman's Journal*, 25 September 1913, 10.

[77] 'Women and Children Fund', *Freeman's Journal*, 26 September 1913, 8.

[78] 'The employers and employed', *Irish Times*, 10 October 1913, 5.

[79] E.P. Culverwell, *The Montessori principles and practice* (London, 1913), vii–xvii.

[80] 'The Peace Committee's report', *Irish Times*, 13 November 1913, 8.

[81] 'Citizens Peace Committee', *Irish Times*, 1 November 1913, 12.

[82] Starkie, *Scholars and gypsies*, 107.

[83] 'Dublin University Gaelic Society', *Irish Times*, 19 November 1913, 9.

[84] TCD, MS 3332/15.

[85] White, *Misfit*, 146–64, 'Dublin Civic League', *Irish Times*, 20 November 1913, 6.

[86] *Irish Times*, 20 November 1913, 6.

[87] McDowell and Webb, *Trinity College Dublin*, 419.

[88] Paul Bew, *Ireland: the politics of enmity* (Oxford, 2009), 370.

[89] TCD, MS 6830/15, Culverwell to Dillon, 1 February 1914.

[90] Jackson, *Home Rule*, 157–9.

[91] TCD, MS 9299/45, Trench to Johnston, 14 March 1914.

[92] TCD, MS 9929/59, Johnston to Trench, April 1914.

[93] TCD, MS 9299/59, Johnston to Trench, undated, ? April 1914.

[94] Dagg, *College Historical Society*, 350.

[95] 'College Historical Society', *T.C.D.*, 27 May 1914, 87–8.

[96] David Murphy, 'Myles, Sir Thomas', in *DIB*.

[97] Owen McGee, 'O'Brien, Edward Conor Marshal', in *DIB*.

[98] Diarmid Coffey, 'Guns for Kilcoole', in F.X. Martin (ed.), *The Howth gun-running and the Kilcoole gun-running 1914* (Dublin, 1964), 116–24.

[99] 'University Philosophical Society', *Irish Times*, 6 November 1914, 7.

[100] TCD, MS 6830/11, Culverwell to Dillon, 11 November 1912.

CHAPTER TWO

Trinity and the First World War

PAX IN BELLUM; or, UNITED KINGDOMERS.

JOHN—"My dear Edward, if you and I ever fight, it will be shoulder to shoulder against any outsider who ventures to attack these islands sacred to both of us."

EDWARD—"My dear old friend, there's my hand on it."

Introduction

> The undergraduate of today can hardly be expected to
> know and love Trinity in the same way as the under-
> graduate of pre-war days. The opportunities are lacking
> to him. University life in its broad sense is dead for the
> time being.[1]

The First World War was the greatest caesura in the life of Trinity College
Dublin. In its infancy, the college had been effectively closed during the
War of the Three Kingdoms in the mid-seventeenth century and again
during the Williamite Wars. The outbreak of war in 1914, however,
marked the first in a series of crises to strike the college; it was equally
deleterious to Trinity's administration, its constituent community and its
place in Ireland and the wider world. Three-thousand and seventy-nine
staff, students and alumni volunteered for service during the conflict. These
figures, tabulated in 1922 and published in the *War List*, are most likely
incomplete, but they record the war service of 869 undergraduates, 993

Opposite: 'Pax in Bellum: or, United Kingdomers', political cartoon published in the *The
Lepracaun* magazine, August 1914, p. 39, Edward Carson and John Redmond agreeing to
fight together against a common enemy.

STUDENT POPULATION, 1913–19

YEAR	MALE STUDENTS	FEMALE STUDENTS	TOTAL
1913–14	1,074	211	1,285
1914–15	844	198	1042
1915–16	611	186	797
1916–17	534	198	732
1917–18	535	186	721
1918–19	567	210	777

SOURCE: *DUBLIN UNIVERSITY CALENDAR*, PT II.

TOTAL MATRICULATIONS, 1913–18

YEAR	MATRICULATIONS
1913	287
1914	279
1915	218
1916	243
1917	228
1918	272

SOURCE: TCD, MUN/V/24/7-8.

NUMBER OF BA DEGREES AWARDED, 1913–19

YEAR	DEGREES AWARDED
1913–14	222
1914–15	192
1915–16	198
1916–17	127
1917–18	112
1918–19	106

SOURCE: TCD, MUN/V/24/7-8.

students and graduates who served on the medical side, 193 chaplains, 27 women and 37 non-academic staff.[2] Four-hundred and seventy-one of them died. The war service—and war losses—of Trinity College Dublin were similar to those of universities in Britain and elsewhere in the empire.[3] Universities tended to provide junior officers for the army who, as leaders of men in the field, were in turn at increased risk of death and casualty. The war was ruinous for educated elites across Britain and the wider world, and Trinity experienced this phenomenon acutely.[4]

The war impacted upon the university as a whole. There was a significant drop in the college's population in the war years; for those who remained the absences were a reminder of the on-going conflict. As might be expected from the diminution of the overall student population, there were consequent reductions in student matriculations and in the number of BA degrees awarded.

The war significantly reduced student numbers at Trinity, but the college was not empty. Trinity's experience was, in this respect, less severe than that of universities elsewhere. For example, the University of Cambridge saw its student population fall from 3,181 in 1914 to 408 by 1918; the fact that conscription was applied in Britain from 1916 undoubtedly had an impact on those numbers. In France, where conscription was applied throughout the war, the population of the Sorbonne fell from 20,000 to 4,000.[5] While the fall in student numbers at Trinity was less than at universities elsewhere, the issue of conscription muddies the comparison. Those who remained in college were not necessarily aware of how Trinity compared to institutions elsewhere in the world, and thus the relative absence of students still had a significant psychological impact.

While Trinity's war experience was similar to that of universities elsewhere in terms of enlistment and casualty rates, it was unique in another way. The First World War transformed universities and accelerated their development into the modern, research-driven and state-funded institutions that we know today. It inaugurated a modern type of warfare; it was a 'total war', in which national resources—economic, industrial and even cultural—were mobilised to ensure its successful prosecution. Universities, as repositories of expert knowledge, were important in this process. Across the world, academic departments and laboratories were harnessed by national governments, and scholars were set to work on specific war-related problems. The consequence was that, following the war, universities were integrated into the apparatus of the state as never before. Trinity, however, as a result of the radicalisation of the political situation in Ireland before and during the war, and because of the Anglo-Irish treaty of 1921, found itself alienated from the new state, rather than further integrated into the old one. Moreover, unlike its peers, Trinity found itself a heartbeat away from actual fighting during the rising of 1916; it was fighting a war abroad and at home.

The First World War was a tragedy for the island of Ireland; in recent decades, a wave of research has shown the depth of Irish involvement in the conflict.[6] Trinity College Dublin was deeply touched by the war in a multitude of ways that perhaps few other Irish institutions were. The war began Trinity's descent from an imperial institution to an impoverished and embattled remnant of the old regime.[7] More than the events of 1916 or 1922, it was 1914 that marked the end of an era for Old Trinity. The war touched every element of the college and had profound consequences for its financial, political and emotional well-being. Exploring Trinity's responses to the outbreak of war, its experiences of war, life on campus in wartime, and its intellectual mobilisation and the end of the war gives a sense of the multifaceted ways in which the war upended the normal life of the college.

The outbreak of war

The outbreak of a European war came as a surprise to most in August 1914, with its course and consequences anticipated by few. A Trinity undergraduate in 1914, Frank Laird recalled that 'no suspicion had crossed my mind that these were the last days of the old order of things'.[8] Another undergraduate, Walter Starkie, lamented years later that 'the College Park never looked more lovely than it did in the summer term of 1914'.[9] Assessing the disposition of the wider student body at the onset of the war is problematic; the conflict broke out during the summer vacation and the first wartime edition of *T.C.D.*, the student newspaper, appeared only in November 1914. Thus, accounts of the outbreak of war tend to be retrospective and coloured by the knowledge of what followed.

The academic year had yet to begin formally, but from its very outset the war nevertheless impacted upon Trinity's cosmopolitan community. Two fellows of the college, George Cathcart and Henry Macran, were away on holidays in Germany and were temporarily interned there.[10] Walter Alison Phillips, the Lecky Professor of History, was also on holidays in Germany and quickly had to make his way home. In a letter to the *The Times* published on 7 August he described the friendliness of the German people during his journey, remarking that 'we have to fight them, but let us do so in the spirit of gentlemen'.[11]

From the outset, the First World War was understood as a cultural conflict. Responsibility for the outbreak of war, as well as atrocities committed by the German army in Belgium in late August 1914 were rallying points for intellectuals to defend their nation and denigrate that of the 'enemy'. Rumours of German brutality in Belgium soon began filtering back to Britain and Ireland. The destruction of the university library of Louvain, which took place between 25 and 28 August 1914, outraged learned communities across the world. As this was a site of cultural, rather than military value, it seemed that Germany was waging war on culture itself.[12] German scholars, previously the envy of the learned world, issued bombastic denials of atrocities such as this and truculent defences of their country's policy.

The response to incidents such as the destruction at Louvain demonstrated once more where Trinity saw itself in the world. The events in Belgium were an outrage to all members of the Republic of Letters, and as had been colourfully demonstrated during the tercentenary celebrations of 1892, this was where Trinity College positioned itself. This was not an unusual response for intellectuals either in Ireland, Britain, mainland Europe or North America. In Dublin, a number of leading intellectuals, both nationalist and unionist, signed a manifesto protesting against the actions of the German army. Names appended to the appeal included Lord Aberdeen (the lord lieutenant), J.P. Mahaffy, J.G. Swift MacNeill (a Trinity alumnus and nationalist member of parliament), George Noble Plunkett (a Trinity graduate, nationalist and the director of the National Museum), and Sir William Thompson (a Trinity physiologist). They decried the events at Louvain as

> An injury to learning, science, and education, to history and art, to religion and citizenship, which is totally without precedent, and which no military exigencies or expediencies can extenuate, much less justify. We regard this act as the gravest injury to the whole fabric and life of European and general civilisation, since it destroys guarantees hitherto respected by combatants.[13]

Student publications too were preoccupied with German atrocities. In December 1914 a poem appeared in *T.C.D.* condemning the German army's actions in Belgium, dismissing Germany as 'the idol that's lost its place in the sun'.[14] This was a common criticism around the learned world; *The Times* famously dismissed the German system of higher education as a 'Fallen Idol'.[15] Trinity did not boast as many connections to the German academy as did Oxford and Cambridge, or even the National University, but there were some German-trained scholars at Trinity. Henry Dixon, Professor of Botany, took his PhD at Bonn, while the historian Walter Alison Phillips was raised in Weimar. Mahaffy, who, as we have seen, was no friend of understatement, liked to speak of his friendship with many European royals, of whom Kaiser Wilhelm II was the most eminent. He affected personal affront at the outbreak of war, remarking that 'the Kaiser is not the man I knew'.[16] This was symptomatic of a wider sense of rupture in the world of universities and was widely articulated by scholars and intellectuals across Britain, France, Italy, Russia, North America and beyond.

Trinity academics became part of the international debate about the crimes of Germany; this discourse simultaneously expressed shock at the course of events and reaffirmed a sense of kinship amongst the transnational community of scholars. Mahaffy wrote to *The Times* in early September, condemning the sack of Louvain. He criticised the German universities and their over-emphasis on intellect, which was to the detriment of religious and moral qualities. With a typical flourish, he dismissed the appeals of the kaiser to God as 'not only ridiculous but profane'.[17] In a public lecture at Trinity in November, Alison Phillips argued that the Germans had brought 'the respectable title of professor into contempt'.[18]

Engagement in this wider discourse took the form not only of public pronouncements, but also private expressions of solidarity. In December 1914 the college board wrote a letter to its counterpart at the Sorbonne in Paris. It expressed a qualified disappointment with German scholars, 'once well-known and respected amongst us', and argued that on account of their being in thrall to 'a mad tyrant', 'the German professors hardly belong to the Republic of Letters'. The letter exclaimed the hope that an allied victory would liberate 'our poor colleagues from the shameful chore of lies which they are forced to set themselves to for the upkeep of Prussian militarism'.[19] The letter, although not signed by an individual, was most likely the work of Mahaffy, and was carefully entered into the minute-book of the University of Paris—one ancient university and member of the Republic of Letters writing to another.

The outbreak of the war led to a reassessment of the high esteem in which German scholarship had been held in the period up to 1914. A flurry of manifestos, vitriolic articles and books followed, and scholars were often asked to lend their names to these. John Joly, the gifted Professor of Geology and Mineralogy, was Ireland's most eminent scientist

Opposite: 'Come into the ranks and fight…', World War I recruitment poster.

Come into the ranks and fight — Don't stay in the crowd and stare.

YOU ARE WANTED
ENLIST TO-DAY

ISSUED BY THE CENTRAL COUNCIL FOR THE ORGANISATION OF RECRUITING IN IRELAND.   LITHOGRAPHED BY ALEX. THOM & CO. LTD. DUBLIN.

at the period; a fellow of the Royal Society, his name carried weight throughout Europe and North America. As such, in the early months of the war he was solicited by colleagues in London who were working for Wellington House, the hub of the British propaganda effort, to lend his name to petitions rebuking German scholars.[20] Joly did so, and the manifesto, entitled 'Reply to German professors: reasoned statement by British scholars', appeared in *The Times* on 21 October. The petition also bore the name of J.E.H Murphy, the Professor of Irish at Trinity; presumably, it was deemed important to append his signature due to the high esteem in which German scholars working in Celtic Studies were held.[21]

More generally, a new and troubling question emerged: what role should a university play in wartime? This issue vexed universities in all belligerent nations, and most improvised their way into war. Trinity was no different. For example, a special commencements ceremony was held on 29 August 1914 for engineering and medical students who had volunteered for active service, allowing them to graduate earlier than was usual.[22] In Britain, letters pages of the newspapers were soon alive with talk of universities and their wartime obligations. Some suggested that universities should be closed altogether and all of their students forced to enlist in the armed forces, provoking a strong reaction in *The Times* from university and college heads.[23] They argued forcefully that, by supplying officers, men of greater moral and intellectual qualities than those in the rank-and-file, universities had an important wartime function.[24] Following strident letters from his counterparts at Oxford and Cambridge, Mahaffy, at the time the vice-provost but effectively running the college due to Traill's illness, wrote to *The Times* in late September to make much the same argument, noting the enthusiasm of Trinity men in enlisting in the armed forces, and adding that 'so far as we can speak for the loyalty of Ireland we are speaking with no uncertain sound'.[25] Mahaffy was appointed provost in November 1914 and would oversee the college's fortunes during the First World War (see Chapter Four).

West Front to Western Front—The military war

In addition to the 3,079 Trinity people who were recorded in the *War List* as having performed service in the First World War, an additional 450, who were not members of the college, received commissions in the army through the university's Officers Training Corps (OTC).[26] OTCs had been set up at schools and universities across Britain from 1907 as part of a programme of army reforms.[27] They were created to give students spe-cialised military training that could result in the attainment of qualifications allowing them to gain commissions quickly in the army, as junior officers. The OTCs quickly became popular for their own sakes. They were sociable, fostered a distinct group identity, and provided stu-dents with a distraction from purely academic matters.[28] Trinity's OTC was divided into four units: an engineer's unit, an infantry unit, a medical unit and an Army Service Corps (ASC) unit.[29]

The Dublin University OTC had been established in 1910 under the guidance of Francis Dixon, Professor of Anatomy.[30] Its commanding officer was Major Robert Tate, Professor of Italian and, from 1914, Public Orator of the university. The OTC established a parade ground on the east end of the College Park and drilled there daily. The OTC was influ-ential: in the years preceding the outbreak of war, it averaged around 400 members, or forty per cent of the male student population.[31] When war broke out, men flocked to the OTC, both from inside and outside of Trinity, recognising that it would provide them with a quick means of gaining a commission for the army. By May 1915 the number of members of the OTC totalled 370.[32] OTCs were also formed at Queen's University in Belfast and the Royal College of Surgeons in Dublin before the war. In 1915, the president of University College Dublin, Denis Coffey, submitted an official request to form an Officers Training Corps there, citing war-enthusiasm amongst his students and staff. The request was denied as no further OTCs were to be formed in wartime.[33]

Walter Starkie recalled that men enlisted in the armed forces in great numbers as early as 4 August. The decision for a civilian to become a soldier is a grave one, and one can imagine is only taken after careful con-sideration and much introspection.[34] Conscription was never enforced in Ireland and all men who enlisted in the armed forces in wartime did so voluntarily. That raises the complex question of why these men chose to enlist.[35] While there was no overwhelming single reason, a number of common threads emerge as having informed the decision of Trinity stu-dents, staff and alumni to go to war. While there were, as we shall see, factors specific to Trinity that impelled men to enlist, often their reasons were no different from those of other Irishmen who decided to fight in 1914, irrespective of class, creed or political views.

Trinity had a long connection to the British empire, through the Indian Civil Service, the Engineering School and the School of Physic (Medical School), and many in the university saw support for the war as a contin-uation of this strong association. Imperial affinity linked political ideologies, professional aspirations and the social identity of students.

This was a common theme in universities throughout the empire. At McGill University in Montreal, for example, home of a large Medical School with strong ties to empire, similar reasons were cited for war enthusiasm: it was an opportunity to demonstrate the accomplishment of these professional schools that traditionally looked to the empire to provide employment for many of their graduates.[36]

The Irish tie to empire had been reinforced by service in the South African War of 1889–1902, which 'bound unionist Ireland to the empire as never before'.[37] Although the (still unclear) numbers who fought in South Africa were much fewer than those who would volunteer from 1914, that conflict was effectively a 'dress rehearsal for Gallipoli and the Somme'.[38] Trinity had been enthusiastic in its support for the South African campaign; however, the board's decision to give an honorary degree to Joseph Chamberlain (the colonial secretary during the conflict) in 1899— and the riots outside Front Gate which accompanied the ceremony—hinted at the potentially polarising impact of support for an imperial war.

Historians have claimed that Irishmen enlisted to fight in the First World War having been influenced by the political ideas invoked at the beginning of the conflict.[39] Superficially conflicting political aspirations —such as unionism (both Ulster and southern) and Redmondite nationalism—found common cause in support for the conflict; in each instance it was an opportunity to prove the loyalty of the respective cause to Westminster, in the hope of gaining favour in return. Trinity was traditionally a strongly unionist institution and it is true that many felt that support for the war effort was in the best interests of maintaining the union between Ireland and Britain. Similarly, the growing number of Home Rulers among the student body felt that support for the war would be a show of goodwill towards the British government. Walter Starkie noted that John Redmond's famous speech in the House of Commons of 3 August—which urged Irish men to serve, as an inducement for the implementation of Home Rule—was very well received amongst his unionist friends.[40] Home Rule was placed on the statute books in September 1914, to become law once the war ended. Thus, the events of 1914 presented a watershed moment in which cooperation replaced antagonism. Factions that had previously been suspicious of one another were seemingly united in the common cause of the war. This blurring of the lines between nationalist and unionist was also experienced at Trinity.

Political motivations were as important to unionists as they were to nationalists in justifying support for the war. John L. Stewart-Moore, a

Opposite: Photograph of members of Trinity's Officers Training Corps lining up in front of the Campanile, 1910.

nephew of Provost Traill, was a signatory of the Ulster Covenant and a member of the Ulster Volunteers. For Stewart-Moore, enlistment was the obvious corollary of his political beliefs. He noted that amongst his regiment, largely composed of working-class Antrim men, most had signed the covenant and 'patriotic and Protestant fervour was at its height'. The unanimity of opinion contrasted with Stewart-Moore's pre-war experiences at Trinity:

> During my years in Trinity I had enjoyed many arguments and debates on politics and religion as well as other topics including of course the burning question of Home Rule. Now at Clandeboye I found myself in a camp of four thousand men where no such debates were possible because everybody thought exactly alike.[41]

Stewart-Moore's recollections underscored the multiplicity of political opinions and positions held amongst the Trinity community in the years before 1914, which had been publicly demonstrated in October and November 1912. As an institution it could hardly remain aloof or insulated from wider political developments and debates; there is a great irony in the fact that Stewart-Moore had to leave Trinity, the constituency of Sir Edward Carson, to meet like-minded Ulster unionists.

P.L. Dickinson, too, cited political motivations for enlistment. Dickinson was not himself a Trinity man, but many of those who enlisted with him were, such as Ernest Julian, the Reid Professor of Law. Dickinson wrote of Redmond's famous Woodenbridge, Co. Wicklow, speech of 20 September 1914, in which he again encouraged nationalists to support the allied war effort, that:

> Numbers of Dublin men, like myself, thought 'Well, I don't belong to his party, but he has done the big thing. Let us shake hands, and we will join up in the Irish volunteers, pledged by John Redmond to the cause of the allies'.[42]

Dickinson's account, like Stewart-Moore's, complicates the traditional binary understandings of both Irish politics and Trinity College's place within it. More pointedly, such accounts speak to the open-endedness and sense of surprise that attended the outbreak of war in 1914. T.C. Kingsmill Moore, who would become auditor of Trinity's Historical Society in 1915, labelled the majority of members of the 'Hist' who volunteered for service either Redmondite home rulers or unionists. In each instance, service could be justified on political grounds, as both sides took Ireland's place within the British empire as a given and regarded service as a 'manifest and compulsive duty'.[43] Noel Drury, who enlisted through Trinity's OTC, noted the unusual change that came about through this sense of shared purpose amongst Home Rulers and unionists in the Spring of 1915:

> Good Presbyterians like myself paraded and marched off to the tunes of the 'Boys of Wexford' and 'A Nation Once Again' and went to chapel for the first and, probably, the only time in our lives. What a change the war has brought over things to be sure. If anyone had told me a year ago that I would have marched to a R.C. chapel to a rebel tune, I would have said they were potty to say the least of it.[44]

Explanations for enlistment cannot, however, be reduced to political beliefs alone; these formed only a part of a much more complex picture. More striking was the group dynamic, a phenomenon that can be seen in schools, universities, clubs and workplaces in all societies where conscription was not enforced and men chose to volunteer.[45] This was very much in evidence in Trinity accounts of the war, and speaks to the intimate bonds of friendship and loyalty that were formed in the course of a university education. The group dynamic was universal; in examining how it was experienced and understood by one intimate Irish community at Trinity College, we can begin to comprehend how millions of men around Europe approached and understood war through a sense of duty to their peers.

Walter Starkie recalled that in 1914 'I followed the example of my college friends and went to a recruiting depot to offer my services', feeling a sense of 'moral obligation'.[46] Frank Laird, described himself as a 'man of peace' but fretted over 'the awkward question of how my friends would regard me afterwards if they found me still at home when the war was over', while also admitting that the war offered him the opportunity of a little excitement.[47] The student community was dispersed by the war, and individuals were transported from the centre of Dublin to foreign climes, many never to return. In light of this, we can understand why many chose to follow their friends rather than stay home, for during the war, home was not really home at all. Noel Drury's experience perhaps illustrates this best. Having reflected on the matter for a number of months, he was unsure why he had enlisted at all.

Join the brave throng th

PUBLISHED BY THE PARLIAMENTARY RECRUITING COMMITTEE, LONDON. POSTER NO. 118.

> None of us knew much about the causes of the war and anything we had heard was all on our side and we knew nothing of the other side's view. Was this, indeed, a vital struggle for our country? Could my individual presence do any good anyhow? Couldn't I stay at home out of it? I wasn't a regular soldier, few of my friends or relatives had been soldiers, why, therefore, couldn't I stay where I was?[48]

Joseph Johnston had recently won a prestigious Albert Kahn travelling scholarship. The scheme, funded by a millionaire French banker and philanthropist, enabled Johnston to travel extensively for a year to further his studies. Johnston wrote in November 1914 that he was glad to begin his travels as 'soon all my friends will be gone'.[49] In the same month, *T.C.D.* made an appeal for men to join the OTC that invoked not a political cause, but group loyalty.

> There are still some Trinity men who have not come forward. This is no time for moralising or for gloomy thoughts, but the time may come when every able-bodied man may have to put his shoulder to the wheel, and the attitude of a College man who, from laziness or other such cause, neglects to avail himself of the opportunity that the Corps affords of receiving military training, is nothing short of criminal.[50]

Above: 'Join the brave throng that goes marching along', poster issued by the Parliamentary Recruiting Committee, London, 1915.

This editorial built on the sense of mutual obligation born of intimate collegiate relations, and invested it with something even more pressing: coercion. Men volunteered for a multitude of reasons and within months enlistment had taken on a momentum of its own, being presented and understood as the duty of all able-bodied men of military age.

In May 1915, the college board approved the proposal of R.M. Gwynn to keep a Roll of Honour, detailing the service of all Trinity men who enlisted in the armed forces.[51] Keeping lists of this nature reflected two linked preoccupations. First, a sense of shared identity amongst members of the college community. Alumni lists were kept in certain schools before the war. The Engineering School, for example, had been producing a detailed alumni directory since 1909, a labour of love that was based, primarily, upon sending thousands of questionnaires to alumni across the empire.[52] This linked to the shared sense of identity and pride in the subsequent careers of Trinity engineers, who found employment around the globe.[53] More pertinently, perhaps, the decision to keep a Roll of Honour demonstrated that something unprecedented was taking place; men were flocking to the colours and it was becoming clear that significant numbers would not return. This sort of inventory-taking became common at universities and similar institutions elsewhere; it reflected a deep anxiety about the destruction wrought by the war and the threat posed to the very existence of the university community itself.

The *War List* was published in instalments in the *Irish Times* during the war, and a final volume appeared in 1922. Such is the nature of the project that it cannot be considered definitive, nor is the information contained within it always consistent. Bearing these caveats in mind, however, some striking trends can be gleaned from the list. The majority of Trinity enlistment took place early in the war. Two-hundred and twenty-five men, or seven per cent of the total to serve in the war, volunteered in August 1914. By the end of 1914, this figure was 738 (twenty-four per cent of the total). A further 792 men enlisted in 1915. Numbers dropped off markedly from 1916, with 289 men enlisting that year; 186 enlisting in 1917; and 135 in 1918.[54] The drop-off in enlistment numbers from 1916 can be attributed to the rising death toll as well as the radicalised domestic situation in Ireland, a consequence of the Easter Rising and its suppression. Broadly speaking, the experience at Trinity overlaps with enlistment patterns in Ireland more generally.[55]

The figures also reflect the power of group loyalty, which was activated in the early months of the war; group loyalties could only be invoked once, and thus the great mass of students followed one another into the army in the first year-and-a-half of the conflict. As David Fitzpatrick has noted, 'loyalty to their friends and families' motivated most men to enlist, allied to membership of paramilitary, sporting, educational or civic organisations.[56] For the students and graduates of Trinity College Dublin, organisational affiliations were deeply embedded. The repercussions were severe.

The information contained in the *War List* is incomplete as already stated, but it still provides an excellent overview of enlistment trends and war experience amongst Trinity staff, students and alumni. Moreover, it also forced M.W.J. Fry, its compiler, to define both what a 'Trinity person' was and what constituted war service. In both instances, the definitions were broad: the *War List* included the names of seven men who had received honorary degrees before the war alongside ninety-six undergraduates who came onto the college books after the war but had no pre-war connection. Service was also broadly defined to include voluntary work alongside service at the fighting fronts. Allowing for these idiosyncrasies, trends emerged in wartime enlistment. Strongest of all was the role of the OTC. Enlistment was strongly distributed along the lines of its four units: 993 men served in the Royal Army Medical Corps, 186 served in the ASC and 173 served in the Royal Engineers. Among infantry units in which Trinity men served, most popular was the Royal Dublin Fusiliers (149 men), followed by the Royal Irish Rifles (82 men) the Royal Inniskilling Fusiliers (77 men), the Royal Munster Fusiliers (53 men) and the Connaught Rangers (47 men). One-hundred and five men served in the Royal Garrison Artillery (RGA), while 102 served in the Royal Field

'What in the end will settle this war?', World War I recruitment poster issued by the Parliamentary Recruiting Committee, London.

What in the end will settle this war ?

TRAINED MEN

It is YOUR DUTY to become one

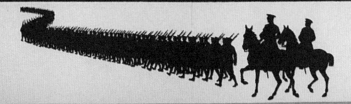

PUBLISHED BY THE PARLIAMENTARY RECRUITING COMMITTEE, LONDON. POSTER No. 94.　　　PRINTED BY JAS. TRUSCOTT & SON, LTD., SUFFOLK LANE, LONDON, E.C.

Artillery (RFA). By the war's end, 70 had served with the Royal Air Force (RAF, formed in 1918) and 51 had served with its predecessor, the Royal Flying Corps (RFC). Service was not restricted to British and Irish units, and Trinity men also served in imperial armies. At least 81 men served in various units of the Indian army, with 31 serving in Australian units, 30 serving in Canadian units, 21 in African units, and 5 in New Zealand units. Finally, one Trinity man served in the French army and another served in the Portuguese army. None were recorded as having served in 'enemy' armies.[57] It should also be noted that men often served in different units during the course of the war.

Just over fifteen percent of those Trinity men who enlisted in the armed forces died, a proportion in line with that of other universities in Britain and higher than the general death rate in the British army, where twelve percent of all mobilised men died.[58] Fitzpatrick puts the general Irish death rate in the war at fourteen percent.[59] Trinity then, suffered in a measure commensurate with its fellow universities, to whom it traditionally looked as peers, and with the rest of Ireland, with whom it had a troubled and complex relationship. The war did not distinguish between these imagined affiliations.

This intimate Dublin community felt the full impact of a global war. Trinity students and graduates died in such diverse arenas as Mesopotamia, German East Africa, West Africa, Egypt, Germany and Italy, as well as in Belgium and France. The systematic study of Trinity's losses in the First World War reveals that there were only three months in the entire conflict when a Trinity person did not lose his or her life in some sort of war service: August 1914, February 1918 and June 1918. A study of these clusters also reveals four periods of intense suffering for the college community. They are May 1915 (19 dead), August 1915 (50 dead), July 1916 (29 dead) and March 1918 (22 dead).[60] The Trinity experience of war was, in this respect, a microcosm of the wider Irish experience; considerable Irish losses were sustained in each of these instances. For Trinity, however, it was more specific; this relatively small and tight-knit community was being eroded, often in the course of a day, sometimes in a matter of hours.

It is a peculiar irony of the war, and the structure of the academic calendar, that the four moments in which there was a major loss of life amongst Trinity men—overlapping, as they did, with severe Irish losses more generally—remain relatively unrecorded in college publications. These major engagements mostly occurred outside of term time, and specifically outside of the publication dates of *T.C.D.*, the student magazine. Consequently, instant reactions from the student body are not available. The month of August 1915 was perhaps the darkest in the college's history. In that single month, at least 50 students, staff and alumni died, the majority of whom (43) perished at Suvla Bay in the Dardanelles in the engagements that followed the allied landings of 7 August.[61] Many, though not all, of these men were members of the 'Dublin Pals', D Company of the 7th Battalion of the Royal Dublin Fusiliers, men who chose not to seek a commission as an officer but to fight alongside their friends. The Pals were formed through the efforts of F.H. Browning, a recruitment activist, Trinity alumnus and president of the Irish Rugby Football Union. Irish engagement at Suvla Bay—being the first deployment of 'national' volunteer divisional formations—was initially seen as a national triumph, but the 10th Division, which made up much of the deployment, was virtually wiped out, and the endeavours of the Irish divisions were soon overshadowed by the radicalisation of Irish politics from April 1916.[62]

For a number of weeks from mid-August 1915, however, no member of the Trinity community could have been unaware of the terrible loss of life that had taken place at the Dardanelles. The *Irish Times* was full of obituaries and death notices, chronicling the destruction of Ireland's middle classes. One the most detailed descriptions of events at Suvla was provided by Poole Hickman, a Trinity graduate, barrister and Wanderers rugby player. His extended account, first published in the *Irish Times* on 31 August 1915, pulled few punches, describing insufferable conditions:

> the sun's rays beat pitilessly down all day long, and where
> the rotting corpses of the Turks created a damnably offen-
> sive smell. That is one of the worst features here—unburied
> bodies and flies—but the details are more gruesome than
> my pen could depict.[63]

Poignantly, Hickman's account was published two weeks after his own death.

The terrible losses of war were experienced in different ways. Shared membership of a small community—such as a college, school, club, or workplace—meant that news of the death of a colleague was cause for intense grief. For some, the grief was familial: the lecturer in history, Constantia Maxwell, lost her brother, Thomas, in September 1916.[64] The Professor of Chemistry, Sydney Young, lost his son at Ypres in 1915.[65] John Henry Bernard, then archbishop of Dublin and future provost, lost

At the Front.

[The following letter from an old member of the O.T.C. will doubtless be of interest to many College men.]

DEAR ——,   22/3/'15.

I have just come back whole (rather to my surprise) from seven days of the " real thing," and am taking the opportunity to let you know how I have been doing, so I hope I won't bore you.

I'll tell you all that has happened since I left, and trust that the Censor won't scratch it all out.

Well, we left Edinburgh on the 4th of March, and eventually arrived at a place called Richebourg at 1 a.m. on the morning of the 12th. Pretty quick, wasn't it? We were only troubled with a little shrapnel on nearing Richebourg, as they have a habit of shelling the roads at night to catch reinforcements coming up.

After having seen my men into terribly damaged billets I was glad to fall asleep on some straw in an old barn.

We were wakened up at 6 a.m. by the village being heavily shelled. During this day and the next two the noise of the artillery bombardment on both sides was something terrific. They say it was the biggest since the war began. We had to stay in that awful village till mid-day, being shelled the whole time (principally shrapnel), and were moved forward to bring reliefs to the support trenches. To do this we had to double along a road for half a mile with full packs (and we doubled willingly ! !). This road was shelled the whole of that day, and the sights I saw there I think I shall remember to my dying day. It was our " baptism " you see, and I saw some of our younger men turn actually green. Personally, I am thankful to say, I was too busy to notice much more than the fact that they were there.

When we did reach the trench we cooled ourselves in cold slimy water, actually up to our waists ; and we cooled with remarkable rapidity. I got my platoon out of the water, after about ten minutes, into some dug-outs, where we had to sit and wait till dark. As our firing line was in front of us we could not retaliate in any way, but just sit and be shelled for about six hours. I can assure you it is a most helpless position. This place to which we had now come is called Neuve Chapelle.

*   *   *   *   *

About 9 p.m. I received orders to support the firing line, and moved my platoon forward in the pitch dark. We had to move along a small portion of the road, and would you believe it that we could scarcely get ground to move along it in single file, as it had been shelled continuously for two days. One of my men fell into a hole in the middle of the road and actually had to *swim* out, the dykes on the edges of the road having met.

I eventually got my platoon behind the firing line, when suddenly the Germans sent up a " star-shell," which lit up the whole country, and a burst of " rapid " told me we had been found.

*   *   *   *   *

We couldn't do much the next day, as the artillery fire on both sides kept the infantry absolutely down in the trenches. They honoured us with shrapnel in certainly beautiful salvos of four, alternated with heavy lyddite, continuously the whole day. During the next few days we did well, however, advancing a good deal, and were specially complimented by Sir Douglas Haig, our Army Corps Commander.

I spent my coming-of-age in the trenches, and the following night—the 18th—we were relieved, and jolly glad we were too.

In the fight for this place—Neuve Chapelle—our brigade captured several German trenches which were wonderful affairs, with wooden floors, pictures on the walls, stoves, etc. But, by jove, it did cost a lot !

Well I hope I haven't bored you with all this, but I like to keep in touch with the D.U.O.T.C.

YOUR OLD " PRIVATE."

Doubt.

My feet have strayed from the highway,
    I have wandered far from the fold ;
The way of peace and my way
    Are severed by space untold.

A wind full of wailing and sorrow
    Creeps over the lonely heath,
Where darkness gives birth to no morrow,
    And the way leads to doubt and to death.

I see the gleam of the fire
    Afar in my distant home ;
I yearn to journey nigher
    The light and no more to roam.

But the night's black pall is flung o'er me,
    The looming mountains enclose,
And dark clouds are piled up stormy
    In skies where no moon glows.

his son, Robert, at Gallipoli in April 1915.[66] William, the son of Trinity surgeon Sir Robert Woods, was killed in October 1916. Mahaffy fretted over the safety of his sons, writing to inform a friend that his son Rob had been shot through both cheeks, had a number of teeth knocked out and could speak only 'with difficulty'.[67] James Campbell, one of the university's members of parliament, worried about his son who was serving in the Dardanelles and wrote to government minister Andrew Bonar Law to see if influence could be brought to have him taken out of the front line and given a safer job elsewhere. He was unsuccessful in his appeal; Philip Campbell was killed at Beaumont-Hamel in November 1916.[68]

Death also occasioned intellectual anxieties. Across Europe a generation of young scholars was being wiped out, and it seemed as though modes of thought themselves were at risk of extinction. The death of the brilliant Oxford physicist Henry Moseley at Gallipoli in 1915 led to outcry from British scientific elites, while the demise of the sociologists André Durkheim and Robert Hertz shook French scholarship. Intellect was assailed in Ireland too; a generation of great minds ran the risk of annihilation. Most famous among these was Tom Kettle, the former Home Rule member of parliament and professor of economics at UCD, killed at Guinchy in 1916, and the poet, Francis Ledwidge, killed at Ypres in 1917.[69] To this list might be added the names of Ernest Julian, the Reid Professor of Law at Trinity, also killed at Suvla Bay in 1915, and Samuel George Stewart, a precocious fellow of the college, killed weeks before the Armistice in 1918.[70] Wartime losses struck at something deeper in the fabric of intellectual life, generating a fear that knowledge itself was being irrevocably lost in the conflict.

There is another narrative of the war, however, which connects Trinity to working-class Dublin. It concerns the college's non-academic staff, 37 of whom volunteered for war. Unlike the students and alumni of the college, these men generally served as privates in the rank-and-file; they became ordinary soldiers. Owing to their social and economic background, they had not previously been integrated into the wider Trinity war story, nor do traces of their experiences remain in the archives. What is known is that three of these thirty-seven men died on active service, including George Marsh, mentioned in Chapter One above. Marsh was reported to have died of 'shell-shock' (post-traumatic stress syndrome) in 1918 at the age of 37. He was not included on the college war memorial when it was inaugurated in 1928, although his name, and those of the

'At the Front', letter from a former member of the OTC, describing the conditions he and his platoon experienced fighting at the battle of Neuve Chapelle on the Western Front in March 1915, published in *T.C.D.: a College Miscellany*, 12 May 1915, p. 63.

two other non-academic staff who died in the war—John Collins and John James Currey—were added later. So, while the wider college community was shaken by the war, its hierarchical structure meant that the voices of some of those lost were not always heard.

Fortunately, the story of the war is not only a story of death. Trinity men who enlisted for active service had a multiplicity of experiences during the war; most of the men who volunteered did not die. Barry Brown, who took his law degree in 1906 and practised in Dublin as a solicitor, went missing on the first day of the Battle of the Somme on 1 July 1916. On this day at least nine Trinity men lost their lives. Brown was wounded and held prisoner in Germany for a year, after which he was evacuated by the Red Cross to a hospital in Poland, where he met and married a local woman.[71] Philip Lyster served in the Royal Field Artillery, was taken prisoner at the Battle of Mons in August 1914 and spent three years in Germany. His transfer to Switzerland was secured in 1917, due to concerns about his health and thanks to the power of the Trinity alumni network. Lyster's mother appealed to Archbishop Bernard, to see if he could exert influence. Bernard contacted Cecil Harmsworth, a Trinity graduate, member of parliament and, briefly, government under-secretary of state in 1915, who was able to arrange for his relocation.[72] Henry Crookshank, who had been wounded at Suvla Bay, was later utilised in Egypt as a censor of soldiers' letters, bemoaning the increase in his workload when new units passed through the city where he was based.[73] He had, in part at least, an intellectually stimulating war, which allowed him to travel and engage with new cultures; from 1917 he was stationed near Jerusalem with 'a nice soft job' and could observe the local Bedouin tribes.[74] Crookshank's war was far from an enjoyable one, however: his brother, Arthur, was amongst the many killed at the Dardanelles in 1915.[75]

Not all men who enlisted in the armed forces did so purely because of political convictions or out of a desire to fight. The university had two schools that produced men who could perform important palliative and altruistic functions in wartime: the Divinity School and the Medical School. Medical students and recent graduates were much valued for their professional and expert knowledge and were desperately needed at the front. Of the 3,000 members of college who served in the war, almost one-third served in the Royal Army Medical Corps (RAMC).[76] Francis Dixon wrote in 1917 that

> the students of the university who intended to enter the medical profession have put the call of duty before their individual interests and have joined the army to take their share in fighting for the Empire.[77]

As a result, Trinity's was the only medical school in Ireland that did not see a significant increase in admissions during the war years.

These men put themselves in positions of grave danger and many distinguished themselves. Adrian Stokes, member of a famous scholarly family, set up the first mobile bacteriology laboratories in France in October 1914, using his motorcycle and some laboratory apparatus that he acquired in Paris.[78] This was soon imitated elsewhere. The war also temporarily transformed the function of medical buildings in Dublin. At Sir Patrick Dun's hospital, the largest teaching hospital linked to Trinity, two wards were turned over to the treatment of wounded soldiers and extra beds added.[79] The hospital also set up a roll of honour to monitor the service of its men in the war, all either Trinity graduates or students.

The Divinity School also played an important role in wartime. Religion offered consolation in difficult times. The challenge of war could, it was expected, make men at the front eager for religious ministration. In the beginning, some army chaplains went to war in the expectation that it might lead to something of a religious revival.[80] Of the Trinity men who enlisted, 193 did so in the non-combatant role of army chaplain.[81] Most notable amongst these was the graduate Edward Campbell, an Anglican chaplain, who was awarded the Distinguished Service Order for his work interring bodies on the Somme. His citation stated that he had performed:

> A most arduous duty, the majority of bodies being in [an] advanced state of putrefaction. Between 5,000 and 6,000 bodies were buried during about 15 weeks. Only Mr. Campbell's determination enabled him to perform the work; his assistants and working parties had frequently to be changed.[82]

Army chaplains also had to perform duties such as writing to the next of kin to inform them of the death of a soldier, as well as holding voluntary services on a Sunday.[83] Not all clergymen opted to serve as chaplains, however. Arthur Aston Luce, a fellow of the college and an ordained clergyman, chose to serve as a combatant in the Royal Irish Rifles.[84] His military and religious experiences were remembered humorously years later in verse:

> As a Captain who fought with the Huns,
> As a Doctor most learned in Divinity,
> Now, as one of the Church's big guns,
> I'm the very best Tutor in Trinity.[85]

Membership of a community or peer group was an important motivation in impelling men to enlist. Once on active service and far from home, friends and family, a soldier's connection to a peer community took on a new importance. A group identity, whether formed at a club, school or university, became a means of normalising an otherwise abnormal situation, and this was the case for belligerents in many countries. For this reason, Trinity men sought each other out at the front, irrespective of whether they had known each other previously.[86] The dispersed college community was a resilient one; individuals on active service sought to repair the breaches in the fabric of college life where they could.

John Stewart-Moore, who graduated in 1913, frequently wrote about the Trinity connection when recording his war experiences. He often referred either to meeting Trinity friends at the front—such as Arthur P.I Samuels (a former auditor of the Historical Society and son of a Trinity MP) and James Hannay (son of the novelist Canon Hannay, 'George Birmingham')—or making the acquaintance of Trinity men whom he had not previously known. These connections were meaningful. Stewart-Moore met the lawyer Barry Brown shortly before the Battle of the Somme in July 1916. Under Brown's guidance, Stewart-Moore made out his will, in which he left all his worldly possessions to his six-year-old nephew.[87] In late 1916, he bumped into an unexpected figure.

> As I made my way through this unknown territory there was an officer standing at the door of a dugout. All officers of course exchanged greetings whether they had ever seen each other before or not so I gave him a polite 'Good morning' and would have passed on had it not been for the warmth and tone of his reply. 'Good morning Stewart-Moore' he said 'I'm glad to see you again.' I stopped abruptly and had a good look at him and there to my surprise under the grime of the trenches I recognised the Reverend A.A. Luce, Fellow of Trinity College Dublin. I had had a nodding acquaintance with him in Trinity as a somewhat aloof figure walking across the front square in immaculate clerical dress with a dog collar that seemed starchier and whiter than anything one would see outside a shop window. Now he had been transformed into a very ordinary infantry officer in the 12th Rifles...He greeted me as an old friend, invited me into his dugout and offered me a glass of whisky. He was glad to have someone to whom he could talk about his troubles, the troubles which afflict an Infantry Officer serving in the front line.[88]

The shared references, acquaintances and stories, all born of a scholarly life in Dublin, begot intimacy and provided solace to men who found themselves in very trying circumstances, hundreds of miles from home. Soldiers held alumni dinners in locations as disparate as Cairo, Jerusalem and Baghdad.[89] The group identity fostered in the course of a university education was durable and meaningful, and men who found themselves at different fighting fronts were perhaps on some level seeking to keep the college community intact as best they could. This was the case also for students and alumni of universities in Britain, France, the United States and Germany, and underlines the important formative influence of college life.

Life in college

Entire societies felt the impact of the First World War; its convulsions rippled out far from the battlefields. In belligerent societies such as Ireland, few towns were unaffected by the flight of young men into the armed forces, the rupture this caused to normal life and the omnipotence of death. This was especially pronounced at universities, with their youthful and male-dominated populations. Across Europe, normal university life ground to a halt; lecture halls and sports fields were devoid of students and the essence of these institutions was in danger of being lost. For this reason, 'business as usual' became the watchword, from the Sorbonne to University College Cork, as universities sought to continue their pre-war function.[90] Trinity was similar to its fellow universities elsewhere in Europe in this respect. *T.C.D.*'s first wartime edition emerged in November 1914, and its editorial had the experience of three months of fighting to reflect upon.

> We have a feeling that events are moving too fast for collegiate experience. Present issues seem too enormous for our dilettante consideration. The hustle and bustle of military effort that has invaded our academic torpor makes us feel ill at ease in College, and begets in us the desire to get away from pursuits and an environment which we have so long associated with careless peace...We used to be a community to ourselves, free from any rude irruptions of outside affairs. These days are past, however, and it will be a long time before College reassumes, if ever it does, its normal aspect...[91]

Student narratives of the war years are difficult to locate; many memoirs were written retrospectively, in the light of subsequent events. However, the pages of *T.C.D.* provide an insight into the workings of a fractured student body seeking to maintain a semblance of normality. By the end of October 1914, thirteen members of the Trinity community had been reported dead and the college was beginning to grasp the severity of the fighting. From late November that year, *T.C.D.* carried the accounts of Harry O'Kelly, a Catholic undergraduate at the front. The tone and content of *T.C.D.* was usually flippant, filled with in-jokes, society gossip and jibes at the college hierarchy. During the war, however, it was not business as usual: O'Kelly wrote of 'men being killed in dozens', 'slaughter', and his own killing of a German soldier.[92] Significantly, O'Kelly's account was serialised in the nationalist *Irish Independent*, where his Trinity affiliation and Catholic faith were emphasised to symbolise the political consensus of 1914, which united unionist and Home Ruler.[93]

The mere articulation of 'business as usual' spoke to the abnormality of the situation. The editors of *T.C.D* struggled with this idea.

> It would appear that the activities of us students cannot continue unabated this session. The best men are away, and the hearts of the rest of us cannot be wholly in our College life. What then is the position of *T.C.D.*? Many of our cleverest and readiest contributors are either now at the front, or have fallen at the front, or are preparing to go to the front. Can we and ought we to continue? … the bare fact is, that in so far as is possible, Trinity College has laid aside the pen for the sword.[94]

The desire for normality came at a cost. It became apparent that wartime sacrifices were not being experienced equally. Indeed, the *T.C.D.* authors suggested that the college board was still disconnected from the reality of wartime life. 'Our motto is "business as usual." As far as we know the Senior Fellows' salaries have suffered no diminution; commons is maintained at almost the usual level of lavishness.'[95] In early 1915, T.B. Rudmose-Brown, Professor of French, reported that he had no students whatsoever for certain classes.[96] Students were the lifeblood of the college and their absence underscored the abnormality of the situation; conversely, the attitude of the board demonstrated its disconnectedness from the students.

Societal life was a casualty of the war, further showing that the policy of 'business as usual' was a difficult standard to meet. In 1914, the Dublin University Experimental Science Association decided to adopt a policy of 'carry on'.[97] This proved too difficult to sustain, however, and the last meeting of the DUESA was held in June 1915. It would not resume its activities again until the end of 1918.[98] This was typical of societal life at universities across Britain too, where societies and sports clubs cancelled their activities during the war owing to lack of numbers. Larger societies found it easier to get by. The Historical Society at Trinity was able to continue its work, but the war pervaded its business. Motions such as 'that this house is of the opinion that lasting international peace can only be secured by the growth of democracy' and 'that this house considers international law can have no binding force in time of war' were debated.[99] The society's life quickly became difficult due to the great numbers of members and committee members who enlisted in the armed forces. As such, it too had to improvise to survive, and adopted new laws in May 1915 allowing officers to retain their positions for multiple years.[100]

The war and its issues trickled down to teaching and examinations. The entrance examination for Michaelmas Term 1915, required that students translate the following passage into Latin.

> The troops began to suffer great hardships, partly because of the chilling frosts and heavy rains, and partly because food became scanty when the roads grew difficult for vehicles by reason of mud. Nevertheless, the undaunted spirit of the general and his officers, and the amazing cheerfulness of the private soldier, made light of all discomforts. They remembered the cause for which they were fighting; they knew that the enemy had suffered great losses during the past year; and they believed that victory would come with the spring.[101]

The English composition component of the same examination gave students the options of writing answers on compulsory national service and wartime economy, amongst other topics.[102] In the same year, questions in logic in the final freshman examination asked students to express statements, such as the following, in the syllogistic form: 'it is to the advantage of mankind to be ruled by the Germans as the superior race'.[103] Examination questions in arithmetic were framed as problems relating to the relative gains of a profiteer in war and peacetime.[104] Meanwhile, examinations in German and French (both set by T.B. Rudmose-Brown) required students to translate passages relating to the war into the relevant language.[105]

The war posed an acute problem for the teaching of German. Universities and academics in Britain and France were quick to distance themselves from their erstwhile colleagues in the Central Powers, while at the same time much wartime propaganda demonised Germany, its history and *Kultur*. Trinity's professor of German, Gilbert Waterhouse, was especially vitriolic in his attitude towards the study of Germany. In May 1917 he gave a public lecture on the subject, in which he argued that he did not 'look forward to any resumption of cordial relations with German scholars after the war'. This was not, however, reason to abandon the study of German outright. Instead, Waterhouse claimed that:

> We do not study German to provide Germans or German-speaking neutrals with comfortable berths in the United Kingdom, nor to flatter German vanity, nor to encourage German trade, nor to aid German propaganda. We study German in order to extract from the language, the literature, the people, and the country the maximum of benefit —moral, intellectual, and material—for ourselves.[106]

The ubiquity of the war and its impact upon all facets of college life was ably described in a poem published anonymously in *T.C.D.* in 1915.

> Now every time I cross the Squares,
> Or wander up my dim-lit stairs,
> I think of the heroic dead,
> And of their narrow Flemish bed.
> The Campanile's sullen bell
> Evokes the guns of Neuve Chapelle.
> Those puddles there of watery mud
> To the mind's eye are pools of blood.
> I have no faith, but sick at heart
> Would from this cursed world depart.[107]

The war challenged traditional gender roles across all sectors of society. As so many able-bodied men of military age were away at the front, women were often left to perform work that had hitherto been the preserve of their husbands, fathers or brothers. In this regard Ireland was no different from the other nations at war. In the history of universities this had a specific relevance: with universities and colleges depopulated, women took on a new and more visible role. The figures presented above of the wartime student population reveal the growing visibility of women in college. Having represented around fifteen per cent of the overall student population prior to the war, they accounted for twenty-seven per cent by its conclusion. As such, the war presented an opportunity for women to challenge some of the limits placed on their participation in college life. As previously stated, although women had been allowed to take full degrees since 1904, they were not equal partners within the college community: they were not allowed to sit for fellowship, to live in college rooms, or to even be present in Trinity after 6 pm.

While it is undeniable that they were not treated equally in day-to-day affairs in college during the war, Trinity was proud of the work undertaken by its female students and graduates during this time. A measure of this can be seen in the *War List,* which includes the names of 27 women, including one who lost her life (see below).[108] The war provided an opportunity for women to perform service (often as medical doctors working in hospitals in Ireland, Britain and in continental Europe), and the university was willing, in this respect, to recognise women's war work as equal to that of men. This was significant and unusual; Trinity's peers in Britain usually chose not to record the work of women when they came to take stock after the war.[109]

There were a number of women-specific war initiatives. A Dublin University Voluntary Aid Detachment (VAD) Hospital was established at Mountjoy Square for war-wounded, under the command of Rachel Mahaffy, the provost's daughter. The hospital was entirely maintained and staffed by graduates and undergraduates of the college, who offered their services for no remuneration. Francis Dixon argued in 1916 that in this respect Trinity led both Oxford and Cambridge.[110] It was ironic that while the college was hesitant about the further integration of women into its community, it could simultaneously invoke wartime progress for women to claim superiority to its traditional rivals.

A number of Trinity women served abroad. Ina Clarke, a demonstrator in Anatomy who was involved in the VAD hospital, also served at the Ulster Volunteer Hospital in Pau, France.[111] Lilian Thompson, daughter of Sir William Thompson, took her degree in philosophy in 1916. Thereafter, she took a war-service job in Paris in order to be closer to her future husband, the previously mentioned A.A. Luce, stationed there on active service.[112] The lone woman whose name features amongst Trinity's dead of the First World War is Louisa Woodcock.[113] She was a 'Steamboat Lady' who was educated at Somerville College, Oxford, but who was able, through a reciprocal relationship between the two universities, to graduate from Dublin University before the war without having attended classes there.[114] Louisa Woodcock was working in the Endell Street Military Hospital in London when she died of illness in 1917.

Monica Roberts, the daughter of William Westropp Roberts, the college's senior lecturer, took it upon herself to organise a society called the 'Band of Helpers to the Soldiers'. While her initial desire was to send items to soldiers at the front, it soon became apparent that the mere act of corresponding was more important to these men, and the collection of letters that she received numbers over 400. The quest for normality in wartime was important, and corresponding—especially with a member of the opposite sex—may have provided a normalising influence for men in the all-male environment of the fighting fronts. Significant too is the fact that Monica Roberts initiated this society herself; while women were taking on important roles in voluntary organisations in wartime, there were still limited outlets for voluntary work. For Roberts, the solution was to take matters into her own hands.

Above: Front of a postcard from Private Edward Mordaunt 8723, No. 6 Platoon, B Company, 2nd Battalion Royal Dublin Fusiliers, he corresponded with Miss. K. Roberts (sister of Monica Roberts) between 18 July 1915 and 21 December 1917.
Right: 'Rules for the Band of Helpers to the Soldiers', instructions issued by Monica Roberts to those intending to join the society she established to send items to soldiers at the front. Following page: 'Gifts for members of the British Expeditionary Forces', page 5 from a leaflet issued by the War Office, titled Letters, Parcels and Gifts for the Army, which Monica Roberts used as the basis for her instructions to members of the 'Band of Helpers'.

RULES FOR BAND OF HELPERS TO THE SOLDIERS.

1. This Society will last during the War, and shall be called "Band of Helpers for the Soldiers".

2. Members pay 3d on being enrolled, which sum will go towards buying comforts, also for postage of goods to the Front.

3. Members to send monthly, addressed to Miss Monica Roberts, Kelston, Stillorgan some contribution, however small, either in money, or any of the following articles, all of which are said to be useful by the War office. Handkerchiefs, boot-laces, chocolate, peppermint, dried fruits, briar pipes and tobacco pouches, tobacco, cigarettes, cigarette-tobacco and cigarette-papers, small tins of boracic ointment or borated vaseline for sore feet, antiseptic powder, post cards, pocket knives, lead pencils etc.

4. These articles will be forwarded monthly to the Dublin Fusiliers, and the Royal Flying Corps.

5. If the Society grows, and receives good support, more regiments could be included, but at present, the above mentioned will be all to whom this Society will contribute.

6. Members are requested to kindly tell their friends about this Society, for as many members as possible are required.

Monica K. Roberts.

III.
GIFTS FOR MEMBERS OF THE BRITISH EXPEDITIONARY FORCE.

Numerous enquiries having been made as to what articles would be useful to soldiers serving with the Expeditionary Force, the following list has been prepared at the War Office for the information of their relatives and friends :—

Housewives.
Handkerchiefs, boot laces.
Newspapers and periodicals.
Chocolate, peppermint.
Dried fruits.
Briar pipes and tobacco pouches.
Tobacco (packed in thick tin-foil if possible).
Cigarettes, cigarette papers and cigarette tobacco.
Safety matches (packed in sealed tins).
Small tins of boracic ointment or borated vaseline for sore feet.
Antiseptic powder.
Pocket-knives.
Postcards and lead pencils.
Warm clothing :—Mufflers, Balaclava caps, mittens, cardigan jackets.

It is unnecessary for the present to send shirts, socks and underclothing, as there are ample reserves of these articles of clothing at the base, whence they can be obtained by the troops as required.

Wines, spirits and matches, other than safety matches packed in tins, should not be sent, neither should fresh fruit, vegetables, or other goods of a perishable nature or likely to cause damage.

Knitted and woven belts and socks, for which a public appeal has been made, should be sent to the Lady-in-Waiting to Her Majesty, Devonshire House, London, W. The object of this appeal is to supplement the provision made by the War Department to meet special winter requirements. The garments will be issued to the troops in November and the following months.

This list does not include articles which would be useful in hospitals, of which lists are issued weekly by the Queen Mary's Needlework Guild, the St. John Ambulance Association and the British Red Cross Society.

The French and Belgian Governments have agreed to admit free of import duty any postal or other parcels containing tobacco, cigars and cigarettes sent for use of British troops at the front. No declaration need therefore be made in this country before despatch, and the public may rest assured that the troops at the front will not be called upon to pay any duty on receipt of the parcels.

The absence of men on campus meant that women became much more visible in day-to-day life. Walter Alison Phillips noted in 1915 that his history classes were reduced to 'four girls and a callow youth'.[115] The pages of *T.C.D.*, traditionally a bastion of male influence and reflective of the composition of the leading college societies, suddenly opened up to women. As early as November 1914, noting the dearth of contributors, the editors called on women students to submit contributions. 'We address our request to the lady students, whose numbers are not so seriously diminished by the war and for whose energies in the literary line we have the highest respect.'[116] By 1918, the enforced change to the college's social make-up fostered by the war had proved to the editors of *T.C.D.* the necessity for radical reform. It acknowledged the second-class status of women at Trinity:

> Women in College have a multitude of grievances. Ever since they have been allowed to take their degree here— some few years ago—they have been made recognise that this was to be almost the only kind concession on the part of Trinity College. They are visitors, but very formal ones, and must on no account prolong their stay beyond 6pm.[117]

The editors called for full integration of women into the societal culture of Trinity. 'Feminism has made and is making giant strides in the world. The women here must only hope that Trinity will not limp too slowly behind the rest of the universe.'[118] Within a week of publishing this, *T.C.D.* was inundated with (unpublished) letters of complaint from fellows of the college.[119] The reformist trail halted there, and for the most part, women would remain 'second-class citizens' until the 1960s.[120] The college occupied a curious space in this period: it led its traditional peers, Oxford and Cambridge, in admitting women in 1904. Both of the latter universities were also shaken by the war, but while Oxford admitted women in 1919, conservative Cambridge remained defiant until 1947. One should not, however, focus solely on the wartime position of women in the imagined community of ancient universities; more recently founded universities, with the NUI to the fore, allowed women full membership of the scholarly community before the war. Moves towards reform at the ancient universities paled in comparison with conventions at newer institutions.

Mobilising the mind

The First World War was a 'total war', in that its prosecution was not re-stricted solely to the realm of the military, but came to impact upon all branches of government and society. Across Europe whole societies were mobilised to fight: as already mentioned, industry, the economy and culture were all reoriented to prosecute this modern war as each belliger-ent nation sought to prevail. The war engaged universities in their entirety; it was, as the British historian H.A.L. Fisher put it, 'a battle of brains'.[121] Fundamentally, it required the enlistment of specialist knowledge, and ac-ademics in Europe and the United States were plucked from their ivory towers to lend their expertise in this sprawling conflict. National govern-ments began making intense demands upon universities. Staff were seconded to government departments; research re-oriented towards war problems; and laboratories requisitioned. This was a revolutionary moment in the history of higher education, especially in Britain and Ireland; governments began funding and directing university research, a trend that has continued to the present day.

While its scientific infrastructure and resources could not compare with those of Oxford, Cambridge or Birmingham universities, Dublin University boasted some brilliant individuals of international standing and a steady flow of accomplished graduates and laboratory assistants who had come under their influence. As a consequence of the under-developed scientific infrastructure of Irish universities, the hallmarks of Irish scientific engagement in the war were individual actions rather than institutional assimilation. There were many motivations for academics to engage in such work. Undoubtedly many professors believed deeply in the allied cause. More often, however, these men, who were not of military age, felt their inability to contribute militarily in acute terms—especially as their classrooms were empty—and sought to serve in other ways. In a sense, this can be regarded as a continuation of the group solidarity that motivated enlistment amongst students and younger alumni.

Small networks of academics were mobilised in novel ways to address the many intellectual problems the war presented; challenges that stimu-lated the academic mind. The natural sciences seemed especially applicable to the problems of modern warfare. When the war broke out, the geologist John Joly was invigorated by the possible applications of his inventive and scientific talents to military matters. Across Europe, scien-tists were alert to the possibilities of applying their talents to war

Opposite: Professor of Geology John Joly, *c.* 1900/1905.

Detecting Enemy Submarines.

————

The following must have been thought of; but as it appears to me to be very important I send it on.

A submarine look-out cell is provided in all large patrol boats. The cell takes the form of a small water-tight compartment with air-lock and a clear opening beneath permitting observation directly downwards beneath the boat.

The cell is worked exactly like a diving bell; compressed air being used to keep out water. A glass floor would naturally be suggested but if it is used means of protecting it from outside must be provided or it will surely get broken if heavy explosions take place in the water beneath.

In another part of the ship a similar cell permits a parallel beam from a search-light to be projected downwards.

The observer in the look-out cell communicates by telephone with the bridge. He should also be able to control the direction of the light-beam.

Mere inspection of the angle of the latter and of his own vision gives a good idea of the depth of a submarine under illumination.

I think it is certain that such a look-out would greatly increase the value of our scouts. Great depths can be explored in this way in clear water. At night time, especially, the gain would be great. A submarine which had dived at the approach of the scout would stand a considerable risk of being detected and mined.

The above seems the best mode of accomplishing the end of good visual inspection of the sea. A specially made boat for the purpose, towed by the patrol, could be used. But this would not be so generally useful and would take more time to bring into use.

J. Joly

March 9th /17

Trinity College Dublin

problems; however, Joly differed in the quantity and variety of inventions that he presented to various authorities, initially at the Admiralty in London and, as the war progressed, in France and the United States. Among his myriad ideas were a shell which, on explosion underwater, would unleash a large net to act as protection against a submarine attack; a means of projecting bombs from aeroplanes; and defences against the use of chemical weapons in trench warfare.[122] In most instances his suggestions were politely declined; some of his ideas were a touch fantastical, while some of the more practical solutions he proposed, such as his method of detecting enemy guns on the battlefield by sound (known as sound ranging), had already been taken up by scientists at the front.[123] Collectively, Joly's papers illustrate the intellectual stimulation of wartime and the brilliant inventiveness of the man. While his own notes perhaps overstate the importance of his work, British archives reveal that a number of his schemes were taken seriously.[124]

Trinity's scientific schools were small in this period. They were staffed by eminent and accomplished men but their resources were limited. Nevertheless, in wartime, their small networks were mobilised effectively. The School of Botany undertook some important research into the relative merits of different timbers used in aeroplane construction and their rates of deterioration due to the presence of fungi and other factors. This work was made possible by the scientific network that existed around Joly and Dixon. Dixon's laboratory assistant in the School of Botany, W.R.G. Atkins, was appointed to a position in the National Physical Laboratory in England in 1916, where he worked in the division for Aeronautical Chemistry.[125] Atkins led the project and was able to acquire different types of timbers from Africa, which were in turn sent to the Botany laboratories in Trinity where Dixon tested them.[126] The result was that Atkins's team was able to establish that 15 per cent of airscrews used in British aeroplanes were unserviceable before use; walnut screws made by a particular manufacturer were especially vulnerable.[127] More importantly, this project demonstrated the power of the scholarly network and the value of research to national governments.

Other departments were equally intellectually stimulated by the war. Emil Werner, Professor of Applied Chemistry, 'carried out work of great importance to the War Office during the war by preparing certain amines in larger quantities and in a much purer state than had been possible previously'.[128] William Ramsden, who was the assistant to the Professor of

Opposite: Letter from Professor Joly to the British Admiralty, 9 March 1917, proposing a method for detecting enemy submarines.

Chemistry Sydney Young, saw combat on the Western Front and also worked on means of countering the effects of specific chemical weapons.[129] The physiologist William Thompson was seconded to the Ministry of Food in London as a consultant for the British government. He drowned on 10 October 1918 when the *RMS Leinster*, on which he was travelling, was torpedoed by a German submarine in the Irish Sea, with the loss of over 500 lives. He had dined on Commons with his son-in-law to-be, A.A. Luce, before he went to Kingstown to catch the ill-fated boat.[130]

Scientific engagement in the war effort was also motivated by international academic politics. The natural sciences remained underfunded and frequently misunderstood at universities across Europe and North America in the early twentieth century. This was acutely felt at universities like Oxford, Cambridge and Trinity, where the classics were firmly entrenched in curricula. In the pre-war years, scientific reformers took aim at the classics as an example of antiquated and esoteric learning with no applicability to modern society. This debate became especially bitter in France.[131] In wartime, scientific reformers felt that the application of scientific knowledge to war problems had demonstrated the utility of scientific research to the nation, and they expected concessions in return. Frequently, however, they were disappointed by the misunderstanding of the scientific method exhibited by government, which meant that their work was being at best inefficiently utilised, and often squandered.

In early 1916 a movement called the 'Neglect of Science' emerged in Britain to call for the full integration of science into school and university curricula as well as army and civil service examinations.[132] The movement's manifesto, signed by over 150 scientists, bore the names of twelve Trinity men, including Dixon, Joly, Werner, Young, Thrift (Professor of Physics), Francis Dixon (Professor of Anatomy) and E.P. Culverwell (Professor of Education). The only other Irish signatories to the manifesto came from University College, Galway. This movement resulted in a number of significant changes in British educational structures by the war's end.[133] In this context, the mobilisation of scientific knowledge in wartime was also a means of proving the utility of scientific research to an otherwise ill-informed government, and a conduit towards gaining better provisions for scientific research and education. It demonstrated the transformative potential of the war for education and society.

The mobilisation of scholarly knowledge had another important consequence for the universities. It entrenched research as a central function; this was especially pronounced at the older British universities, which had originally developed to train men for professional or religious vocations. Research for research's sake was not a priority, and was associated more with the German universities. Trinity, the NUI, along with virtually all British universities adopted the PhD degree in 1919.[134] This was an important development in the modernisation of universities through the affirmation of research as a central priority. Crucially, it owed its origins to wartime cultural politics.

Universities were, in the main, beholden to the wider political and military dynamic of the war. This was again demonstrated in 1917 when the United States entered the conflict on the side of the allies. One of the most important initiatives of this period was the British Educational Mission—comprised of eminent scholars from Britain and Ireland—which toured American universities in late 1918. This high-profile initiative was simultaneously an act of cultural diplomacy and an expression of a desire for reform. The mission sought to build links between British and Irish universities and their American counterparts. The representative of Irish universities was John Joly.

At Columbia University in New York, Joly spoke of Trinity, invoking Goldsmith, Lecky, Hamilton and Burke, and Trinity's architecture, but pointedly contrasted the university's heritage with its wartime losses. 'What is our fame in science, in literature, or in art compared with the glory of the supreme sacrifice of our simple, lovable boys?' Joly argued that peace in the world could be facilitated by the greater exchange of students. 'This is the highest and, I take it, the ultimate reasons for our mission to your university.'[135] The introduction of the PhD was a direct result of this mission; its introduction in Britain would allow students from the United States and other allied nations to spend time at British and Irish universities in the course of graduate study. While the initial hopes of the reformers for the large-scale movement of graduate students were unfulfilled, the introduction of this higher degree became an integral part of the modern university.

A further example of the importance of this form of cultural diplomacy came in October of 1919, and concerned relations with the other great First World War ally, France. A reciprocal exchange of readers, or junior scholars, was established between Trinity and the École Normale Supérieure in Paris, which produced the political and academic elites of France.[136] While a low-level exchange between two academic institutions may seem innocuous, this particular exchange proved of much importance in Irish intellectual history, as it later enabled Samuel Beckett, Thomas MacGreevy and Owen Sheehy-Skeffington to travel to Paris and further their scholarly interests. Thus, the wartime reconfiguration of international scholarship had many unanticipated but important repercussions, not least of which was enabling the development of Beckett's distinguished literary career.

Ending the war

The continuation of the war and the growing death toll led to much anxiety at Trinity, and would be exacerbated by the Easter Rising and its aftermath (see Chapter Three). In May 1917, an anonymous letter to *T.C.D.* suggested that the college, being 'a university unassimilated by a nation, itself unassimilated by an empire, in its turn unassimilated by the world' should do something to engage with the wider world.[137] A satirical rebuke appeared in the following issue, which argued that for Trinity to engage fully with the wider world as then constituted, would necessitate that 'a system of well-traversed trenches, with wire and No Man's Land complete, ... be constructed in the Bay, and all students (except scholars) would be required to reside in these during term', and that daily practical demonstrations in asphyxiating gases and heavy bombardments take place.[138] The point was that, with Europe being destroyed, perhaps Trinity's assumed aloofness was not an altogether bad thing. While Trinity's attitude may always have been somewhat aloof, it too was feeling the impact of the war acutely.

The armistice that ended the war was signed on 11 November 1918. News of its signature was no immediate cue for celebration in Trinity, for there was little to celebrate. Some students allied with their counterparts in the College of Surgeons and staged an informal rag, commandeering cars and staging a procession in which an effigy of the kaiser, wrapped in a Sinn Féin flag, was drawn behind a hearse from Grafton Street to Sackville Street.[139] The end of fighting went conspicuously unremarked upon in *T.C.D.*, which was perhaps all too happy that the cessation of hostilities would—it hoped—allow it to resume its traditional 'no politics' platform. The armistice did not immediately make a substantial difference to the life of the college. While it took the men who were at the front away from immediate danger, the college itself remained under-populated and would continue with wartime improvisations into the early months of 1919. The fact that a baseball game took place amongst the traditional events of Trinity Week in 1919—a consequence of the fact that significant numbers of American soldiers were being temporarily housed in universities across Europe before continuing home at the end of the war—aptly demonstrates this.[140]

A better measure of reactions to the end of the war can be seen in the attempted transition from wartime contingency back to to pre-war normality. It was in these moments that the measure of the change wrought by the war could be felt most acutely. In January 1919, the Historical

Society held its first inaugural meeting since 1914; a sure sign of efforts to return to normal. The event was labelled a 'Peace Inaugural Meeting', and the *Irish Times* noted that many of the participants had 'been face to face with the grim realities of war, and they will find now that they cannot escape the grim realities of peace'.[141] *T.C.D.* wrote a month later of the contradiction of trying to recapture the pre-war sensibility: 'while Trinity is thus engaged in seeking the Old Spirit, the world is endeavouring to create the New Spirit'.[142] This theme was prevalent in memories of university and intellectual life produced throughout the 1920s, especially at Oxford and Cambridge; it pervades the writings of a generation of middle-class writers who came of age and went to university after the war and finds perhaps its best expression in Evelyn Waugh's *Brideshead Revisited*. This longing for the pre-war world would also be a strong theme at Trinity College Dublin in the decade following the conflict.

Adding to the sense of rupture was the wider Irish context, which is discussed at length in Chapter Four below. The political situation in Ireland after the end of the First World War was unrecognisable when compared with 1914. Trinity men volunteered and fought in that war for disparate reasons; those who were politically motivated did so to reassert their unionist or Home Rule credentials. Those who fought out of a sense of group solidarity found that their choice had become politicised; participation in the war was not congruent with the rise of Sinn Féin and separatist nationalism in the aftermath of 1916. In 1919, Trinity faced an uncertain future on many fronts; the beginning of this uncertainty, and the death of Old Trinity, began in 1914.

Shortly before his death in May 1919, Mahaffy had made elaborate proposals for a war memorial, which was to take the form of a replica of the Niké of Samothrace, the famous Greek statue of the goddess of victory. This statue was to be of 'colossal size' and would stand in the middle of Front Square, its design being completed using the evidence from ancient coins.[143] The proposal, enthusiastically embraced by students immediately before Mahaffy's death, was quietly dropped thereafter. The proposed memorial would have reflected many sides of Mahaffy's career; it echoed both his love of the classics and ancient history, his proclivity for ostentation, and the way in which he was seen—and saw himself—as towering over Trinity. The war changed this; in 1919, the mood was sombre, with almost 500 members of the college community dead, many disabled, and, crucially, Ireland drifting into a secessionist war. There was little appetite for such a monument.

NOTES:

[1] Editorial, *T.C.D.: a College Miscellany*, 28 November 1917, 1.

[2] *University of Dublin, Trinity College. War List* (Dublin, 1922), v–vi.

[3] Trinity had the sixth-highest enlistment rate of any university in Britain and Ireland, and suffered the sixth-highest losses. J.M. Winter, *The Great War and the British people* (London, 1985), 94–5.

[4] Jean-François Sirinelli, *Génération intellectuelle: khâgneux et normaliens dans l'entre-deux-guerres* (Paris, 1988), 26–30; Richard Carr and Bradley W. Hart, 'Old Etonians, Great War demographics and the interpretations of British eugenics *c*. 1914–1939', *First World War Studies* 3 (October 2012), 217–40; Samuel Hynes, *The Auden generation: literature and politics in England in the 1930s* (London, 1976), 17–37.

[5] 'Academica', *Cambridge Magazine*, 26 January 1918, 338; Elisabeth Fordham, 'The University of Paris during the First World War: some paradoxes', in Trude Maurer (ed.), *Kollegen – Kommilitonen – Kämpfer: Europäische Universitäten im Ersten Weltkrieg* (Stuttgart, 2006), 91–106: 93–4.

[6] See, for example, John Horne (ed.), *Our war: Ireland and the Great War* (Dublin, 2008); John Horne and Edward Madigan (eds), *Towards commemoration: Ireland in war and revolution 1912–1923* (Dublin, 2013).

[7] R.B. McDowell and D.A. Webb, *Trinity College Dublin 1592–1952: an academic history* (Cambridge, 1982; new edn, Dublin, 2004), 480.

[8] Frank M. Laird, *Personal experiences of the Great War (an unfinished manuscript)* (Dublin, 1925), 1.

[9] Walter Starkie, *Scholars and gypsies: an autobiography* (London, 1963), 120.

[10] Macran was held in Germany from the outbreak of war until the turn of the New Year in 1915, when he was released in an exchange of prisoners, the consequence of Mahaffy's political lobbying; see British National Archives, Kew, FO 383/21.

[11] 'Travelling from Germany', *The Times*, 7 August 1914, 3.

[12] Alan Kramer, *Dynamic of destruction: culture and mass killing in the First World War* (Oxford, 2007), 27–30.

[13] 'Louvain: a protest', *Irish Times*, 3 September 1914, 6.

[14] 'A hymn of culture', *T.C.D.*, 9 December 1914, 173.

[15] 'The fallen idol', *The Times*, 5 January 1915, 9.

[16] W.B. Stanford and R.B. McDowell, *Mahaffy: a biography of an Anglo-Irishman* (London, 1971), 93.

[17] 'Letters on the War: the sack of Louvain', *The Times*, 1 September 1914, 12.

[18] 'The War and Great Britain: modern history lectures in Trinity College', *Irish Times*, 5 November 1914, 6.

[19] Archives Nationales (AN), Paris, AJ/2589, Conseil de l'Université de Paris, Meeting of 18 December 1914, 371.

[20] TCD, MS 2314/4/43, Joly Papers, Circular letter to Joly, 6 October 1914.

[21] The petition, which was signed by the most eminent names in the British scholarly world, also included the signature of J.B. Bury, Regius Professor of History at Cambridge and once of Trinity. 'Reply to German professors—Reasoned statement by British scholars', *The Times*, 21 October 1914, 10.

[22] 'University of Dublin: conferring of degrees for Volunteers', *Irish Times*, 30 August 1914, 3.

[23] 'Fill up the ranks!', *The Times*, 29 August 1914, 9.

[24] 'Cambridge University and the War', letter of W. Durnford and H.J. Edwards to *The Times*, 3 September 1914, 9, 'Universities and the War,' *The Times*, 7 September 1914, 4.

[25] Mahaffy claimed that 200 men had been accepted for commissions by that point. 'Dublin University and the War', quoted in *Irish Times*, 25 September 1914, 7.

[26] *War List*, v.

[27] Hew Strachan, *History of the Cambridge University Officers Training Corps* (Tunbridge Wells, 1976), 121–2.

[28] Thomas Weber, 'British Universities and the First World War', in Maurer (ed.), *Kollegen – Kommilitonen – Kämpfer*, 75–90: 77–8.

[29] Roger Willoughby, *A military history of the University of Dublin and its Officers Training Corps* (Limerick, 1989), 2.

[30] Editorial notes, *T.C.D.*, 9 February 1910, 192; Editorial notes, *T.C.D.*, 23 February 1910, 21.

[31] Willoughby, *A military history of the University of Dublin*, 9. Student population figures are derived from *Dublin University Calendar*, 1910–14.

[32] 'O.T.C. notes', *T.C.D.*, 3 March 1915, 37.

[33] NLI, MS15177/3, Redmond Papers, Coffey to commander of armed forces in Ireland, 7 April, 1915.

[34] David Fitzpatrick, 'The logic of collective sacrifice: Ireland and the British Army, 1914–1918', *Historical Journal* 38 (4) (December, 1995), 1017–30: 1017.

[35] Keith Jeffery, *Ireland and the Great War* (Cambridge, 2000), 9.

[36] R.C. Fetherstonhaugh, *McGill University at war 1914–1918, 1939–1945* (Montreal, 1947), 2–14.

[37] Alvin Jackson, 'Irish Unionists and the Empire', in Keith Jeffery (ed.), *An Irish empire? Aspects of Ireland and the British Empire* (Manchester, 1996), 123–48: 136.

[38] McDowell and Webb, *Trinity College Dublin*, 354.

[39] Jeffery, *Ireland and the Great War*, 12–14.

[40] Starkie, *Scholars and gypsies*, 131.

[41] National Army Museum, London (NAM), 7707–76, Random recollections recorded by J.M. Stewart-Moore at Drumtullagh, Commencing Tuesday, 27 January 1976, 2.

[42] P.L. Dickinson, *The Dublin of yesterday* (London, 1929), 120.

[43] Account of T.C. Kingsmill Moore, Auditor 1915–19, in Declan Budd and Ross Hinds (eds), *The Hist and Edmund Burke's club* (Dublin, 1997), 185.

[44] NAM, 1976–07–69, Papers of Noel E. Drury, Book 1, 21.

[45] Fitzpatrick, 'The logic of collective sacrifice', 1029–30.

[46] Starkie was refused on medical grounds. Starkie, *Scholars and gypsies*, 131.

[47] Laird, *Personal experiences of the Great War*, 3.

[48] Laird, *Personal experiences of the Great War*, 29.

[49] TCD, MS 11398/24, Joseph Johnston to Clare Johnston, 8 November 1914.

[50] 'D.U. Officers' Training Corps and the War', *T.C.D.*, 11 November 1914, 129.

[51] TCD, MUN/V/5/21, 91.

[52] School of Engineering, Trinity College Dublin, *A record of past and present students* (Dublin, 1909).

[53] Fitzpatrick, 'The logic of collective sacrifice', 1029–30.

[54] The remaining 772 had enlisted in the armed services before the war.

[55] Fitzpatrick, 'The logic of collective sacrifice', 1020; Fitzpatrick; 'Militarism in Ireland, 1900–1922', in Thomas Bartlett and Keith Jeffery (eds), *A military history of Ireland* (Cambridge, 1996), 379–406: 388.

[56] David Fitzpatrick, 'Home Front and everyday life', in Horne (ed.), *Our war*, 131–42: 134.

[57] All figures are derived from the *War List*.

[58] Winter, *The Great War and the British people*, 92.

[59] Fitzpatrick, 'Militarism in Ireland, 1900–1922', 392.

[60] *War List*.

[61] Gerald Morgan, 'The Dublin Pals', in Sarah Alyn-Stacey (ed.), *Essays on heroism and sport in Ireland and France* (Lampeter, 2003), 101–35: 126.

[62] Stuart Ward, 'Parallel lives, poles apart: commemorating Gallipoli in Ireland and Australia', in Horne and Madigan (eds), *Towards Commemoration*, 29–37: 31; Fitzpatrick, 'Militarism in Ireland 1900–22', 391.

[63] 'Irish valour in Gallipoli', *Irish Times*, 31 August 1915, 5.

[64] *War List*, 139.

[65] W.R.G. Atkins, 'Sydney Young, 1857–1937', *Obituary notices of fellows of the Royal Society* 2 (6) (January 1938), 373.

[66] R.B. MacCarthy, *John Henry Bernard 1860–1927* (Dublin, 2008), 23.

[67] Woods Family Papers - Private collection, Mahaffy to Lady Woods, no date.

[68] Parliamentary Archives, BL 51/18, Campbell to Bonar Law, 21 September 1915; *War List*, 29.

[69] Philip Orr, '200,000 volunteer soldiers', in Horne (ed.), *Our War*, 67–70.

[70] Julian's last words are reputed to have been 'I am glad I did my duty'. NLI, MS13487, TP Gill papers, Folder 10, Account of Dardanelles Expedition, 20 August 1915.

[71] NAM, 7707–76, Stewart-Moore reminiscences, 36.

[72] National Archives of the United Kingdom (NAUK), FO 383/267, Bernard to Harmsworth, 25 May 1917.

[73] TCD, MS 11290/1, Crookshank to his Mother, nd.

[74] TCD, MS 11290/8, Crookshank to his Mother, 2 November 1917.

[75] Morgan, 'The Dublin Pals', 130.

[76] *War List*, vi.

[77] TCD, MS 2388/110, Letter of Francis Dixon, 22 February 1917.

[78] S. Lyle-Cummins, 'The Late Professor Adrian Stokes', *British Medical Journal* 2 (3489) (19 November 1927), 956.

[79] *Annual Report of Sir P. Dun's hospital Grand Canal Street, Dublin, for the year ended December 31, 1914* (Dublin, 1915), 6–7.

[80] Edward Madigan, *Faith under fire: Anglican army chaplains and the Great War* (Basingstoke, 2011), 90.

[81] *War List*, vi.

[82] Madigan, *Faith under fire*, 104.

[83] Madigan, *Faith under fire*, 107–8.

[84] Luce was one of three fellows to serve in the war. The other two were Francis la Touche Godfrey and Samuel George Stewart.

[85] Jack Point (pseud: Joseph Johnston), *The compleat anglers: a brazen monument immortalising the tutorial system* (Dublin, 1935), 8.

[86] This happens in the letters of Henry Crookshank (TCD MS 11290), Joseph Johnston (it is a feature of letters he received; he did not enlist; TCD MS 11398), Patrick Hone (TCD MS 11274), as well as in the pages of *T.C.D.*

[87] NAM, 7707–76, Stewart-Moore reminiscences, 33.

[88] NAM, 7707–76, Stewart-Moore reminiscences, 44.

[89] NLI, MS22902.

90 Ann and Dermot Keogh, *Bertram Windle, the Honan bequest, and the modernisation of University College Cork 1904–1919* (Cork, 2010), 158.

91 Editorial, *T.C.D.* xx (359) (11 November 1914), 126.

92 H.K. O'Kelly, 'Letter from the front', *T.C.D.*, 25 November 1914, 152.

93 *Irish Independent*, 30 December 1914, 3.

94 Editorial, *T.C.D.*, 10 November 1915, 121.

95 Editorial, *T.C.D.*, 9 June 1915, 100.

96 TCD, MUN/V/21, 91, Minute of 27 February 1915.

97 TCD, MUN/DUESA/4, Meetings of 18 September 1914 and 12 November 1914.

98 TCD, MUN/DUESA/4, Meeting of 9 December 1918.

99 Both of the named debates were decided in the negative. T.S.C. Dagg, *College Historical Society, a history (1770–1920)* (Cork?, 1969), 353–4.

100 Account of T.C. Kingsmill Moore, in Budd and Hinds (eds), *The Hist and Edmund Burke's Club*, 186–7.

101 *Dublin University Calendar, 1916–17*, pt I, v–vi.

102 *Dublin University Calendar, 1916–17*, pt I, vii.

103 *Dublin University Calendar, 1916–17*, pt I, xxix.

104 *Dublin University Calendar, 1918–19*, pt I, i.

105 *Dublin University Calendar, 1916–17*, pt I, lxxxiv; xc.

106 Gilbert Waterhouse, *The War and the study of German, a public lecture delivered in Trinity College, Dublin, on Tuesday, May 29th, 1917* (Dublin, 1917), 3.

107 'In a College Doorway, 1915', *T.C.D.*,16 June 1915, 115.

108 *War List*, vi.

109 See *University of Edinburgh, roll of honour 1914–1919* (Edinburgh, 1921); *University of St. Andrews, roll of honour and roll of service, 1914–1919* (Edinburgh, 1920); *The war list of the University of Cambridge, 1914–1918* (Cambridge, 1920); *Oxford University roll of service, 1914–1916* (Oxford, 1916).

110 'Dublin University VAD Hospital', *Irish Times*, 30 June 1917, 6.

111 *War List*, 33.

112 J.V. Luce, 'Introduction: a memoir of A.A. Luce', in A.A. Luce, *Fishing and thinking* (Shrewsbury, 1990, originally published 1959), i–ix: iii.

113 *War List*, 220.

114 Parkes, *A danger to the men*, 87.

115 Bodleian Library Special Collections (BLSC), MS Fisher 61/61–62, Alison Phillips to H.A.L. Fisher, 2 December 1915.

116 Editorial, *T.C.D.*, 11 November 1914, 128.

117 Editorial, *T.C.D.*, 5 June 1918, 109–110.

118 Editorial, *T.C.D.*, 5 June 1918, 109–110.

119 Editorial, *T.C.D.*,12 June 1918, 115.

120 Lyndall Luce, who came to Dublin and Trinity in 1948 as the wife of Professor J.V. Luce, used this term. Parkes, 'The 1940s: College during the Emergency and after', in *A danger to the men*, 164.

121 H.A.L. Fisher, Preface to *British universities and the war* (Boston and New York, 1917), xi–xiv: xiii.

122 TCD, MS 2303a.

123 TCD, MS 2303a/48, Ernest Rutherford to Joly, 18 September 1915.

124 NAUK, WO 106/342.

125 H.H. Poole, 'William Ringrose Gelston Atkins: 1884–1959', in *Biographical memoirs of fellows of the Royal Society* 5 (February 1960), 3.

[126] Atkins, 'Henry Horatio Dixon', 85–6.

[127] Dixon Papers, School of Botany, Trinity College Dublin, W.R.G. Atkins, 'Aircraft Timber'.

[128] TCD, MUN/DUESA 4.

[129] TCD, MUN/DUESA 4, DUESA meeting of 30 January 1923.

[130] 'Sir W. Henry Thompson', *British Medical Journal* 2 (3016) (19 October 1918), 451–2.

[131] George Weisz, *The emergence of modern universities in France, 1863–1914* (Princeton, 1983), 341–68.

[132] 'The neglect of science', *The Times*, 14 January 1916, 9.

[133] *The neglect of science* (London, 1916), 7.

[134] TCD, MUN/V/5/21, 362, Board meeting of 21 November 1919.

[135] TCD, MS 2313/3/9, Address of John Joly, *Columbia Alumni News*, 'Foreign visitors', 18 October 1918, 10, 3, 136–7.

[136] AN, AJ/16/2890, Minister of Education to Vice-Rector of the Academy of Paris, 24 October 1919. It seems that the most likely facilitator of this exchange was Joseph Johnston, who was well connected to French intellectual elites through his experiences with the Fondation Kahn, which had sponsored his round the world trip in 1914–5. Another individual who was important in this connection was Émile Borel, an associate of Johnston through the Kahn Foundation and the sous-directeur of the École Normale Supérieure; he was given an honorary degree by Trinity in 1921. Robert William Tate, *Orationes et Epistolae Dublinenses (1914–40)* (Dublin, 1941), 43.

[137] *T.C.D.*, 23 May 1917, 147.

[138] *T.C.D.*, 6 June 1917, 167–8.

[139] 'End of the Great World War', *Irish Independent*, 12 November 1918, 3.

[140] 'Trinity Week', *Irish Times*, 16 June 1919, 4.

[141] 'Universities and Labour', *Irish Times*, 30 January 1919, 4.

[142] Editorial, *T.C.D.*, 19 February 1919, 49.

[143] Editorial, *T.C.D.*, 12 March 1919, 68; Editorial, *T.C.D.*, 21 May 1919, 79–80.

CHAPTER THREE

Inter arma silent leges
Trinity and the Easter Rising

Introduction

Historians may say that Trinity backed the wrong horse;
but at the time there was only one course of action open
to law-abiding citizens in College.

A.A. Luce. [1]

The Easter Rising was the defining event of modern Irish history; it provided the founding narrative for the modern Irish state and became a
reference point for all that followed.[2] Much of the rising's power came
from its symbolism, either through the occupation (or attempted capture)
of iconic sites around Dublin or the 'martyrdom' of the rebel leaders. The
rising was inherently theatrical; Patrick Pearse styled himself on romantic
martyrs like Tone and Emmet whose immediate battles were doomed to
failure but whose sacrifices were necessary to awaken the nation and earn
posthumous reward. The event itself was staged for maximum dramatic
impact.[3] In a theatrical reading, Trinity College played out its historic role

Opposite: 'The birth of the Irish Republic – 1916', poster depicting the Easter Rising, from
the Samuels ephemera collection.

as the pantomime villain, locking its gates and providing a base from which the British army could suppress the rebellion from the Wednesday of Easter Week, while leading college figures issued condemnatory missives in newspapers and journals. As such, the rising served to confirm many of the widely-held criticisms of Trinity made over the previous decades; the symbolic closing of the doors reinforced the college's image as an establishment fortress, and the centrality of the rising to the subsequent narrative of Irish history ensured that Trinity continued to be seen as an oppositional force in Irish national life and politics.

Trinity has demonstrated a deep unease about its actions in 1916 over the subsequent century. Trinity-based or trained scholars, such as F.S.L Lyons, Roy Foster, David Fitzpatrick and Peter Hart have contributed significantly to a greater understanding of the revolutionary decade with all of its contradictions and complications; they helped move the historiography of the period forward considerably from the narrow and hagiographical 'Whiggish' accounts of the period that characterised the first half-century of scholarship following the rising. The college itself, however, has remained virtually silent about its role in the period. The three official college histories published since 1922—those of McDowell and Webb, Kenneth Bailey and John V. Luce—devote only eight pages between them, from over a thousand, to Trinity and the rising.[4] This was not for a want of sources. As we will see, those within the college wrote extensively of their experiences and impressions of the events of Easter Week.

Trinity's silence is explicable in the context of Irish secession from the Union; from 1922, the college, crippled by wartime debts and eager to reconcile itself to the new Free State government in the hope of securing financial aid, began a careful policy of quiet cooperation with the new powers. Both the government and the college were initially suspicious of each other but slowly came to a solid working relationship, which is explored at length in the Epilogue below. While this process was on-going, however, there was little discussion of Trinity's role in the rising. During the 1960s, as the fiftieth anniversary of the rising loomed, Trinity decided to record the reminiscences of its veterans of the week who were still alive, but the ultimate plans for these accounts are unclear.[5] Public silence prevailed.

For Trinity College, the rising's outbreak must be seen in the wider context of the war. Indeed, many immediate reactions in the college, as elsewhere around Dublin and Ireland, assumed that the rebellion was directly initiated by Germany. Trinity was, as we have seen, deeply embedded in the prosecution of the war; the conflict pervaded university life. The OTC was actively preparing men for commissions in the army, classes were under-populated, and people craved news of those at fighting fronts in far-flung parts of the globe. In April 1916 many contemporaries initially felt that the war had come to Trinity College, and the week of hostilities in Dublin presented those who were left behind with a terrible taste of the front. Whereas the universities that Trinity saw as its peers experienced a sense of rupture in their normal life on account of the war, only a handful, such as the University of Louvain in Belgium in 1914 and the Sorbonne for a period in spring 1918, were directly menaced by conflict. Trinity joined that short list, and gained the curious distinction of having the only Officers Training Corps in Britain or Ireland to see active service during the war years—although ironically, not in the First World War itself.

Trinity's experience of the events of Easter Week—broadly defined— is a complex web of often contradictory motivations and reactions, public gestures and private ruminations, and occasionally erroneous recollections. The college's experience of the week served both to reinforce the symbolic and physical separation between Trinity and the city of Dublin, and to break it down altogether.

The Easter Rising

Trinity was, like the rest of the city of Dublin, caught unawares by the events of the morning of 24 April 1916. The college was virtually empty, with most people away for the long weekend, compounding Trinity's under-population on account of the war. Some members of the college community were attending the races at Fairyhouse that Monday. The main focus of the university's activity was to be an election, triggered by the appointment of one of the university's MPs—James Campbell—to the position of attorney-general for Ireland, which was scheduled for that week.[6] Some examinations were also due to take place. The Professor of Geology and Mineralogy, John Joly, later wrote that Monday, 24 April looked 'a day of peaceful thoughts if ever there was one'.[7]

The seizure of the General Post Office—the symbolic inauguration of the rising—seems to have gone unnoticed by people in Dublin city centre, many of whom were informed by word of mouth after midday.[8] The exception to this was the Professor of German, Gilbert Waterhouse, who heard 'fairly heavy firing from a southerly direction'—presumably St Stephen's Green—from his rooms at 34 New Square.[9] Arthur Aston Luce, one of three fellows of the college on active service in the war, found himself home in Dublin on leave. He too was oblivious to events escalating around him, and walked John Gwynn, the octogenarian Regius

Professor of Divinity, from Christchurch Cathedral to Sackville Street, where he was to catch a tram. On their way they were warned not to venture too far up the street, as Luce's army uniform might bring unwanted attention. Luce walked Gwynn to his tram, turned to face the GPO, and only then saw that 'the windows were sand-bagged, and rifles looked out'. Almost immediately, 'a small troop of horse cantered up on the far side of the road; rifles rang out, and one or two horses and riders fell'.[10] Luce then made his way to Trinity.

As word of a rebellion began to trickle in, the few present in college, without knowing details of what was happening, sought to make it secure. The Chief Steward, 70-year-old Joseph Marshall, took care of this:

> I took from my Office a large padlock with a strong chain attached and put it on the [Front] gate myself, together with arming the Porters with Fenian Pikes, which I had seized while in the DMP [Dublin Metropolitan Police] in 1867. I also directed the Porters to invite into College all passing soldiers for safety, many of whom entered College and became very useful later on in defence of the College when armed at OTC Headquarters.[11]

Marshall also arranged for the porters to lock Lincoln Gate—at the college's east end—and a sentry was placed on duty there, while the chief steward armed himself with an 'old historic revolver and my Tipperary Blackthorn, which I brought into use in the Wild Riots in Dublin in September 1913'.[12] While the OTC had ammunition and weapons stored at the other end of the campus, Marshall seems to have been happy to make do with his own private store of assorted weapons.

There is perhaps an irony that it was the porters, who existed somewhat apart from the main body of college's academic community, who were the ones to defend its interests. As has been demonstrated in Chapter One, however, even if Trinity's non-academic staff were not wholly integrated into the academic community, they were relatively well remunerated for their work and likely felt their own sense of institutional loyalty. Moreover, their response was no different from that of the majority of Dublin's population, irrespective of class, who initially did not support the outbreak of hostilities and the breakdown in law and order that followed.

In the opulent surrounds of the Provost's House, John Mahaffy's daughters, Elsie and Rachel, were making plans for their servants' outing. Elsie was filled with 'happy thoughts' when one of the porters, George Crawford, arrived to announce that a rebellion had broken out, that the

Front Gate of college had been locked, and that the gates to Number One Grafton Street (the Provost's House) should be locked and all west-facing shutters pulled.[13] Like Waterhouse, Elsie Mahaffy soon heard shots from the south, which she reckoned to have come from St Stephen's Green.[14] Elsie, unmarried and aged 47 in 1916, began recording events in a notebook as they unfolded and collecting related ephemera, which she pasted into the notebook alongside her written account; in doing so she emerged from her father's considerable shadow as a remarkable witness to epoch-defining events.

Almost unthinkingly, members of the college community descended upon Trinity on hearing the news of the rising. It seems that people were instinctively drawn to the campus. Gerald Fitzgibbon, a 49-year-old bar-rister and Trinity graduate, had joined the OTC in 1914 in anticipation of a German invasion. When he heard of the rising, he, 'knew everyone would be wanted there', and within minutes he was summoned to Trinity by E.H. Alton, a fellow of the college and a captain in the OTC. Being the highest ranking officer present, Alton took command on his arrival. He and Fitzgibbon found 'about a dozen [men] collected, and at once got out rifles and ammunition [from the OTC stores] and served them out'.[15]

The men who assembled were a disparate crew. Aside from OTC members like Fitzgibbon and Alton, there were men from many different regiments who happened to be on leave in Dublin and had quickly de-camped to Trinity, knowing its wartime military ethos and assuming it to be a safe-haven. James Glen was an OTC member and young artillery officer who, like Luce, inadvertently walked past the GPO in the early af-ternoon of Easter Monday. Both he and the friend accompanying him were in uniform and, coming under fire, had to run away. Perhaps the war really had come to Dublin. Glen described the situation:

> We realised that we were probably the target and ran down to O'Connell Bridge, where we were joined by about half a dozen soldiers (Australians and, I think, one or two South Africans) who were on leave and had been attracted by the firing. My friend and I ... took the party into College.[16]

Those assembled in college on the Monday came from across Ireland, Britain and the empire. Fitzgibbon estimated that they were five ANZACS (Australian and New Zealand Army Corps), two or three Canadians and nine South Africans, as well as men from different British regiments.[17] For these men who had come from the front, the rising was another battle

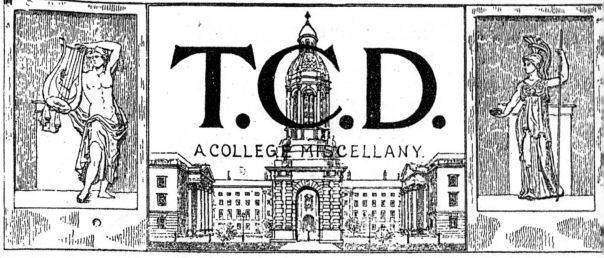

T.C.D.

A COLLEGE MISCELLANY.

Vol. XXII. No. 388   MONDAY, JUNE 19, 1916.   **Price Threepence.**

NOTICES.

"T.C.D." is published every Wednesday during the six weeks of Lecture Term.

Applications for Advertisements should be addressed to the Treasurer, " T.C.D.," Trinity College. Dublin.

The Subscription is (post free) **2/6** for the year; for ten years, **20/-**. To residents in College, **6d.** per Term. **Subscriptions for the Present Term must be paid at once to the Secretary. "T C.D.," Trinity College.** Colonial Subscription, **3/-** per year; for a period of ten years, **25/-**.

All Contributions for insertion should be addressed :— "The Editors, ' T.C.D.,' Trinity College, Dublin," and, if intended for publication in any particular Number, should reach us not later than the FRIDAY before publication.

Since our last issue the rebellion has come and gone, and in that rebellion Trinity College, true to her traditions, has played a worthy if an unacceptable part. To be called on to defend our University against the attack of Irishmen, to be forced in self-defence to shoot down our countrymen—these are things which even the knowledge of duty well fulfilled cannot render anything but sad and distasteful. Trinity College has always held men of every shade of religious and political thought, but all alike have held staunchly to the ideals of loyalty, and have foreseen for Ireland a brighter future as one of the mother countries of a mighty Empire than as an isolated and impotent state. Though the College vigorously opposed the Act of Union, and though it was their applause of a patriotic speech of Grattan's that lost the students their time-honoured privilege of free admission to the Irish Parliament by merely holding up their gown, yet we find College Volunteers helping to quell the rebellion of '98. "They took part in all the military movements around Dublin," and their banners, moth-eaten and begrimed with age, now hang in the entrance hall of the Provost's House.

Nor is this the first time that Trinity College has been in the hands of the military. James II. and his army occupied it in 1689, and relieved the College of much of its property. The soldiers followed the example of their commanders, for we read that "The garrison destroyed the doors, wainscots, closets and floors, and damnified it in the building and furniture of private rooms to the value of two thousand pounds." Luckily in the last occupation the property of students and College, with a few exceptions, remained unhurt.

Yet in all the disturbances of the past centuries Trinity has never passed a more anxious time than on that fateful first night of the rebellion, when the houses held by the enemy loomed ominously over the low building, where a handful of students watched and waited for an attack; while the tramp of rebel feet and the sound of rebel challenges came clearly being fought in unfamiliar surrounds. Members of the OTC were both impressed and taken aback by their battle-hardened professionalism.

The locking of the front gate was a symbolic act; there was still much crossover between those outside and those within. Ernie O'Malley, a medical student in UCD, found that he had a choice to make. He had bumped into two Trinity students who promised him a rifle and convinced him to join the defence of the college. O'Malley first went home, and on his way met a friend from the School of Art who changed his mind. His friend perceptively argued that

> it's not your university. Remember you'll have to shoot down Irishmen, your own countrymen. You bear them no hatred. If you go in there you cannot leave; and, mark my words, you'll be sorry ever afterward. Think it over.[18]

O'Malley later rose to prominence as a republican during the War of Independence; but for two chance meetings, things could have been different; such was the contingent nature of Easter Week.

Sentries were posted on the various gates around the college. John Joly, aged 59 in 1916, arrived at Trinity at 4 pm on the afternoon of Easter Monday and found the college 'almost without defenders', save for the small band under Alton, Luce and Waterhouse.[19] Provost Mahaffy did not betray any outward signs of anxiety.

> He seemed as he walked up and down the garden to be as calm and free from alarm as if nothing exceptional had been happening, and as if there was nothing to prevent his enjoying studious ease in an academic bower.[20]

The garrison quickly organised itself, and Luce recalled that 'sentries were posted at the Regent House windows, and outside on the roof, and at other key points. There were snipers in the Nassau Street windows, and crossing the [College] Park was not safe.'[21] The colonial soldiers were placed on the roof of Trinity's West Front, facing onto College Green, while other members of the ramshackle garrison were placed elsewhere in the college grounds. On the night of 24 April, there were 44 men inside.[22] John Joly wrote:

Opposite: 'Editorial', from T.C.D.: *a College Miscellany*, vol. 22, no. 388, 19 June 1916, in the aftermath of the rising, noting the extent of Trinity's involvement.

Night now slowly closed in. The city without was plainly in a state of chaos. Shots rang out every now and again. Distant shouts and challenges were heard. Sometimes a more rapid succession of shots suggested more serious fighting. Slowly the precincts around became indistinct. Impending dangers, unknown disasters, seemed to fill the gloom. Was this indeed to be, perhaps, the last night of our ancient University? The question is no mere extravagance of the imagination, for so much of the very existence of so venerable a foundation is bound up with its century-old buildings, with its literary and artistic treasures, that sack and conflagration in a single night might obliterate practically, all but its memory from the earth. So might perish Ireland's most priceless treasure— the University of Berkeley, Goldsmith, Burke, Hamilton, and Lecky.[23]

The defence of Trinity College?

Accounts of the period, written at the time and subsequently, referred to the 'defence' of college. One of the first scholarly accounts of the revolutionary period, written in 1923 by Trinity historian Walter Alison Phillips, claimed that 'a feeble attack on Trinity College was beaten off by a few soldiers and cadets of the Officers Training Corps', and this image has prevailed.[24] However, it was not accurate. The motley crew present in Trinity on Easter Monday made preparations for an attack, but none ever came. The front-like experience of those inside of the college, in addition to the incessant sound of gunfire heard from outside, fostered the idea that the university was under siege, but the attacks were metaphorical rather than literal; there was little defending to be done. Trinity's story of 1916 was, initially, a non-event, and this came as a great surprise to those present.

Gerald Fitzgibbon wrote of his reaction to events. 'We were lucky to have held it [College], I doubt if we could have stuck out for twenty four hours with the means at our disposal if we had been seriously attacked.'[25] He added that if the rebels 'had come any time after midday on Tuesday it would have been a merry fight. Before that, we would have been scuppered'.[26] Many years later James Glen recalled that

> The insurgents erred badly in not trying to rush the College early on Monday and in not including it among their strong-points...Failing an initial rush, a determined attack during the first night might well have been successful.[27]

Major Harris of the OTC wrote that the college was especially vulnerable from the east side, where it was relatively exposed at Westland Row. The rebels held many houses on that street as well as the railway bridge that overlooked the College Park and, crucially, the OTC Parade Ground. A rebel prisoner later explained to Harris that the sight of sandbags led them to believe that Trinity was better defended than it actually was and, therefore, they did not feel that they could successfully enter or occupy it.[28]

There was reason to believe that Trinity may be attacked, as many of those present seemed to assume. It was widely regarded as a symbol of ascendency, elitism, inequality and the Union itself. It embodied everything that political and cultural nationalists claimed to stand against and was frequently cited as an example of British misrule and misunderstanding of Ireland. These characteristics were frequently unrepresentative of the university as a whole; nevertheless, they still retained an important rhetorical value. The Trinity 'other' helped give definition to political and cultural nationalists. Following this line of thinking, an attack on Trinity would be an attack on all elements of British rule, be they cultural, military or political. Trinity College was not the only strategic or symbolic site in Dublin to go unmolested, however: Dublin Castle, the Bank of Ireland on College Green, and the Custom House were all also notable for their strategic importance and were for the most part unscathed by the rising.[29]

Planning of the rising was clouded in secrecy and, thus, the intentions of the rebels remained unclear both to contemporaries and to historians.[30] Moreover, organisation of the rising was ramshackle at first. That said, Trinity occupied one of the most strategic points in the city, and occupying it certainly might have been within the rebels' plans, given that it stands almost equidistant from Dublin Castle, St Stephen's Green and the GPO. The importance of Trinity in breaking lines of communication would prove integral to suppressing the rising, underlining this strategic value.[31]

What is more, from the outbreak of war it was assumed by many that the minority Volunteers—who had split with John Redmond in 1914—could stage a rebellion.[32] Trinity College was known to have stores of ammunition that were held by the OTC; indeed the Irish Volunteers had undertaken reconnaissance of Trinity to assess the viability of raiding these ammunitions stores in early 1916, when a post office employee called John Brophy was able to access the college grounds in his capacity as a telegraph messenger and drew detailed sketches of the campus. On the basis of this information, his commandants Éamon Ceannt and Cathal Brugha decided that a raid on Trinity was not viable due to the difficulty of escaping the grounds.[33] While a raid was far from a full-on assault, this anecdote suggests that Trinity was perceived as a difficult site to hold. The high walls and wrought-iron railings were frequently invoked as metaphorical evidence of Trinity's fortress mentality; perhaps this also factored into the military perception of the rebels.

In his account of Easter Week, Joly was deeply troubled about the potential destruction of college buildings and the cultural heritage they represented.[34] This was a legitimate concern and one that needs to be put in historical context. One of the developments of the First World War that marked it out as a new departure in warfare was cultural vandalism. As already noted, in late August 1914 the German army burned down the seventeenth-century library at the University of Louvain (where Mahaffy had been given an honorary degree). This attack, coupled with the shelling of Rheims Cathedral in France that September, not only outraged the academic world, but became a rallying point in popular representations of the war. As these were sites of cultural, not military, significance it seemed as though the symbols of learning—indeed, culture itself—were targets in this brutal war.[35] The controversy surrounding the actions of the German army scandalised international opinion, especially in neutral countries such as the United States. Stories of German atrocities committed in Belgium were a focus for Irish support for the war effort in 1914 and 1915 and even became a galvanising myth at Patrick Pearse's St Enda's School in Rathfarnham.[36]

A number of the rebel leaders had Trinity connections and sometimes complex relationships with the college. Pearse frequently railed against Trinity's un-Irish attitude in his periodical writings.[37] He had briefly attended lectures at Trinity in 1900 while training to be a barrister at the King's Inns and, unsurprisingly, found the atmosphere oppressive.[38] At the same time, two of his greatest political inspirations were Trinity men: Thomas Davis and Robert Emmet. Douglas Hyde was also an important guiding figure in cultural matters. During Easter Week a bizarre rumour began circulating amongst Dublin's Protestant population: Pearse wanted to be installed as provost of Trinity.[39] While this was nothing but a curious aside to the week's events, it was suggestive of a degree of respect the rebels may have held for Trinity and its potential in a new Irish Republic. More than that, it showed the insecurity of those connected to the college, who suddenly had to make sense of huge disruption to their normal lives that was, it was becoming clear, predicated on a rejection of the values for which they stood.

Other rebels had stronger links to Trinity than Pearse. Éamon de Valera had been on the books at Trinity in 1905–6, attended lectures in mathematics and sat three college examinations before taking up a teaching post at Carysfort College in September 1906.[40] John Henry Bernard later wrote, with a dismissive flourish that would have made Mahaffy proud, that de Valera's academic failure was 'so complete that immediately after the scholarship examination he abandoned the idea of distinguishing himself in the world of learning, and turned to Irish politics'.[41] Joseph Mary Plunkett was the son of a Trinity graduate, George Noble Plunkett, who had in turn been sworn into the Irish Republican Brotherhood in April 1916.[42] And, as we have seen, Thomas MacDonagh applied for Dowden's chair of English in 1913. All of this demonstrates that the pre-war arguments that posited that Trinity was cut off from the rest of Dublin and Ireland did not hold up to closer scrutiny; there was much crossover between the population of the college and the rest of the city; even the rebel leaders had first hand experience of that.

Inside and outside the walls

The story of the 'defence' of college is only part of the story of Trinity and the Easter Rising. Dublin was paralysed for a week as telegram lines were cut and trams did not run. Simply getting about was fraught with danger, but there was still much movement around the city. Many rumours circulated and information became a valuable commodity. On Tuesday, 25 April, martial law was declared in Dublin.[43] Beyond the four walls of college, Trinity's wider community, scattered across Dublin, Ireland and beyond also became part of the story of the rising. Some members of the college community, like Monica Roberts, daughter of William Westropp Roberts, the Senior Lecturer, were stranded outside the city in the family home at Stillorgan. William was able to telephone college on Easter Monday to ascertain that examinations would not be held; shortly after the lines were cut and the Roberts family would experience the week's hostilities through the sound of distant explosions, flashes on the horizon at night and rumour.[44]

Walter Starkie cycled around the city throughout the week, although by the Friday his movements were curtailed. On Easter Monday, he had the misfortune to come across the aftermath of the ambush of the 'Gorgeous Wrecks' of the Home Defence Force at the intersection of Haddington and Northumberland Roads. This band of often elderly

Dubliners was drawn from the business elites of the city. They were too old to enlist in the armed forces but frequently drilled unarmed; on this occasion, they were returning from exercises near Kingstown, carrying rifles without ammunition.[45] Among their number was Major Harris, of the OTC, and F.H. Browning, Trinity graduate and president of the Irish Rugby Football Union. Browning, as noted in the previous chapter, had been instrumental in organising the Pals battalion that had been destroyed at Suvla Bay in August 1915. Harris managed to escape the Easter Monday ambush unscathed but Browning was not so fortunate. Starkie was shocked by the 'insanity [that] prompted the rebels to kill unarmed old men'.[46] Another shocked eye-witness wondered what the 'horror of it all' could mean.[47] Danger and death quickly made themselves felt, even away from the rising's main theatre of operations.

For Harry Nicholls, a nationalist and graduate of the Engineering School (1911), the experience of Easter Week was different from that of most of his fellow alumni. Born in Derry to a conservative Protestant family—his father was a self-described imperialist—Harry was politicised by his brother, George (Seoirse), another Trinity graduate and language activist. A third Nicholls brother, William, was a lifelong unionist.[48] Harry, a civil engineer in Dublin Corporation, joined the Volunteers in 1913 and participated in the Howth and Kilcoole gun-runnings in 1914. His engineering background was important, as he lectured to others in his company on the application of engineering to military preparations. He claimed to have been 'ready to go' when the initial Volunteer mobilisation was called off by Eoin MacNeill's countermanding order on Sunday, 23 April. The next day, still awaiting mobilisation orders, he went to St Stephen's Green and presented himself to the Irish Citizen Army there. Later in the week he was placed in charge of the nearby Turkish Baths and was subsequently deported for his part in the rising.[49] Nicholls was the only Trinity graduate to fight with the rebels during Easter Week, and this says much about the prevailing political outlook of the college community. While there was much dissent and a growing constitutionalist nationalist body within Trinity, radical republicans were few in number. There was great irony in the fact that on Easter Monday, the day on which Nicholls went to St Stephen's Green, another engineer, nineteen-year-old undergraduate John A. Thompson from Enniskillen, home on leave from the front, was killed in Dublin.[50]

Opposite: Notice declaring the imposition of martial law in Dublin city and county in response to the outbreak of the rising.

G. R.

PROCLAMATION.

WHEREAS, in the City of Dublin and County of Dublin certain evilly disposed persons and associations, with the intent to subvert the supremacy of the Crown in Ireland, have committed divers acts of violence, and have with deadly weapons attacked the Forces of the Crown, and have resisted by armed force the lawful Authority of His Majesty's Police and Military Forces.   AND whereas by reason thereof several of His Majesty's liege Subjects have been killed and many others severely injured, and much damage to property has been caused.

AND, whereas, such armed resistance to His Majesty's authority still continues.   NOW, I, Ivor Churchill, Baron Wimborne, Lord Lieutenant-General and General Governor of Ireland, by virtue of all the powers me thereunto enabling **DO HEREBY PROCLAIM** that from and after the date of this Proclamation, and for the period of One Month thereafter (unless otherwise ordered) the **CITY OF DUBLIN** and **COUNTY OF DUBLIN** are under and subject to

MARTIAL LAW

AND I do hereby call on all Loyal and well affected Subjects of the Crown to aid in upholding and maintaining the peace of this Realm and the supremacy and authority of the Crown.   AND I warn all peaceable and law-abiding Subjects within such area of the danger of frequenting, or being in any place in or in the vicinity of which His Majesty's Forces are engaged in the suppression of disorder.

AND I do hereby enjoin upon such Subjects the duty and necessity, so far as practicable, of remaining within their own homes so long as these dangerous conditions prevail.

And I do hereby declare that all persons found carrying Arms without lawful authority are liable to be dealt with by virtue of this Proclamation.

Given at Dublin this 25th day of April, 1916.

WIMBORNE

GOD SAVE THE KING.

Diarmid Coffey, who was active in the college Gaelic Society before its suppression, was distraught by what was happening in the city. A Redmondite, he was at the family home at Harcourt Terrace during Easter Week. He wrote of feeling 'cut up' by the outbreak of the rising, and that it 'seems awful sitting here doing nothing while people are killing each other in the streets'.[51] People were anxious for news of the rising and for members of the Trinity community it soon became apparent that information could be gleaned at their alma mater, located as it was at the heart of the hostilities.

In her account of Tuesday, 25 April, Lil Stokes, part of a famous Trinity family, noted that all communication lines had been cut, so she made her way to the Provost's House, where the Mahaffys welcomed her and where she could apprise herself of the situation.[52] Elsie Mahaffy noted that the house had become 'practically an inn', with people passing through on a regular basis for meals, security and out of a sense of kinship with the others present.[53] The young medical student, Dorothy Stopford Price, also wanted to go to college to attend a Botany laboratory on the Tuesday but was advised against doing so, instead spending the remainder of Easter Week at the Viceregal Lodge with Sir Matthew Nathan, the under-secretary for Ireland.[54]

It was not just the Provost's House that became a hive of activity. On Monday, the OTC set up a Medical Unit, initially in House Six (in the rooms of the Elizabethan Society), and later in rooms in Botany Bay. Casualties were brought into the improvised hospital from every street in the vicinity of college, and a report written once hostilities had ended noted with pride that not one wound treated by the unit had become septic.[55]

Despite Trinity taking measures to repel an anticipated attack, there was still traffic passing through college. It was occasionally distressing. Elsie Mahaffy recalled a sudden commotion in the Provost's House at 4 am on Tuesday morning. It was Alton and Sheppard.

> Together they opened the hall door into the street front; more people came running through to carry through our hall after a short while a dead Sinn Féiner on a stretcher... He had been shot from the roof of Trinity College; one of three rebel despatch riders on bicycles. His comrades only redoubled their speed and left him lying on the road.[56]

The despatch rider's name was Gerald Keogh. He was recorded as the Medical Unit's first casualty but died before reaching them. Gerald Fitzgibbon witnessed the incident; the sharpshooting of the ANZAC snipers having delivered the fatal shot and dispersed the two other riders accompanying Keogh.[57] The body remained in a room in college for three days before it was temporarily buried in the garden of the Provost's House. Elsie Mahaffy wondered who he was, and was surprised that someone from a middle-class background could be part of the rising. 'During the fortnight while he lay in College, though well dressed and from a respectable street, no one ever came to ask for his body.'[58] Ever inquisitive, John Joly went to see the body and was deeply troubled by what he found:

> Later I saw him. In no irreverent spirit I lifted the face-cloth. He looked quite young; one might almost call him a boy. The handsome waxen face was on one side concealed in blood. Poor boy! What crime was his?[59]

A.A. Luce, the Church of Ireland clergyman who was home from the front, gave Keogh a full Christian burial.[60] Keogh's death put a human face on the rebellion and on the 'enemy', and the reaction of most Trinity people who witnessed it was humane but condemnatory of the cause which he represented. Keogh's death was also a stern warning for those wishing to cross College Green and an indication of the terrible accuracy of the battle-hardened colonial soldiers stationed on top of the college's West Front.

Two other notable events took place on Tuesday, 25 April 1916. James Campbell was re-elected as the member of parliament for the university, as planned. Mahaffy, the returning officer, entered the Examination Hall at 11 that morning. Campbell was proposed by Louis Purser and seconded by Sir William Moore, a notable Dublin doctor, and, as he was the only candidate, was deemed to be re-elected.[61]

Shortly afterwards, a small group of junior sophister (third year) students, mostly women, assembled on the steps of the Dining Hall in the full anticipation that they would be sitting their scheduled exams. Remarkably, they had made their way across the city to Trinity, risking sniper fire along the way.[62] One of them, Eileen Corrigan, had travelled from Belfast the day before especially to sit the examination. From the beginning of her written examination at 9.30 until it finished three hours later, firing could be heard. 'We got so much accustomed to it that we did not even lift our pens from the paper when it would re-commence after an interval of silence.'[63] Afterwards, Mahaffy took the four women for lunch in the Provost's Garden, but this was far from idyllic. Elsie Mahaffy recalled that they were deafened by constant firing, which left her feeling 'terrified'.[64] Corrigan and her fellow students were due to be examined orally—a *viva voce*—on Wednesday. Luce wryly recalled that he was asked to conduct a *viva voce* in logic but was—for rather obvious reasons—'obliged to decline'.[65] The provost personally examined the students. Eileen Corrigan passed her examinations, although a number of the men failed. Many, understandably, did not show up and had their examinations rescheduled for a later date.[66]

Both events were a striking, but muted, expression of Trinity's desire for business as usual. For all of this obstinacy, however, the stress was clearly taking its toll on those in the college. Elsie Mahaffy wrote of the constant din of firing: 'How I longed for the arrival of soldiers, to hasten the end of this bewildering and terrible war!'[67] Her hopes were soon realised. On Tuesday, Brigadier-General W.H.M. Lowe, commander of the 3rd Reserve Cavalry Brigade at the Curragh, arrived in Dublin. He later based himself in Trinity and, in the words of historian Charles Townshend, he launched the operations that shaped the battle for the next five days.[68] The tide would soon turn, but, paradoxically, this would mean the end of the 'business as usual' attitude at Trinity.

Wednesday saw the end of the duties of the motley Trinity garrison; they were relieved by troops of the Leinster Regiment who arrived with two machine guns. In addition, four ominous eighteen-pound field guns arrived from Athlone. The strategic importance of Trinity once more became manifest; it would be the hub from which the rising would be suppressed and was transformed into a veritable barracks for weeks to come.

The arrival of troops in substantial numbers completely disrupted the college's normal life. There is no record of a formal written arrangement being reached between the college hierarchy and the military authorities; the arrival of troops in Trinity was, it seems, improvised, and understood by all concerned to be a necessary wartime measure. That is not to say that people welcomed the disruption. Alton later recalled with some dissatisfaction that 'soldiers invaded the sacred glass plots, horses and mules kicked up the time honoured cobbles, and impetuous Tommies brushed aside impatiently the most august of our academic figures'.[69] In contrast, Eileen Corrigan wrote that 'the sight of hundreds of troops' in college on Wednesday 'gave us courage'.[70] However, Elsie Mahaffy's hopes that the arrival of troops would lessen her feelings of terror were misplaced.

> Very early on Wednesday morning we heard the noise of the heavy guns coming near to Trinity College with many men driving the mules. At a little after 7.30 the 'pounding down' of Liberty Hall began. It lasted some half an hour and was indeed terrible; even the solid Provost's House

Extract from a letter written by Miss K. Price to Trinity student Eileen Corrigan, 11 May 1916, expressing relief that Eileen and three other female students had made it into college safely to sit their exams during the rising, despite the dangers, and noting that a number of male students had not turned up at all on the second day of the exams.

trembled and in the garden all the birds who had sung and warbled sweetly through all the previous noises became mute; huddling together in terrified clusters, the terrible noise was made by an '18 pounder' run out of College at the last moment into a place prepared for it in Tara Street and from the guns of the 'Helga' gunboat on the river below the Custom House.[71]

James Glen was among those responsible for firing one of the 18 pounders. He had handled heavy guns on the Western Front and was chosen to help set up these guns on D'Olier Street. The target was a building on the corner of Bachelor's Walk and Sackville Street:

Postcard from Eileen Corrigan, 24 April 1916, reassuring her family in Belfast that she had reached Dublin safely on Easter Monday despite the rising, and noting that troops were expected from the Curragh the following day.

Rathmines, Y.W.C.A.
Dublin / 24th april.
1916

Just a line to let you know I arrived safely, in case the papers should make you anxious. All communication is stopped from Dublin, but a lady promised to post this to-morrow from the north. Everything will probably be all right to-morrow, as the military are coming from Curragh. With love Frog.

5 T. C D

20/5/16

Results of S Second
just out. You have
passed all right, &
so have the other three.
Marks not yet available,
we shall send them
later

E. M. Hanan

Postcard, 20 May 1916, informing Eileen Corrigan that she and her three female colleagues had passed their junior sophister exams.

> My friend and the gun crew…manhandled the gun out
> through the Front Gate and along College St; the limber
> was cast off; the trail was dropped into position; my
> friend took careful aim on the first floor window; a round
> was loaded and the gun was fired.[72]

The reinforcements who came from England arrived in Kingstown late on Tuesday evening. Two infantry brigades were sent—the 176th and 178th—which comprised two battalions of Sherwood Foresters, young recruits who had only been in uniform for eight weeks and some of whom had never even fired a rifle.[73] Monica Roberts received the news excitedly and went to the roadside with her father to watch them pass by and give them cigarettes. 'A cheery word and a smile from all. It was grand to see our Tommies and they gave one a great feeling of security.'[74]

The brigade, marching in two columns of two battalions each, marched west, presumably destined for Trinity. They made their way past Beggars Bush down Northumberland Road, where they were ambushed at Mount Street Bridge, sustaining devastating casualties: a 'near-unimaginable disaster', in the words of Charles Townshend.[75] On nearby Grand Canal Street, Margretta Thornton, the matron of Sir Patrick Dun's, Trinity's main teaching hospital, reported that

> heavy firing was heard coming from the direction of
> Ballsbridge, and we knew that the Military, who were
> trying to force their way along Northumberland Road,
> were being attacked by the rebels in the adjoining houses.[76]

As luck would have it, the nurses home for Sir Patrick Dun's was located nearby at 97 Mount Street, from where the nurses inside 'could see the soldiers falling, and they felt they must go out and try to rescue them'. Initially, nurses from number 97 braved the bullets to try and tend to the wounded soldiers; they were soon supported by the resident doctors and students from the hospital. Over the course of four-and-a-half hours, 80 soldiers and three civilians were brought into the nurses' home. There, they were treated by the staff of the hospital, including Sir James Craig and Sir Robert Woods, both of whom held professorships at TCD, and both of whom would later represent the university constituency in different parliaments.[77] From the nurses house the patients had to be moved to various hospitals around the city that were fit to care for them.[78]

Back at Trinity, the college continued to fill with soldiers. The College Park, Engineering School and part of the Dining Hall were made available to the troops.[79] The 3rd Royal Irish Regiment arrived on Wednesday.[80] Conn O'Grady, a UCD student and son of the writer Standish O'Grady, volunteered as an orderly at Trinity for the week. He reported to Diarmid Coffey that

> all troops there [in Trinity] Irish and not at all bitter against the volunteers though no question of not obeying orders. He says officers more intransigent. All unanimous in praising the fighting of the volunteers.[81]

By Thursday, the transformation was complete. Trinity accounts of 1916 tend to become less detailed and less voluminous from this point forth, perhaps as events were now literally beyond their control. The college was taken from the Trinity community.

> The front court of Trinity College grew fuller and fuller of soldiers, here, at all hours we could see, weary boys, sleeping on the grass, in the sun, or footsore men who had marched into Dublin, washing their feet under the antiquated water taps; others eating 'bully' beef and hard biscuit.[82]

Joly awoke on Thursday morning to an 'extraordinary appearance':

> Some 4,000 troops were stationed in the College. Horses tied to the chains which enclosed the grass plots gave the place the appearance of a vast open-air stable or horse fair. Men stood in ranks or sprawled on the pavements or on the doorsteps—anywhere—sometimes closely packed and fast asleep in every conceivable attitude. Many of them had put in a hard night's work.[83]

The human cost of the rising was also becoming apparent to those within the college. First, two dead British soldiers were brought in on Thursday, one being buried in the Fellows' Garden, the other in the College Park, according to the rites of the Church of Ireland. A small plaque was erected on the Nassau Street wall, marking the spot where Private A.C. Smith was temporarily buried.[84] Later that day, a small boy was brought in on a stretcher by his father. He had been shot through the hand on Monday and his father feared that the wound would become infected. Both were prevented from proceeding far inside Front

'Field kitchens for the troops in Trinity College', photograph published in *The 'Sinn Féin'
revolt: an illustrated record of the Sinn Fein revolt in Dublin April 1916*, p. 16, of some of
the soldiers garrisoned in Trinity during the rising.

Gate, but there they met John Joly and informed him that the child had
not eaten since Monday. He ensured that the boy was given 'internal
and external remedies' (food and treatment for his wound), before being
sent on his way again.[85] The 'most terrible tragedy' was yet to come: a
woman was brought into college in an ambulance. Her stretcher dripped
with blood. A glance showed that 'death was not far from her'. The
woman, the victim of a rebel bullet, to Joly's estimation, 'had done no
wrong. She was probably seeking food for her six little children when
death met her'. Cumulatively, these events showed 'that great total of

'The morning wash—Troops in Trinity College', photograph published in *The 'Sinn Féin' revolt*, p. 16.

human sorrow which the mind cannot evaluate or even conceive'.[86] Students and dons saw at first hand ordinary Dubliners and troops from exotic climes who had been injured in the course of the week. In this sense, the college's assumed isolation from the city was broken down but, paradoxically, at the same time reinforced by the fortress like appearance of the campus.

William Evelyn Wylie, a Trinity-trained lawyer, had been on holiday in Kerry when the rising broke out. On Tuesday he made for Dublin, finally arriving two days later. A member of the OTC, he immediately called Trinity to see what he could do and was ordered to report to Ballsbridge to serve with a brigade of the Royal Inniskilling Fusiliers freshly arrived from Britain. Wylie returned to Trinity with the Fusiliers on Friday. There, he was shocked by the appearance of the campus, with field guns in the squares, troops in the college rooms and machine guns on the roofs of college buildings.

The imposition of military forces on the academic oasis was beginning to vex the college hierarchy, and Wylie became a key liaison. A Trinity alumnus, he could act as a link between the occupying military forces and the college authorities, as relations were becoming strained. Mahaffy, so annoyed at the disruption caused to his academic idyll, threatened the recently arrived General Carleton, of the 177th Infantry Brigade, that all troops would have to leave the college. Wylie was asked to mediate and did so successfully.[87]

The incoming British commander-in-chief in Ireland, General Sir John Maxwell, arrived in Dublin on Friday, but there is no account of him coming to Trinity while the rising was still being fought, nor of a formal arrangement being thrashed out between the academic and military authorities.[88] Throughout this period, General Lowe remained in Trinity, and on the early afternoon of Saturday, 29 April, his telephone rang. Dublin Castle was on the line to tell him that Elizabeth O'Farrell, a member of Cumann na mBan, had brought a message from Pearse, informing Lowe of his terms of surrender. At 3.30 that afternoon, Pearse gave his formal surrender to Lowe on Parnell Street and the beginning of the end was in sight.[89] The remaining garrisons—at Boland's Bakery, the South Dublin Union, the Royal College of Surgeons and Jacob's Biscuit Factory—surrendered the following day.[90]

On 30 April, a 21-year-old Trinity student called Philip Addison Purser was killed; the official Trinity *War List* noted that his death took place during 'civil disturbances'.[91] Purser was initially buried in the grounds of Dublin Castle before being reinterred at Grangegorman military cemetery in 1963.[92] The names of the two Trinity students to die during the rising— Thompson and Purser—were listed on the walls of the college's First World War memorial when it opened in 1928, alongside their colleagues who died much further from home. The deaths of Purser and Thompson bookended Dublin's—and the college's—bloody week.

The defining characteristic of college experience in the period from Wednesday until the surrender of the rebels on Saturday, 29 April was passivity. Trinity had to cast aside all normal functions in the face of military imperative. Its primary utility in these days was strategic; its location in the heart of the city meant that it could cut communications between

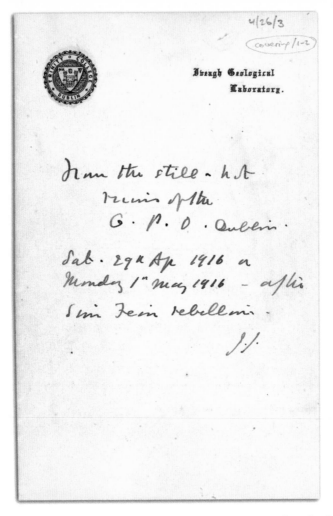

'From the still-hot ruins of the G.P.O. Dublin', note written by John Joly on headed paper from the Geology Department, and one of a selection of partially burnt documents he rescued from the ruins of the GPO (following page) on 29 April and 1 May 1916. The date stamp on the partially burnt document overleaf is 4 August 1914, the day that Britain went to war with Germany.

rebel bases in north and south Dublin, and its size, coupled with its many empty buildings and student rooms, meant that it was an ideal staging post for troops to suppress the rebellion at most locations in the city.

The surrender allowed people to take stock of what had just happened and try to piece the events together. Immediately, John Joly made for the GPO where he gathered together charred papers 'from the still-hot ruins'.[93] Trinity people began to learn more about the rebels and their motivations. Lil Stokes noted in her diary that 'the leader in Boland's [Éamon de Valera] was a fine looking man called the Mexican, he is educated and speaks like a gentleman'.[94] Others came even closer to the leaders. At least three Trinity-trained doctors tended to the wounded James Connolly: Henry

4/26/1

Pruna [illegible]

Postmasters.—No. 14.

DELIVERY RETURN.

Office Stamp. HILLSBOROUGH.D.O.DUBLIN PM 15 4 AU 14

Postman, No. 130

No. of Delivery 3 finished at H. 4 M. 15

Pouch delivered at

Town Sub-Office at H. M. or posted in

Charlotte St Letter Box at H. 4 M. 20

	Number.
Undelivered Postal Packets	2
,, Cash on Delivery Packets..........	
,, Parcels..........	
For particulars see back. ,, Registered Letters..........	
,, Registered and Insured Parcels, including Foreign Parcels	
For Delivery. Number of Registered Letters	
,, ,, ,, Parcels	
,, ,, Ordinary ,, ...	
Receipts for Registered Letters Delivered	
A.R. Forms..........	

	Amount. £	s.	d.
Uncollected Postage..........			

Postman's Signature [illegible]

Checked at Head Office by

(1339). Wt.655—53. 250,000. 5/'13. C.&Co.,Ltd. Sch

Stokes[95], J.C. Ridgway[96] and William Boxwell.[97] When Harry Nicholls was arrested following the rising, some of the detectives of G-Division of the Dublin Metropolitan Police recognised him at Richmond Barracks, and wondered how a respectable professional with a promising engineering career could have been caught up in the fighting.[98] Many of his former engineering classmates may have wondered the same.

William Wylie had the closest interaction with the rebel leaders of all Trinity figures of the period. As he was a King's Counsel, Wylie was retained for 'dealing with rebel prisoners'.[99] He was sent to Richmond Barracks, where the leaders were being held, and charged with preparing their prosecution. Throughout, Wylie was the epitome of humanity, decency and the voice of leniency amongst the military prosecutors. He wrote at length of the human qualities of the leaders, describing Pearse and Thomas Clarke, in particular, as decent people. He noted that Pearse's statement in the dock was 'very eloquent speech of which I always call the Robert Emmet type'.[100] Pearse would have appreciated the comparison.

The executions of Pearse, Clarke and Thomas MacDonagh left Wylie unhappy. He seems to have had a genuine empathy for the condemned men and felt that execution was in certain instances, especially that of MacDonagh, unnecessary. Moreover, the legal process was highly flawed. Wylie wrote to James Campbell, the attorney-general for Ireland and, as we have seen, one of Dublin University's two parliamentary representatives in Westminster, to demand that the accused be allowed to offer a defence. Campbell denied this request, however, and urged retribution against the rebel leaders. He was not alone in this: on 3 May the Protestant archbishop of Dublin, John Henry Bernard, a former Archbishop King's lecturer in Divinity at Trinity and later provost, wrote to *The Times* urging 'punishment, swift and stern'.[101] Such rhetoric appeared often in the popular press—both unionist and nationalist—in the days following the surrender, making Wylie's moral stand all the more remarkable.

Aftermath

The weeks that followed the surrender of the rebels allowed for members of the Trinity community to reflect on the events and attempt contextualising them. The board met on 8 May and passed a resolution thanking the OTC and members of the college community for their part in the defence of the college and for their full cooperation with the armed forces during the week.[102] On the same day Trinity re-opened to students, much to the relief of the studious Dorothy Stopford Price, but she recorded in her diary that it still resembled a barracks more than a college.[103] At a board meeting the following week bonuses were voted to the kitchen staff and porters for their work during the occupation of college.[104] Not long after, however, the board became preoccupied with the rather more mundane business of seeking remuneration from the military authorities for losses sustained during the same occupation.

The rising caused an internal reassessment of Trinity's place in the city. While it had not been attacked directly, the probability of an assault in the near future seemed heightened by the rising. Therefore, a College Defence Committee was formed, consisting of Sir Robert Tate (Commandant of the OTC, who was stranded outside of Dublin during Easter Week), Major Harris, E.H. Alton and John Joly. They recommended that one company and two machine guns would be required in the event of a repeat of the rising.[105] Later in the summer, loop-holes were created in the walls of college buildings across the campus, and ladders and planks were placed on the roofs of a number of buildings to facilitate easy movement if sentries or snipers would once again have to take up positions there.[106] Within weeks of the cessation of fighting, a number of businesses in the vicinity of college had written either to the board or to the OTC to thank them for their role in protecting their property.[107] Dublin business-owners also published a number of letters of thanks in the *Irish Times*.[108]

The majority of those associated with Trinity whose reactions are recorded viewed the events of late April and early May 1916 as a human and a political tragedy. John Joly's account was typical:

> Hundreds of the untimely dead lie beneath us in the stricken City. Upon hundreds of others the shades of death are even now closing. The ruined, unhappy leaders are there—now at length seeing all their own mischance. The pitiful dupes who took their word for the future of the 'Irish Republic'; and now only look forward to death or penal servitude! Others, just as guilty lurking in hourly fear of detection! The orphaned children crying for mother and father! Ruined lives and ruined business! All this and far, far more make up the tragedy at our feet. And the future? Nothing can be more gloomy save the miserable present. Does anyone believe that this is indeed the end of madness in this unhappy land?[109]

Elsie Mahaffy wrote of the waste and misguided motivations of the rebel leaders. 'Ireland has lost in some of her rebels men of real intelligence—whose clear brains and deep—if misguided love of her she can ill afford so to lose.'[110] Alton, the most senior member of the OTC present in Trinity during Easter Week, wrote in a typically measured fashion that 'it is difficult yet to take a dispassionate survey of the events of that week. The scenes unroll themselves in memory like the mad unrealities of a nightmare.'[111] Perhaps the most evocative response to the rising was an editorial written for *T.C.D.* in its first post-rising edition by T.C. Kingsmill Moore. In one sentence, Kingsmill Moore summed up the central tragedy of Trinity's role in 1916.

> To be called upon to defend our university against the attack of Irishmen, to be forced in self-defence to shoot down our countrymen—these are things which even the knowledge of duty well fulfilled cannot render anything but sad and distasteful.[112]

Others were less circumspect. The *Church of Ireland Gazette* congratulated Trinity for its role in protecting the city during the violence of Easter Week.

> Our own clergy will have learned with lively satisfaction by this time of the epic part which Trinity College played in the insurrection. Dublin can congratulate herself on the fashion in which she faced the upheaval.[113]

William Ridgeway, a Trinity-educated classicist working at Cambridge wrote that 'I am truly proud of my old university for the splendid part it has played in saving Dublin.'[114] Writing from Nairobi where he was on active service, the Trinity graduate George Pim told his mother that the rising was a 'sickening thing' and hoped that 'no sentimental clemency' would be shown to the perpetrators.[115] Noel Drury, who was stationed in Salonika, felt as early as 29 April that the rising was 'a regular stab in the back for our fellows out here', and feared that Irish troops would be viewed with suspicion by their fellow soldiers in the British army.[116] In the immediate aftermath of the rising, Trinity figures tended to eschew talk of politics; it was almost as if a collective shock inhibited rational thought on the political future of Ireland. As such, it took a number of months before prominent college figures began talking of the future. Chapter Four deals with this in more depth.[117]

Very early on Wednesday morning
we heard the noise of the heavy guns coming
into Trinity College with many mules driving
the mules. At a little after 7.30. the "pounding
down" of Liberty Hall began - it lasted
over half an hour. and was indeed
terrible. even the solid Provost's House trembled
& in the garden. all the birds, who had sung
& warbled sweetly through all the previous
noises, became mute, huddling together in
terrified clusters. the terrible noise was made
by an "18 pounder" run out of College at
the last moment into a place prepared
for it in Tara St and from the guns of
the "Helga" gunboat on the river below the
Custom House: The rebels - were evidently
not surprized; as very few were in Liberty
Hall at the time. our soldiers were very
anxious & secure any information they could
from Liberty Hall - & the save any papers
which might be there; so it was not actually
blown down. The outer walls remain.
Many of my acquaintances, have since
visited it and found interesting books
& pamphlets.

On Thursday afternoon the naval guns
far down the river. Battered as home on
Ormond Quay. There the green flag was
flying. and proved to be full of rebels -
(I believe it must have been one of the rebel printing
houses 18 upper Ormonde Quay) They saw nothing
as two bridges hid the "Helga", suddenly
Shells began to fall upon their lair & shattered it
I believe also a good deal of fighting
went on round Bolands Bakery. and
on this day also the terrible battle on
Lr Mount St Bridge took place -
The rebels were entrenched in the 4 corner
houses commanding the bridge - in one
they certainly had a machine gun
The "Sherwood Foresters" being marched
into Dublin from Kingstown walked into
this trap, in a very few minutes they had
150 casualties. Civilians, who had some
pity & tried to carry the wounded into
safety, or went bind up their wounds
were fired upon without mercy, and a
poor boy. aged 15, giving a drink.
to a dying soldier was shot dead.

Elsie Mahaffy's description of the shelling of the centre of Dublin by the *Helga* and the battle at
Mount Street Brigdge on Thursday, 27 April 1916.

O Rahilly was found afterwards wrapped up in the celebrated "flag of the Irish Republic" which existed for only 48 hours.

Romantic ladies thought this incident "most touching" until it became known that under the flag he was stark naked. His watch, his pearl pin, his clothes were all rifled off his dead body by his followers. So he had escaped thus narrowly from "dying for Ireland". Common decency I suppose made them anxious to cover the poor body — the flag came in usefully.

While at dinner news was brought in to General Carleton that the rebels in Jacob's Factory — under McBride & Thomas MacDonagh had fired on a business motor lorry. Killed one man & badly wounded two. Such was the way these "gallant" men treated unarmed, non combatants of their own class.

This night the city fires

In the weeks and months that followed the rising, Trinity sought to portray itself as an establishment institution, one that had been loyal to government and Crown in their time of need. On 13 May both General Maxwell and Herbert Asquith, the prime minister, who was in Dublin to assess the city in the aftermath of the rising, came to Trinity to inspect the OTC, who paraded in the College Park.[118] When Maxwell finally left Ireland in November of 1916, he wrote to Mahaffy to convey to him his thanks for 'the loyal and cordial assistance you have so willingly rendered to me in particular and His Majesty's forces in Ireland in general'.[119] This link was further underscored that summer when Edward Carson presented the OTC with a silver cup as a permanent memorial to the part they played in the rising.[120]

In late May 1916, a number of local businesses organised a committee to raise funds in thanks to the OTC for defending their property during the rising, ultimately presenting it with £700.[121] The OTC used this money to make their own silver cups, which were presented to a number of key individuals associated with the defence of the college in Easter Week. There were six in total; while it was not explained why these particular six men merited this special award, the list included James Glen, suggesting that perhaps the cups were presented to those who undertook dangerous tasks such as wheeling the 18 pound guns to D'Olier Street.[122] Replica cups were issued to 138 men and women; virtually every member of the OTC and college staff present during Easter Week (both academic and non-academic staff), as well as family members—wives and daughters—who were present, received the replica cups.[123]

Trinity also began trying to identify and track down the colonial troops who came into college during the Monday and Tuesday; these numbered thirteen in total, with addresses in South Africa, Canada, Australia and New Zealand.[124] In addition, seven ceremonial swords were issued to men who had played a conspicuous role (again unspecified) during the week, including Alton, Wylie and Waterhouse.[125] While there were clearly political overtones to the recognition of the 'defence' of college during the rising, the inclusiveness and egalitarianism demonstrated in the award of replica cups spoke to the sense of camaraderie and communality born of an extraordinary shared experience. The inscription on these cups claimed to memorialise the 'defence of T.C.D'; the reality was there was little need to defend Trinity during Easter Week. The defence was largely an imagined one.

Opposite: Elsie Mahaffy describes how Michael O'Rahilly's body was found 'wrapped up in the celebrated flag of the "Irish Republic" which existed for only 48 hours...under the flag he was stark naked. His watch, his pearl pin, his clothes were all lifted off his dead body by his followers, who escaped thus narrowly from "dying for Ireland"'.

Conclusion

The rising saw Trinity play out its historic role as an establishment institution. While it was a practicality given the breakdown of law and order, the symbolism of the locking of the gates on Easter Monday reinforced the idea that Trinity was cut off from Dublin and Ireland, and this meaningful gesture—allied to the radicalisation of Irish national politics which followed—informed Trinity's sense of unease at the time and its historical silence regarding the events of the week. As A.A. Luce noted in 1965 with the benefit of hindsight, Trinity undoubtedly backed 'the wrong horse'. Most of the Trinity protagonists at the time, however, would have seen it as a one-horse race. Trinity had slowly brought itself to co-exist with constitutional nationalism; the rising was something that none had foreseen and few could, at first, comprehend. The desire to defend the college from the events unfolding on Easter Monday 1916—and the assumption that it would require defending—was perhaps understandable in the context in which the rising began; people reacted instinctively, knowing little but fearing the worst. The consequences of Easter Week would radically alter the political ground on which Trinity—and many of its constituent community—stood, and informed the college's development in the half-century to follow.

NOTES:

[1] TCD, MS 4874/2, Recollections of A.A. Luce, 14 October, 1965.

[2] Michael Laffan, 'Insular attitudes: the Revisionists and their critics', in Máirín Ní Dhonnchadha and Theo Dorgan (eds), *Revising the rising* (Derry, 1991), 106–21: 107–8; Clair Wills, *Dublin 1916: the siege of the GPO* (London, 2010), 2.

[3] Wills, *Dublin 1916*, 2–5; Ben Levitas, *The theatre of nation: Irish drama and cultural nationalism 1890–1916* (Oxford, 2002), 225–6.

[4] R.B. McDowell and D.A. Webb, *Trinity College Dublin 1592–1952: an academic history* (Cambridge, 1982), 420–1; K.C. Bailey, *Trinity College Dublin 1892–1945* (Dublin, 1947), 4, 47–8, 158; J.V. Luce, *Trinity College Dublin: the first 400 years* (Dublin, 1992), 130–1.

[5] TCD, MS 4874/2, 4875, 4456.

[6] The election was a formality; Campbell could hold both positions but having been appointed attorney-general had to be re-elected to his university seat. 'Trinity College election', *Irish Times*, 19 April 1916, 5.

[7] John Joly, 'In Trinity College during the Sinn Fein Rebellion', in Joly, *Reminiscences and anticipations* (London, 1920), 218–64: 218.

[8] TCD, MS 2783/19/1, MS 4873.

[9] TCD, MS 4875.

[10] TCD, MS 4874/2.

[11] TCD, MS 2783/19/1.

[12] TCD, MS 2783/19/1.

13 TCD, MS 2074, 2.

14 TCD, MS 2074, 3.

15 TCD, MS 11107/1, Fitzgibbon to William Hume Blake, 10 May 1916.

16 TCD, MS 4456/1.

17 TCD, MS 11107, Fitzgibbon to Blake, 10 May 1916, 1.

18 Ernie O'Malley, 'A student and the Rising', in Roger McHugh (ed.), *Dublin 1916: an illustrated anthology* (New York, 1980), 126–44: 129.

19 Joly, 'In Trinity College', 222–4.

20 J.G. Swift MacNeill, *What I have seen and heard* (London, 1925), 58.

21 TCD, MS 4874/2.

22 Joly, 'In Trinity College', 223.

23 Joly, 'In Trinity College', 227–8.

24 Walter Alison Phillips, *The revolution in Ireland 1906–23* (London, 1923), 99.

25 TCD, MS 11107/1, Fitzgibbon to Blake, 10 May 1916.

26 TCD, MS 11107/2, Fitzgibbon to Blake, 15 May 1916.

27 TCD, MS 4456/4–5.

28 TCD, MS 2783/64.

29 Charles Townshend, *Easter 1916: the Irish rebellion* (London, 2006), 162–3.

30 Townshend, *Easter 1916*, 152–82; Fearghal McGarry, *The Rising. Ireland: Easter 1916* (Oxford, 2010), 120–4.

31 McGarry, *The Rising*, 120–1; Townshend, *Easter 1916*, 163–4.

32 Townshend, *Easter 1916*, 122.

33 BMH, WS 307, Statement of Thomas MacCarthy.

34 Joly, 'In Trinity College', 222–3.

35 Alan Kramer, *Dynamic of destruction: culture and mass killing in the First World War* (Oxford, 2007), 6–30.

36 Catriona Pennell, 'Going to War', in John Horne (ed.), *Our war: Ireland and the Great War* (Dublin, 2008), 35–48: 41–2.

37 See Séamas Ó Buachalla (ed.), *A significant Irish educationalist: the educational writings of P.H. Pearse* (Dublin, 1980).

38 Ruth Dudley Edwards, *Patrick Pearse: the triumph of failure* (Dublin, 2006; originally published 1977), 40.

39 Joost Augusteijn, *Patrick Pearse: the making of a revolutionary* (Basingstoke, 2010), 323; Starkie, *Scholars and gypsies*, 145.

40 David Fitzpatrick, 'Eamon de Valera at Trinity College', *Hermathena: a Trinity College Dublin Review*, 133 (1982), 7–14.

41 BL, Add, MS 52784/75.

42 D.R. O'Connor Lysaght, 'Plunkett, Count George Noble', in James McGuire and James Quinn (eds), *Dictionary of Irish Biography* (Cambridge, 2009).

43 McGarry, *The Rising*, 167.

44 Dublin City Archives (DCA), Monica Roberts Collection, vol. 8, 2–22.

45 Max Caulfield, *The Easter rebellion* (Dublin, 1963), 102–3.

46 Starkie, *Scholars and gypsies*, 143.

47 Caulfield, *The Easter rebellion*, 103.

48 Martin Maguire, 'Harry Nicholls and Kathleen Emerson: Protestant Rebels', *Studia Hibernica* 35 (2008–2009), 148–50.

49 Military Service Pensions, 34 REF 15964, 1–2.

50 Tom Turpin, 'Trinity's engineering losses in the Great War', unpublished research paper, 13.

51 NLI, MS21193, 2.

52 UCD Archives, de Valera papers, 'Account of Miss L. Stokes', P 150/522.

53 TCD, MS 2074, 3–8.

54 Anne MacLellan, *Dorothy Stopford Price: rebel doctor* (Dublin, 2014), 30.

55 'The Medical Unit, DUOTC, and its work during the Rebellion', *T.C.D.*, 19 June 1916, 251.

[56] TCD, MS 2074, 11–12.

[57] TCD, MS 11107/1, Fitzgibbon to Blake, 10 May 1916.

[58] TCD, MS 2074, 12.

[59] Joly, 'In Trinity College', 235.

[60] Luce recalled a 'British Soldier' being killed in College Green and brought into college. His is the only account to mention this specific set of events and it must be assumed his memory was mistaken almost 50 years after the event; see TCD, MS 4874/2. This supposition is verified by the contemporary account given by George Crawford, the acting porter, TCD, MS 2783/20.

[61] R.B. McDowell and W.B. Stanford, *Mahaffy: a biography of an Anglo-Irishman* (London, 1971), 231.

[62] McDowell and Stanford, *Mahaffy*, 231.

[63] Georgina Fitzpatrick, *Trinity College and Irish society 1914–1922* (Dublin, 1992), 14.

[64] TCD, MS 2074, 13.

[65] TCD, MS 4874/2.

[66] TCD, MS 3987a/3, Lucy Gwynn to Eileen Corrigan, 10 May 1916.

[67] TCD, MS 2074, 14.

[68] Townshend, *Easter 1916*, 186.

[69] 'Work of the OTC', *T.C.D.*, 19 June 1916, 252.

[70] Fitzpatrick, *Trinity College and Irish society*, 14.

[71] TCD, MS 2074, 20.

[72] TCD, MS 4456/3.

[73] Townshend, *Easter 1916*, 195.

[74] DCA, Roberts, vol. 8, 10.

[75] Townshend, *Easter 1916*, 196–7.

[76] Royal College of Physicians of Ireland Archives (RCPIA), *Annual report of Sir P. Dun's Hospital Grand Canal Street, Dublin, for the year ended December 31, 1916* (Dublin, 1917), 12.

[77] Woods was Honorary Professor of Laryngology and Otology, while Craig was the King's Professor of Medicine.

[78] RCPIA, *Annual Report for 1916*, 13.

[79] Joly, 'In Trinity College', 244–5.

[80] Townshend, *Easter 1916*, 208.

[81] NLI, MS21193, 2.

[82] TCD, MS 2074, 30.

[83] Joly, 'In Trinity College', 248.

[84] Having been heavily eroded over time, it was replaced in 2007 with a new plaque. A.C. Smith was reinterred in Grangegorman military cemetery.

[85] Joly, 'In Trinity College', 249.

[86] Joly, 'In Trinity College', 250–1.

[87] León Ó Broin, *WE Wylie and the Irish revolution* (Dublin, 1989), 6–18.

[88] Townshend, *Easter 1916*, 207.

[89] Caulfied, *The Easter rebellion*, 273–7.

[90] McGarry, *The Rising*, 247.

[91] *University of Dublin, Trinity College, War List, February 1922* (Dublin, 1922), 170.

[92] 'Remains of British Officers reinterred', *Irish Times*, 18 May 1963, 7.

[93] TCD, MS 2313/4/26/1–3.

[94] Michael Purser, *Jellett, O'Brien, Purser and Stokes: seven generations, four families* (Dublin, 2004), 164.

[95] Purser, *Jellett, O'Brien, Purser and Stokes*, 164.

[96] BMH, WS 1431.

[97] NLI, MS21193, 5.

[98] Maguire, 'Harry Nicholls and Kathleen Emerson', 147–8.

[99] TCD, MS 2783/48.

[100] Ó Bróin, *W.E. Wylie*, 21.

[101] This letter originally appeared in *The Times* of 5 May but was reprinted in the *Irish Times* the following day. 'Dublin—The next phase. Archbishop Bernard's views', *Irish Times*, 6 May 1916, 3.

[102] TCD, MUN/V/5/21, 182, Board resolution of 8 May 1916.

[103] MacLellan, *Dorothy Stopford Price*, 35–6

[104] TCD, MUN/V/5/21, 183, Board resolution of 13 May 1916.

[105] TCD, MUN/V/5/21, 188, Board meeting of 3 June 1916.

[106] TCD, MS 2309a/13.

[107] TCD, MS 2783/34–6.

[108] 'Trinity College and the rebellion: the city's thanks', *Irish Times*, 17 May 1916, 5; 'Trinity College OTC and the rebellion: appreciation of their services', *Irish Times*, 19 May 1916, 4.

[109] Joly, 'In Trinity College', 263.

[110] TCD, MS 2074 'Introduction'.

[111] 'Work of the OTC', *T.C.D.*, June 1916, 252.

[112] T.C. Kingsmill Moore, 'Editorial', cited in D.A. Webb (ed.), *T.C.D. an anthology, 1895–1945: extracts in prose and verse from 'T.C.D., A College Miscellany'* (Tralee, 1945), 90–1.

[113] *Church of Ireland Gazette*, 28 April to 5 May 1916, 320.

[114] TCD, MS 2075/233, Ridgeway to (unspecified) Mahaffy daughter, 23 May 1916.

[115] Liddle Collection, Leeds University Library (LCLUL), AFE 24/58–59, George Pim to his mother, 28 April 1916 and 11 May 1916.

[116] National Army Museum (NAM), London, 1976–07–69, 130, Papers of Noel E. Drury, book two, entry for 29 April 1916.

[117] J.P. Mahaffy, 'The future of Ireland', *Blackwood's Magazine*, MCCXII, October 1916, 548–55.

[118] 'OTC: Inspection by Sir John Maxwell', *Irish Times*, 13 May 1916, 2; George Arthur. *General Sir John Maxwell* (London, 1932), 258.

[119] TCD, MS 2074, Maxwell to Mahaffy, 10 November 1916.

[120] TCD, MUN/V/5/21, 194, Board meeting of 1 July 1916.

[121] Roger Willoughby, *A military history of the University of Dublin and its Officers Training Corps* (Limerick, 1989), 22.

[122] TCD, MS 2783/27.

[123] Willoughby, *A military history of the University of Dublin*, 23; TCD, MS 2783/28.

[124] TCD, MS 2783/35.

[125] TCD, MS 2783/87.

CHAPTER FOUR

The Politics of War and Revolution, 1914–19

Introduction

John Pentland Mahaffy's years as provost—from November 1914 until April 1919—were some of the most tumultuous and eventful in the history of the college. This had little to do with Mahaffy's actions; he was active in public life for most of this period and felt himself qualified to speak out as the voice of learning and common sense while Ireland and the world descended into a cycle of bitter violence, but few people listened. Mahaffy's voice became increasingly irrelevant as the situation in Ireland radicalised; his pontifications and obfuscations lost whatever charm they may have had before the war and he was superseded by politically astute university representatives. With the unionists split between Ulster and the south, the southern unionists in turn divided, and the Irish Parliamentary Party on the run from a rampant Sinn Féin, Ireland was politically transformed. The college community was, in turn, divided in myriad ways. The situation called for careful political manoeuvring, which Mahaffy, by the time of his death in 1919, was unable to provide.

Less than five years previously, Mahaffy had stood confidently as the new provost of Trinity College Dublin, belatedly achieving his life's ambi-

Opposite: John Pentland Mahaffy, professor of Ancient History from 1871 and provost from November 1914 to April 1919.

tion.[1] A few weeks before his official appointment to the post he was in-volved in an incident that, retrospectively, became part of the lore of Ireland's decade of war and revolution. In October 1914 the college Gaelic Society planned an event to mark the centenary of the birth of nationalist icon Thomas Davis, the poet and journalist who had founded the Young Ireland movement in the 1840s and provided a blueprint for an inclusive independent Ireland. Davis was a Trinity alumnus and a figure to whom Trinity nationalists clung. As we have seen, the Gaelic Society, founded by language enthusiasts in 1907 (the same year in which an equivalent society was founded at UCD), had become a hub for student radicals of all per-suasions, and was at the centre of labour disturbances in college in 1913.

To mark the Davis centenary, the Gaelic Society had invited and re-ceived confirmations from two speakers, the poet W.B. Yeats and the educationalist and Irish language enthusiast Patrick Pearse. Mahaffy had agreed to take the chair.[2] With the outbreak of war, however, Pearse had begun agitating against recruitment to the British army, and for this reason Mahaffy forbade the society from holding its event, writing to it that 'a man called Pearse' was not welcome to disseminate his 'traitorous views' in Trinity College.[3] Given the college's commitment to the war, allowing an anti-recruitment activist to speak was deemed anathema by Mahaffy. This placed the Gaelic Society in a bind. Meetings were held, deputations were sent to meet with Mahaffy, officers resigned, and meetings were re-convened. All of this activity was recorded not in the usual society minute-book, but on a separate sheet of paper—the reverse of an anti-recruitment flyer published by Sinn Féin. The society's decision to record the events on the back of this flyer—which was then carefully pasted into the minute-book—was subtly subversive.[4]

Less subtle in its subversion was the decision of the committee to release all of its correspondence with Mahaffy to the press, and it was duly published in the *Irish Times* on 14 November.[5] This act of dissent was brutally punished: the college board swiftly and unanimously resolved that 'the Dublin University Gaelic Society be suppressed'.[6] The Davis cen-tenary meeting ultimately went ahead, but in the rooms of the nearby Antient Concert Hall. As the event had become notorious, however, it proved difficult to secure a chair, as Mahaffy's eminent friends—such as Douglas Hyde, Canon Hannay and Sir Horace Plunkett—did not want to be seen to be publicly rebuking their colleague.[7] In November 1914 Mahaffy could stand confidently by his decision knowing that his milieu—drawn from different political backgrounds—would support him. At the event itself, Yeats criticised Mahaffy for having broken 'the truce of the Muses', and expressed his disappointment that politics could not have been put to one side for the sake of literature.[8] The final speaker, Tom Kettle, a former nationalist member of parliament and lecturer at UCD, showed up inebriated, wearing a British Army uniform; he was repeatedly heckled, observers deeming it inappropriate that he discuss the poetry of Davis while so attired.[9]

By 1919 things had changed. Pearse was martyred, a legendary figure. In that year, his first full-length biography emerged, entitled, knowingly, *The man called Pearse*.[10] Mahaffy's dismissive words were remembered; to many, the epithet bore testament to just how out of touch Mahaffy and Trinity as an institution had been, if not to the contingency of intervening events. Pointedly, less than a year after Mahaffy's death, a new society called the Thomas Davis Society was formed in college. It boasted many of the same preoccupations as the Gaelic Society that preceded it.[11] Ironically, not many years later, Great Brunswick Street, the location of the Antient Concert Rooms, would be renamed Pearse Street, while a pub called Mahaffy's on the corner of the street would face the site of the famous meeting. The folk memory of this incident was strong.

Mahaffy's provostship frames this chapter. It takes the rapidly changing political situation as its focus, from the outbreak of the war, through the rising, the Irish Convention of 1917–18, and the armistice that ended the war. The events of 1916 led to a radicalisation of Irish politics and produced widespread support for an Irish republic, quickly undermining the position of constitutional nationalists and seeing the remarkable rise of Sinn Féin. This further entrenched the Ulster unionist position and, at a stroke, the irreconcilability of the two sides undermined the political consensus of 1914, rooted in support for the war. Trinity College Dublin was left in an uncomfortable position; traditionally, it found solace in its political influence and friends in Westminster. Ironically, the deteriorating Irish situation was being driven by Sir Edward Carson, the university's own parliamentary representative, who refused to participate in the 1917–18 convention held at Trinity to find a constitutional settlement between nationalists and unionists.

All of this demonstrated that the college was losing the political influence that underwrote its privileged position in Ireland. Trinity, its parliamentary representatives and its political alumni sought to exert their influence on events, but the university's traditional political power was undermined by both the rise of Sinn Féin and the intransigence of the Ulster unionists. This ultimately played out in an unseemly public spat between Mahaffy and Carson in late 1918, which ended the latter's 26-year career as a member of parliament for Dublin University.

Politics before the Rising

The outbreak of war in 1914 seemed to have resolved the impending crisis provoked by the Home Rule controversy and the arming of volunteers, north and south. Both constitutional nationalists and unionists of all persuasions were, as we have seen, united in their support for the allied cause. Two men who had been educated at Trinity were central to this Irish political truce whereby all parties had pledged in 1914 to support the war: Sir Edward Carson, the parliamentary representative of Dublin University, and John Redmond, leader of the Irish Parliamentary Party (IPP).[12] The necessity of galvanising support for the war—and winning it—overrode all other concerns, and had the consequence of lessening the antipathy between Home Rulers and southern unionists.[13] Southern unionism, the political outlook most common at Trinity, was increasingly divided over the issue of Home Rule. Some switched from an outright 'negative' unionism, condemnatory of nationalism, to a more positive vision of Ireland united through mutual cooperation on both sides, while others remained deeply hostile to Home Rule.[14] As we have seen, Home Rule was placed on the Westminster statute books in September 1914 and was to become the law of the land once the war—in which nationalists and unionists alike were playing their part—had ended. Southern unionism struggled to reconcile itself to this development and to Ulster opposition to it, and developments at Trinity in this period illustrate the dilemmas and divisions of southern unionists well.

Mahaffy's accession as provost added to the sense of political uncertainty. His predecessor, Anthony Traill, was a committed Ulster unionist and signatory of the Ulster Covenant in 1912. Traill died in October 1914 and his demise following the death of Edward Dowden in 1913 meant that two of Trinity's most outspoken and politically engaged scholars were gone. Mahaffy differed from both Traill and Dowden in that he was not ostensibly political. He had political opinions, which he frequently trumpeted in public, but he did not profess to speak for any political grouping or to represent any established position. As with much of his public life, Mahaffy's political outlook was often contradictory, misrepresented and provocative. As already noted, he was one of two senior fellows to vote against the Campbell amendment of 1912. While his refusal to let Pearse speak in October 1914 was seen, retrospectively, as symptomatic of his unionist credentials, at the time, many unionists, including Carson, feared that Mahaffy was a closet advocate of Home Rule.[15]

Historians have argued that the period prior to the Easter Rising marked a rapprochement between constitutional nationalists and southern unionists, with the national question being sidelined in the face of wartime exigency. Trinity, of course, still had a significant Ulster representation, which meant that divisions did not disappear outright, and Carson's position as both the figurehead for Ulster unionism and Dublin University's senior member of parliament at Westminster, further complicated this picture. When the coalition government was formed by Prime Minister Herbert Asquith in the spring of 1915, Carson was appointed attorney-general, a position that he took with a 'lack of zeal' and held until October of that year.[16]

The jostling for positions prompted by the formation of the new government showed where the university's political power lay; after all, the unionists had now joined the Liberals in government and their leader, Andrew Bonar Law, who was appointed colonial secretary, became the channel through which Trinity and its representatives sought to further their position. Bonar Law was a staunch opponent of Home Rule and had backed Carson's leadership of the Ulster unionist movement, as well as giving his full support to the arming of the Ulster Volunteers.[17] The formation of the new coalition exposed fissures in both the Trinity hierarchy and the college community more generally. Asquith agreed to appoint Campbell, the university's junior member of parliament, as lord chancellor of Ireland.[18] Campbell had followed Carson in signing the Ulster Covenant in 1912. John Redmond, who himself refused to accept a ministerial post in the new government, was outraged. In a letter to Asquith Redmond claimed that Campbell's proposed appointment negated the consensus in place since the outbreak of hostilities in Europe in 1914. 'We cannot', he wrote, 'and will not, agree to this. A truce by all means; but, if this appointment is made, it means a deliberate breach of the truce.'[19] The IPP submitted a formal protest to the prime minister, citing its opposition not only to the proposed appointment of Campbell, but also 'the appointment as Attorney-General of a gentleman [Carson] who for some years has openly preached defiance of the law by physical force'.[20]

The two parliamentary representatives of Dublin University were held up by Redmond and his party as examples of political bad faith and a threat to the wartime political truce. Campbell was untroubled by this and wrote continually to Bonar Law attempting to solicit the job of lord chancellor. Campbell was in no doubt that nationalist opposition to his appointment was because he was 'anti-Home Rule', which made him 'disqualified to hold office under a coalition'.[21] The nationalist press mobilised in opposition to Campbell's proposed appointment and it created a political controversy. Asquith, seeing the potential for revolt by the IPP in Westminster, switched positions, and decided to oppose Campbell's appointment.[22] His ambitions temporarily thwarted, Campbell dismissed the nationalist press as 'a rotten lot'.[23] He did not, however, cease in his campaign to lobby Bonar Law privately for appointment to high office, and continued his letter writing well into 1916.

The high-profile wrangling over Campbell's appointment had another important consequence at Trinity. The issue threatened to trigger an election, because if he became lord chancellor, Campbell would need to be replaced as a member of parliament for the university. Mahaffy sounded out his friend, Sir Horace Plunkett, to stand for the vacant seat. At the turn of the century, Plunkett had been a southern unionist. His position had, however, like Mahaffy's own, become more conciliatory towards Home Rule, and by the outbreak of war he supported Dominion Home Rule.[24] Sixteen fellows of the college, led by S.B. Kelleher, the lone Catholic in their ranks, wrote with Mahaffy's encouragement to Plunkett, inviting him to stand in the election. Arthur W. Samuels, a leading Dublin barrister and unionist who had unsuccessfully contested the Dublin University seat in 1903, had learned of a movement of 'indignant' fellows who felt that Plunkett's running in that constituency would pose 'a severe blow to the unionist cause'.[25] He informed Carson of the behind-the-scenes lobbying of Plunkett and declared his intention to stand if the seat became available.

Carson wrote—without a trace of irony—to Mahaffy to warn him against proposing Plunkett.

> As Sir Horace is an avowed Home Ruler this would necessarily force a contest in the university which I think would be deplorable having regard to the truce which has been observed since the war began by all parties.[26]

Pointedly, he remarked that 'however you may agree personally, as I believe you do, with Sir Horace's political views', it would be wrong for Dublin University to break the truce. So, on both sides, with the proposed appointment of Campbell and his mooted replacement by Plunkett, Trinity risked upsetting the precarious wartime political balance, and was cautioned by actors on each side not to do so. The incident was compounded by the personal antipathy between Carson and Mahaffy. Ultimately, the issue resolved itself following Asquith's decision not to appoint Campbell to the lord chancellorship.

Carson resigned his post as attorney-general in October 1915 in the wake of the disastrous Gallipoli campaign.[27] By early 1916 the political scene—as it pertained to Trinity—was quiet. The Campbell incident demonstrated that Trinity was beholden to political events elsewhere; its fortunes would rise and fall with governments. With wartime the turbulence—and consequently the potential for change—was great. At the same time, most people were too focused on the imperative of winning the war to expend too much time on national political concerns.[28] The consequence of this was that, while southern unionism remained divided, many of its adherents developed a largely unspoken acquiescence to the idea of Home Rule.[29]

The Rising and after

The protagonists present in Dublin during the rising rarely reflected upon its political ramifications at the time. Their immediate concerns were for the restoration of law and order. It was not until a number of weeks—or even months—after the cessation of hostilities in Dublin that people began trying to make sense of what had happened and what this in turn meant for the future of Ireland and, in the case of the Trinity community, for the college. The radicalising power of the rising quickly shifted the ground on which Trinity stood. Before 1914 the main cause of anxiety in Trinity was Ulster; the unionist community was increasingly split between anti-Home Rule and pro-partition northerners and anti-partition southerners who were better disposed towards Home Rule. While Ulster unionism had defined itself clearly during the crisis of 1912–14 and had come to stand for the permanent exclusion of six Ulster counties from a Home Rule settlement, southern unionism struggled to redefine its own political culture in the context of developments in Ulster and the more long-standing decline of the landed classes, who traditionally formed the basis for much of its support.[30]

The rising marked the dawn of a new reality: militant southern separatism. This development seems genuinely to have surprised the college hierarchy.[31] It took some time before members of the Trinity community knew both who was responsible for the rising and for what they claimed to have fought. William Ridgeway, the Regius Professor of Greek at Cambridge, a Trinity alumnus and well-connected unionist figure, was in no doubt: Germany was acting through Sinn Féin.[32] In the months following the executions, however, the rebel leaders became mythical figures; their faces, names, actions and writings were widely disseminated and they became icons for an invigorated separatist movement. In the year that followed a new movement began to take shape; leaders, hierarchies, platforms and tactics emerged.[33]

3/ or two poor fellows have lost relatives in this scandalous affair.

We just have had some men returned off leave, and they tell us that Dublin is in ruins, it is awfully hard to lose one's life out here, without being shot at home. The Sherwood's lost heavily but I expect the rebels got the worst of the encounter, We of the 2nd Battn the Dublins would ask for nothing better than the rebels should be sent out here and have an encounter with some of

Pages from a letter to Monica Roberts from Private Joseph Clark(e) 18369, No. 7 Platoon, B Company, 2nd Battalion Royal Dublin Fusiliers, writing from France, 11 May 1916, describing the reaction of members of the platoon to the news of the Easter rising, which he calls a 'scandalous affair'. He suggests that the rebels are 'pro-Germans' and that no Irishmen would be sorry if they were executed.

4/

their "so called Allies"
"the Germans") I do not
think anything they have
done will cause any
anxiety to England or
her noble cause, We will
win just the same, these
men are pro-Germans pure
and simple and no Irish-
-men will be sorry when
they get justice meted out
to them which in my opinion
should be Death. by being
shot.

I was glad to hear
you came to the rescue
and gave the troops some
refreshments for I know

Following the rising, Carson reported that he felt as if he had 'a nail through his heart' and urged that an immediate resolution be reached between the Home Rulers and the Ulster unionists. The executions of the leaders of the rebellion helped turn the public mood against the government and in favour of the rebels; the nationalist MP John Dillon, perhaps sensing a sea-change that would undermine the constitutional nationalist movement, made a strident speech in Westminster in which he condemned the executions and compared the qualities of British soldiers unfavourably with those of the insurgents. In his response to the rising, Mahaffy did not demonstrate the tact shown by others. He turned on Dillon, his erstwhile neighbour in North Great George's Street, accusing him of supporting the rebels. Mahaffy was outraged that any respectable politician could sympathise with the perpetrators of the rising, for they had fought 'a mean and cowardly fight'. Specifically, he wrote of how:

> Members of the Veterans' Corps, coming home from a route march, without a cartridge in their possession, were shot in the streets. Women and children were hit by the stray bullets of snipers occupying roofs in many respectable parts of the city.[34]

Moreover, the rebels had done nothing to prevent the looting of businesses in the city centre, unlike Trinity's OTC. The *Freeman's Journal*, the organ of constitutional nationalism, directed a very pointed response at Mahaffy. It started by comparing the current provost with his predecessor a century earlier who had condemned Robert Emmet. Mahaffy's letter, it continued

> should be studied as a good example of a rat in a panic. It is not long since Provost Mahaffy was represented by his friends to be a Unionist 'on the move'. The credulous would have us believe that he had found salvation. Even the Celticists imagined that he had at last discovered that Gaelic literature was not all stupidity and indecency. But Provost Mahaffy has recanted all the heresies of the Professor, and resumed his old form.[35]

A few weeks later, many of Ireland's leading scholars—including a sizable contingent from Trinity—met in their guise as members of the Royal Irish Academy, an institution that traditionally prided itself on its non-political character. Indeed, Mahaffy himself described it as being 'in

'Surrendered', editorial cartoon by John Scott Clubb, published in the *Rochester Herald*, 2 May 1916, the day the last of the rebels surrendered after the rising. The newspaper summarised the drawing as follows: 'A man lies face down, dead, amongst the ruins of a thatched cottage representing the shambles made of the attempt to create an Irish Republic'.

a sort of backwater, outside the rush and turmoil of the torrent'.[36] The meeting of 1 June was attended by Mahaffy and his fellow Trinity members Westropp-Roberts, Fry and Alton; the presidency of the academy at the time was held by John Henry Bernard, the aforementioned Church of Ireland archbishop of Dublin. In the course of this meeting it was resolved that Eoin MacNeill, founder of the Volunteers, Celtic scholar and professor of Irish at UCD, should be deprived of his membership of the academy, owing to his being 'found guilty of crimes against the peace of His Majesty the King and of this Realm'.[37] The resolution cited a precedent from the aftermath of the 1798 Rebellion. The prominent role played by Trinity men in ostracising MacNeill from the academic establishment again seemed to confirm Trinity's anti-Irish status. In the summer of 1916, the Trinity establishment did not seem to grasp the widening appeal of republicanism.

Proposed political settlements

The rising and its aftermath undermined many certainties. Ever perceptive, and seeing the potential for imminent radicalisation, Joseph Johnston wrote to the *Irish Times* urging the formation of a new wartime administration for Ireland, with Carson as lord lieutenant and Redmond as chief secretary. This temporary wartime measure would, in Johnston's view, prevent further deterioration in public support for the state.

> If the present situation is not handled with diplomacy and tact, large sections of the Irish people, who naturally and somewhat perversely sympathise with the under dog, will experience a revulsion of feeling in favour of these criminal lunatics.[38]

It was noticeable that Culverwell, who often intervened in difficult political and social issues, maintained a public silence through these fraught times.

Herbert Asquith's government and his Minister of Munitions, David Lloyd George, sought to find a resolution quickly. Lloyd George opened negotiations—separately—with Redmond on one side and Carson on the other in the last week of May. He resolved that the 1914 Government of Ireland Act should be enacted as soon as possible for 26 counties, with six Ulster counties being excluded. Redmond understood this exclusion to be temporary, while Carson was persuaded that it would be terminated only with unionist consent.[39] More than ever, the British government needed shrewd observers who were well connected in Dublin to furnish them with sound information on Irish opinion and constructive policy. Trinity's parliamentary representatives were important in this respect; the leading unionist politician Walter Long wrote to Lloyd George that while Carson and Campbell were not entirely representative of Dublin's unionists, 'if you have the approval of these two leading Irishmen…you will have an immense force on your side'.[40] Another important and increasingly influential figure was Cecil Harmsworth. He was the London-born and TCD-educated brother of the press proprietor Lord Northcliffe, and a figure on whom Lloyd George relied.[41] Harmsworth visited Dublin at the end of May and reported back to Lloyd George, highlighting the swing of public opinion in favour of the rebels, warning against punishment of their rank-and-file and advising that a strong garrison be maintained in the city.[42] Harmsworth's standing would rise with Lloyd George's, and he would emerge as an important advocate for Trinity in Westminster in the years to follow.

James Campbell, who been one of Asquith's guides in Dublin during his visit in the aftermath of the rising, wrote a long memorandum to the prime minister in June of 1916, interpreting the public mood and opposing Lloyd George's proposed settlement. Like many southern unionists, he opposed partition, fearing that a settlement on that basis would leave them exposed as a minority in the south. On this point too, however, the southern unionists were split, weakening their position.[43] Campbell wrote that:

> So many Irishmen of all creeds and classes in the Empire's great struggle for victory had materially softened and assuaged, leading many here, like myself, to the belief that out of it might arise a new spirit of conciliation and compromise which might after the conclusion of the war lead Irishmen to accept a generous and comprehensive scheme of self-government for the whole of Ireland, and I was prepared to work day and night for such a consummation.[44]

Partition would, he argued, lead to bitterness across the board; among nationalists in Ulster, unionists in the south and those in the three border counties. He continued:

> Neither in Ireland nor America will a people, with the ideals that prompted a rebellion at a time when they actually had a Home Rule Bill for the whole of Ireland on

the statute book, ever consent to accept in its place a mutilated bill for a dismembered Ireland. Englishmen may well think that the experiment is worth the risk, but no Irishman who is conscious of the dreadful results that must inevitably follow from its failure can regard it as anything short of a desperate and dangerous gamble, while its success must permanently divide the Irish nation into two hostile sections, each bearing the statutory brand of distinctive religion and sentiment.[45]

During the negotiations, another important Trinity figure was sounded out by Lloyd George. John Henry Bernard was, as we have seen, the archbishop of Dublin, president of the Royal Irish Academy, and deeply embedded in the college community. At Lloyd George's request he prepared a detailed memorandum in early June 1916, which would begin his ascent as an important political figure. Bernard agreed with Campbell that 'separatist legislation for Ireland will injure Ireland's higher interests'.[46] While he disagreed with the proposed legislation, he asserted that it was the duty of every good citizen to try and make it work 'if it is forced upon us'.[47] Bernard argued that partition was undesirable in the abstract, but if it must happen, he offered practical suggestions as to how it might be made workable. For example, he suggested following pre-existing geographical boundaries in each instance, ensuring that a large Catholic and nationalist minority remain in Ulster and a large Protestant and unionist minority remain in the south.[48] This would, he argued, ensure reciprocal good faith. Following this line of thinking, the southern unionists must be adequately represented in both houses of a Dublin parliament.[49] Bernard argued that the southern unionists were 'ready to make great sacrifices to ensure any stable form of government, under which life and property shall be secured'.[50] With southern unionists remaining deeply polarised, however, and the issue of partition proving especially divisive, Lloyd George's plan was dropped by July following intense opposition from the anti-partitionist southern unionists.[51]

Bernard's ascent was mirrored by Mahaffy's eclipse. Mahaffy was not consulted by the British government regarding the proposed Irish settlement in 1916, and he seems to have been out of touch with the prevailing mood of the southern unionists. This was perhaps natural for such an individualist. Indeed, he claimed that

Detail from 'The Kidnappers' by Henry Mayer, published in *Puck*, vol. 76, no. 1953, 8 August 1914, centrefold; the vignette shows Edward Carson kidnapping Ulster from 'Home Ruled Ireland'.

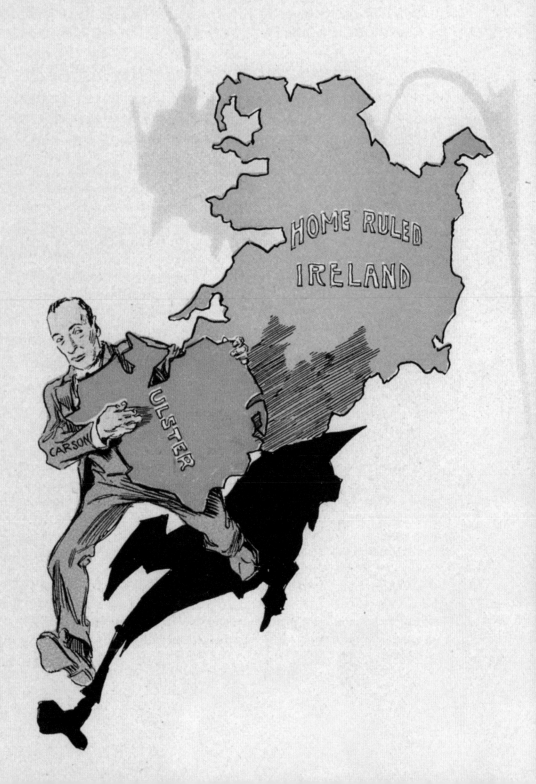

... I am constantly being asked for my opinion, and above all, the fact that I belong to no party, and hence may be expected to have an unbiased judgment. But for that reason my opinion carries no weight whatever in the counsels of the nation.[52]

Mahaffy used his column in *Blackwood's Magazine* in October 1916 to berate the Catholic Church for its stranglehold on primary education and, by association, for fomenting sedition. His article expressed little in the way of constructive solutions, except for an expression of admiration for Canada's dominion status, which reconciled Catholics and Protestants alike.[53] The *Catholic Bulletin*, known for its extreme views, dismissed Mahaffy as an 'ambitious wayfarer' and his opinions as 'bovine'.[54] Pointedly, Mahaffy remained apart from the larger debates about the future of Ireland.

In the midst of all this, the ambitious Campbell continued to petition Bonar Law for promotion to the position of lord chancellor. As we have seen, he was appointed attorney-general in April 1916, and his formal re-election as member of parliament for the university took place while the rising was still on-going. In November 1916 he was appointed lord chief justice for Ireland, meaning that he had to vacate his parliamentary seat. Despite the promotion, within weeks he was writing once more to Bonar Law to say that 'in all fairness I should now be returned to the position of Lord Chancellor here'.[55] The importance of his appointment for the college was that it triggered a by-election, the conduct of which presented a snapshot of the college community in transition at a crucial juncture in Irish history.

Running as the establishment candidate was Arthur Samuels, a barrister, unionist and imperialist, and typical of Trinity's previous parliamentary representatives. In his election address he stated that he wished not to represent any party, but the university. However, his party allegiances were clear.[56] The surprise candidate was Sir Robert Woods, Honorary Professor of Laryngology and Otology at Trinity, who had tended to the wounded soldiers in the aftermath of the Battle of Mount Street Bridge during the rising. Woods's candidacy caused a shock. He did not belong to a political party and was not a member of the Irish bar. Since the union was enacted, only W.E.H. Lecky had represented the university without this legal credential.[57] Woods claimed first and foremost to stand for Trinity's overlooked medical students and graduates, who formed almost one-third of the university's total contribution to the war effort.[58] In his policy statement on Ireland, Woods set himself against any attempt to coerce Ireland into a wartime settlement that it did not desire, and stated, rather vaguely, his commitment to a solution freely arrived at by all parties.[59]

Woods's candidacy constituted a break with tradition. More to the point, there were many within the college who wondered if Woods actually did have political allegiances—to Home Rule. William Ridgeway wrote privately that he would support Samuels, as 'Woods is being run by Kelleher, who is I believe, a strong Home Ruler, and from Woods' address, I infer that he is a disguised Home Ruler. This further justifies my support of Samuels.'[60] S.B. Kelleher was, as we have seen, the sole Catholic fellow of Trinity.

There seems to have been much suspicion of Woods among large parts of the electorate. At the same time a letter from a graduate was published in the *Irish Times* asserting that until Woods proclaimed his mantra to be 'The Union, the whole Union, and nothing but the Union', he would be supporting Samuels.[61] Joseph Johnston offered his perspective in a letter to the *Irish Times* on 3 January. Woods found himself in an 'unfortunate' position because, Johnston claimed, 'Home Rulers say that he is a Unionist and Unionists say that he is a Home Ruler'. This was the consequence of the emergence into politics of 'a man whose mind is too broad to fit the narrow mould of party'.[62] A number of Woods's supporters pledged their vote to him on the basis of his medical background but remained unsure of whether he was a Home Ruler or a unionist.[63]

While supporters of Woods argued that the issue was whether 'the legal monopoly in the representation of the university is to continue or not', his opponents saw it in party political terms only.[64] His supporters portrayed him as a progressive and broad-minded candidate, arguing that Samuels was the candidate of reaction and vested interests.[65] Indeed, many of Woods's backers wrote privately of their desire to end Trinity's position as a 'lawyer preserve', stating that 'the reputation of the university has been for too long in the hands of the lawyer'.[66] Woods's entry into the contest further complicated the issues at stake in late 1916. While most electors cited either Home Rule or professional affiliation in making their decision, others had more complex motivations. John Joly wrote that he required three issues to be addressed by any university representative: 'the Empire, the Union, and the recognition of science in the older universities'.[67]

In the event, although Woods polled well Samuels was elected by a ratio of just over 2:1. Woods managed to attract a significant minority in a short period of time, which he saw as vindication of his decision to run.

> I take this as proof that there is growing rapidly in this con-
> stituency a feeling among the electors of conviction that at

this crisis in the history of the Empire there ought to be some test for fitness to be a representative in the Imperial Parliament other than that of a party political one.[68]

The election showed growing divisions within the Trinity community that were not necessarily due to the changing political context but were certainly informed by it.

In December 1916 the Liberal David Lloyd George supplanted Asquith as the prime minister and led a coalition government. Soon after his appointment, Lloyd George decided to release all remaining Irish internees held since the aftermath of the rising; a key moment in the revival of the separatist movement. Even more important was a by-election that took place in February 1917 and turned out to be one of the most important in modern Irish history.[69] George Noble Plunkett, a scholar, papal count, Trinity graduate and father of a signatory of the 1916 proclamation, was elected in North Roscommon for Sinn Féin, and declared his intention to abstain from Westminster, in keeping with Arthur Griffith's original Sinn Féin policy.[70] Plunkett briefly became a figurehead for the party, but more importantly, his electoral victory spurred the separatist movement on and ensured its spread across the country.[71] Éamon de Valera, one of the 1916 leaders who had not been executed, was elected to the East Clare constituency in July 1917, and the following October Sinn Féin was reconstituted as a reinvigorated and reorganised secessionist political party. De Valera became the new Sinn Féin president.[72]

In addition to Count Plunkett's important electoral victory, Trinity's connections also radiated in other important directions after the rising. Lloyd George appointed Carson as first lord of the Admiralty in his new coalition government in December 1916. While Carson joked that he was 'all at sea' with his new appointment, he was generally popular with his colleagues.[73] Carson remained in this position until July 1917 without distinguishing himself before being promoted to the War Cabinet as minister without portfolio. While he did not achieve a great deal in this period, the situation itself was striking: Dublin University's senior member of parliament was at the very pinnacle of the British government's war planning.[74] At the same time, he was becoming increasingly distanced from his constituents.

The Irish Convention

At the beginning of 1917 there was no sign of a resolution to the Irish problem. In parliament, Lloyd George sought to reconcile the interests of constitutional nationalists and Ulster and southern unionists, all in the hope that the imposition of a settlement would quell growing unrest in Ireland. In May 1917 he announced that 'Ireland should try her hand at hammering out an instrument of government for her own people'. To do so, he declared his intention of summoning a convention of representative Irishmen to solve Ireland's problems themselves, and find a means of introducing Home Rule that was amenable to all parties.[75] The result was the Irish Convention, which sat for almost a year at Trinity. It was, in the words of its historian R.B. McDowell, owing to its composition and the stakes at play, a 'brilliant failure'.[76] Others, such as David Fitzpatrick, have been less kind: he has described it as 'utterly futile'.[77] Nevertheless, the convention was important in demonstrating how constitutional political movements in Ireland had lost their effectiveness and how the British government had yet to comprehend this crucial change. It was emblematic of a wider political transformation.

From the beginning, the convention was restricted in what it could achieve. Sinn Féin refused to participate, as did some Ulster unionists, including Carson.[78] With Sinn Féin's growing support across Ireland and the concomitant undermining of Redmond's constitutional nationalists, the party's non-participation rendered the convention effectively impotent from the beginning. The same was true of the absence of Carson and his colleagues.[79] The convention was populated by the Irish middle classes—intellectuals, clergymen, businessmen and local government officials—who were predominantly representative (with some exceptions) of either constitutional nationalism or southern unionism. These were the parties with most in common, and also those facing declining political significance. Mahaffy's friend, Sir Horace Plunkett, was appointed the convention's chairman.

In June 1917 Mahaffy offered the use of the Regent House in Trinity to the British government for use by the convention. The *Irish Times* took the offer as evidence that he was 'a good Irishman'.[80] This gesture of public good faith was, however, also an act of self-interest. Walter Starkie recalled that his godfather was more concerned to have the 'dilapidated old hall' spruced up. 'With great satisfaction', Mahaffy told Starkie how

> he had persuaded the Government authorities to select
> Trinity College as the locale of the Convention, and he

chuckled at the thought that the British Government were defraying the cost of renovating the dingy Regent House which had been the eyesore of the College.[81]

T.P. Gill, secretary to the Department of Agriculture, was an astute figure who advised the British government on the convention's structure and related issues. A pragmatic and realistic Home Ruler, he was well connected in the literary and academic worlds of Britain and Ireland. Gill's common sense can be seen in a number of his recommendations. For example, he advised the government to appoint Diarmid Coffey, late of the Gaelic Society, to the convention's secretariat. Coffey had contact with

> all sections of politics, especially with the young men—including the Sinn Féiners—by whom he is respected. On the other hand he is connected by relationship with some of the leading unionist families in Ireland, by whom he is also much thought of for his abilities and his character.

Here, a Trinity nationalist was a useful hybrid figure, possessing the knowledge, contacts and respect of all sides.[82]

Pointedly, Gill warned against accepting Mahaffy's offer to use Trinity, which he feared—owing to both its history and reputation—would undermine the convention from the outset. Gill wrote to Francis Hopwood, the civil servant appointed secretary to the convention, urging him not to select Trinity as a site for the meetings.

> Trinity is a centre of controversy and of bitter jealousy and very bad feeling on the part of large numbers of people in this country. All this has been greatly aggravated since the rebellion by Trinity's action on that occasion and by Mahaffy's offensive letters and speeches. The would-be wreckers of the Convention are saying nothing against this place of meeting, for they are hoping it will be selected.[83]

For Gill, the oft-invoked image of Trinity as the bastion of Protestant Ascendency, conservatism and establishment, all buttressed by the perception of Trinity's stance in 1916, threatened to undermine the convention before it even started. The fact that its meetings were to be held in Trinity, allied to the non-participation of Sinn Féin and some in the Ulster unionist hierarchy, the convention appeared stuck in the politics of the nineteenth century.[84]

Predictably, for a conference that sought to resolve a problem already superseded by new political forces, Trinity and its milieu were well represented at the convention. The Anglican archbishops of Armagh and Dublin, both graduates, were prominent delegates; John Redmond, the emasculated leader of the IPP was present; as were Bertram Windle, the president of University College Cork (another Trinity graduate), and Provost Mahaffy.[85] The convention sat for almost a year from July 1917. It produced much paperwork, but little in the way of consensus. The question of control of customs and excise in a proposed Home Rule settlement, allied to the refusal of the Ulster delegates present to accept any all-Ireland settlement, were the final sticking points.[86] As it happened, these discussions were increasingly academic, as at the time Sinn Féin was supplanting an increasingly discredited IPP; Home Rule was no longer enough for much of the Irish population; and the British government's plans to introduce conscription in April 1918 only exacerbated the situation. John Redmond's death on 6 March 1918 was symbolic of the demise of his movement.

All that said, the convention was still of much interest for Trinity. Having been invited to attend in his capacity as provost, his participation at the convention showed that Mahaffy carried little political influence. The former *bête noire* for nationalists was a somewhat peripheral figure, at a conference which was itself peripheral. In his first major speech to the convention, in August 1917, Mahaffy asserted his political beliefs and confirmed Carson's long-held views: he had, over the previous twenty years, 'drifted over towards Home Rule'.[87] This public declaration, which might have been startling three years previously, barely registered in mid-1917. Mahaffy's interventions were frequently out of keeping with the general discussion at the convention, but he remained idiosyncratic to the last, advocating a federalist solution to the Irish problem modelled on the constitution of Switzerland (which was, as he pointed out, the land of his birth). Referring to one of Mahaffy's interventions, an unnamed observer remarked to Stephen Gwynn, the nationalist MP, that 'it's only the Provost, and nobody minds him'.[88]

As the convention was struggling to reach a solution in the spring of 1918, Mahaffy stood to give his final speech, delivered, he declared, with 'greater anxiety' than he had experienced in relation to any previous speech in his career. In it he expressed his fear that sectarian divides might indefinitely inhibit Ireland, and he made a plea for minority safeguards.

Following pages: Delegates to the Irish Convention, which was instituted by Prime Minister Lloyd George with the aim of finding a resolution to the issue of the governance of Ireland and which sat in Regent House, TCD, from July 1917 until March 1918. John Henry Bernard, John Redmond, John Pentland Mahaffy and Sir Horace Plunkett are seated fourth, sixth, seventh and eighth from the right, respectively, in the front row.

As long as Roman Catholics and Protestants exist in Ireland, it makes and emphasises the contrast not only of two creeds, but two breeds, of two ways of thinking, of two ways of looking at all the most vital interests of men.[89]

Privately, Mahaffy sought to secure better relations with the Catholic Church. In May he wrote to William Walsh, the Roman Catholic archbishop of Dublin, about plans for the construction of a new Roman Catholic cathedral in the area destroyed in 1916 near Sackville Street. 'I for one, though a Protestant, should willingly subscribe to the carrying out of the plan.'[90]

A more important consequence of the convention was the rise of John Henry Bernard. Bernard emerged as a significant political figure during the course of the convention, and by its conclusion was ensconced as one of the leaders—if not *the* leader—of the southern unionists. His colleague, the Earl of Midleton, described him as 'probably the most distinguished Irishman of the day' present in Regent House.[91] Bernard was pragmatic, dignified and statesmanlike. Seeing both the decline of constitutional nationalism and the threat to the southern unionist position, he was 'judiciously conciliatory' at the convention.[92] He supported Midleton's plan for the implementation of Home Rule, which would involve all parties surrendering some interests, while customs duties would remain under imperial control and safeguards would be introduced for minorities.[93] Bernard's growing political importance saw him summoned to London—along with Midleton—to discuss a potential settlement with the prime minister in December 1917.

The London trip was one of many that Bernard would make in the next half-decade to negotiate with the British political establishment on behalf of both the southern unionists and Trinity. In the meeting of December 1917, he and Midleton reiterated their belief that all sides should make concessions; one concession that could not be made, however, was partition. Bernard argued that this would reduce any proposed scheme to 'waste paper'.[94] Bernard, Midleton and Lord Desart would go together to London in February 1918 for one meeting with the War Cabinet and another with Lloyd George on his own.[95] The question of partition would remain a fundamental sticking point that divided southern unionists.[96] Bernard's emergence as a respected political figure would prove invaluable for Trinity in the years to come as the influence of the university's parliamentary representatives waned.

The final and most important consequence of the convention was that it brought the developing breach between Trinity and Carson into the open. Trinity in 1914 was, as we have seen, a predominantly unionist institution in the south of Ireland, not a southern unionist institution. It tolerated and fostered many shades of unionism, from resolute Ulster militancy to more conciliatory southern unionism. Traditionally, Trinity drew large numbers of students from Ulster and, of course, Carson was the leader and inspiration for the Ulster unionist movement. However, the threat of partition altered this balance. With Lloyd George's desire to implement a settlement as soon as possible, and his promise of partition to Carson in the summer of 1916 (as well as Redmond's acceptance of at least temporary partition), Trinity faced an uncomfortable reality: it could soon be a minority institution representing a fading minority class under a Home Rule parliament in the south. The rise of Sinn Féin suggested that the new powers would be hostile to Trinity. The convention—at which Carson and Sinn Féin were noticeable through their absence—showed how isolated the southern unionists were, despite their influence at Westminster. Minority safeguards and self-preservation became the order of the day. While Campbell became, like many southern unionists, more pliable, Carson's position—as the university's parliamentary representative—was increasingly untenable. His political interests were no longer those of his constituents, the university community.

The 1918 election

The 1918 election demonstrated how the political ground on which Trinity stood was shifting. Ireland was growing increasingly lawless; the British government's threat to impose conscription on the country in the spring both fanned the separatist flames and created a temporary unity between constitutional and advanced nationalists against it.[97] Even before this, however, disorder was on the rise. In February 1918 a petition signed by high sheriffs for counties and cities in Ireland, bearing Mahaffy's signature in his capacity as the high sheriff for Monaghan, reached Lloyd George, and told of 'crimes which are being perpetrated daily...which seem to us to be animated by a strong pro-German sympathy'.[98]

Once more, Trinity connections used their position to inform the prime minister of the state of opinion in Ireland. Cecil Harmsworth wrote to Lloyd George that 'to impose conscription on Ireland against the goodwill of the Irish people...would be a mistake of the first magnitude'.[99] Arthur Samuels, who was both a university representative in Westminster and also at this point the attorney-general for Ireland, wrote a long memorandum to Lloyd George in May 1918. It made for stark reading.

The country is in a most dangerous condition. Treason
and sedition is being openly promulgated. There is grave
and well-grounded anxiety that it is on the verge of a civil
war, and that it will be a war of religion, like previous
Irish rebellions.[100]

Enforcement of the law had become impossible, a second memorandum
claimed, as no jury would dare convict those guilty of wrongdoing. Sinn
Féin was preparing for another rebellion, Samuels warned, and the imposition of Home Rule on Ireland would not solve anything; consequently, it
should be dropped. He reasoned that Sinn Féin would never accept it and
the Ulster unionists were more steadfast than ever against it.[101] The overwhelming sense coming from Trinity's politically connected representatives
was one of powerlessness. The situation continued to radicalise and to
threaten the college's position. Indeed, the armistice that ended the First
World War went unacknowledged in the minutes of the board; the imminent general election was of much greater importance. It was to sweep
'most of the constitutional nationalists out of parliamentary life'.[102]

The 1918 election resulted in a final breach between Carson and
Trinity. Carson had long been suspicious of Mahaffy's affinities for Home
Rule; he had softened in his attitude towards the teaching of Irish after
1908, and he was close to a number of Dublin-based constitutional nationalists, such as Archbishop Walsh and Douglas Hyde as well as to
Dominion Home Rulers like Sir Horace Plunkett. At the convention,
Mahaffy had made his support for Home Rule a matter of public record.
Ulster unionists, who Carson still led, increasingly viewed the exclusion
of six Ulster counties from the control of a Home Rule parliament as a
safe, if not entirely desirable outcome, while the southern unionists were
themselves fragmenting between those who could tolerate Home Rule
without partition and those who opposed it outright.[103]

Carson's position was, in the aftermath of the convention, no longer
the Trinity position; it was a purely Ulster position. Moreover, he was increasingly disconnected from Trinity issues, due to both his position in
the War Cabinet as minister without portfolio and his preoccupation with
Ulster politics. In January 1918, 22 members of Trinity's academic staff
(sixteen fellows and six professors) sent a petition to Carson, asking for
his guidance—as the University's senior member—before a presumed settlement emerged from the convention.[104] They suggested that he had
neglected university issues.

In the run-up to the election of November 1918, rumours began to
circulate that Carson would run in an Ulster constituency. Samuels wrote

'I'm afraid I'll have to drop my parcel', political cartoon *c.* 1918, depicting John Redmond and the Irish Party running from Sinn Féin ahead of the 1918 election; £400 per year was an MP's salary at the time.

to Bernard to inform him that Carson was coming under 'the strongest possible pressure' to do so.[105] This would be, Samuels continued, a tremendous loss to Trinity's influence in Westminster, especially in the knowledge of the 'big problems' facing the college. Samuels was clearly angry at the prospect of Carson's 'desertion'. He claimed that Carson 'owes everything to Trinity' and that if he left it would be seen as a sign that, for Trinity and unionism in the 26 counties, 'the game was up'.[106]

Bernard was left in a difficult position. While he had emerged as a leader of the southern unionists following the convention and was deeply embedded in the Trinity community, he was, first and foremost, archbishop of Dublin, and as such did not wish to interfere. He was adamant that the partition of Ireland would be 'very injurious to Trinity College', and that 'it will be a very serious thing, if the members for Dublin University commit themselves…to the dismemberment of Ireland. That is to abandon the Union quite definitely, and to secure the interests of Belfast at the expense of unionists in the South and West'.[107] He continued:

When a man has the affectionate confidence of a constituency for 26 years, courtesy at least obliges him to give
due notice of his intentions to sit for another constituency,
and in other interests. I recognise the difficulty of his position, but it has been apparent since he agreed to
partition in 1916. So I don't quite think that it is for us to
write to him; it is for him to write to us, and as soon as
possible. He is a very old and very dear friend of mine,
and I cannot imagine why, if he is in any perplexity as to
his position at Trinity, he has not written to me.[108]

Carson should have written to the provost—as returning officer for
the constituency—to announce that he would not stand in the forthcom-
ing election. Instead, he told Samuels privately of his intentions before
writing in affectionate terms to Bernard. In this letter he stated that he
had felt for some time it would be a 'contingency' that he move to a
Belfast constituency.[109] There followed a terse and official notification to
Mahaffy, in which Carson stated that 'it is right that the University should
be represented by a member who is not so closely connected with the
Ulster position'.[110] Privately, Carson wrote that 'the south of Ireland
people are very angry with us'.[111] His decision had left Trinity in the tricky
position of having three weeks to find a suitable candidate to replace him.
Samuels feared that a non-unionist could be elected.

Mahaffy responded provocatively and publicly. Perhaps taking his cue
from the Gaelic Society four years earlier, he released the correspondence
from Carson to the press, adding that this late notice put him as returning
officer, as well as the wider university community, 'to the utmost incon-
venience he could possibly have devised for us'.[112] The spat continued;
Carson wrote, in a public letter a few days later, that 'Dr. Mahaffy has
never been a supporter of mine, and, indeed, his action at the Convention
was one of the chief elements that impelled me to come to the conclusion
that I did'.[113] Mahaffy responded the next day, exercising restraint and
attempting to remain above the fray. 'As Returning Officer for Dublin
University, I am obliged to deny myself, for the present, the extreme pleasure of replying to Sir Edward Carson'.[114]

On announcing the election results in late December, Mahaffy directed
a few parting shots at Carson. He had greatly inconvenienced the college
and its global electorate by his late announcement. Twisting the knife,
Mahaffy informed the gathered crowds that in the 26 years that Carson
represented Trinity, he never once voted for him. Damningly, Mahaffy
claimed that Carson had bartered 'his high and important seat as repre-

sentative of this great constituency for what most of them present would call a very new seat in the slums of Belfast'.[115]

The election itself presented a new challenge. Trinity needed wise and experienced politicians to guide it through the impending strife. Samuels sought re-election and Sir Robert Woods also returned to the ballot. Joining them were two new names who showed the fracturing of the politics of the time. One was William Jellett, son of a former provost, described by the *Irish Times* as 'an uncompromising Unionist' who had repudiated the conciliatory line towed by Bernard.[116] He was firmly anti-Home Rule and anti-partition. The other was Stephen Gwynn, part of a famous Trinity family and educated at Oxford. Gwynn had served as a Home Rule MP for Galway, was a captain in the 16th (Irish) Division during the war, and had been a delegate to the convention. He decided to contest the seat as an independent nationalist and his candidacy caused disgruntlement in the Trinity community. Henry Dixon, the Professor of Botany, wrote privately that of the four candidates his preferred order would be 'Samuels 1., Woods 2., Jellett 3 and—The Devil take the hindermost!'[117]

The election results presented a snapshot of Trinity in transition. Samuels was easily re-elected. Woods took the second seat, edging out Jellett. In the context, Woods's non-traditional background was overlooked where it had not been in December 1916. Jellett's hard-line Unionist stance had limited appeal as Trinity confronted its own isolation in a future partitioned settlement. Gwynn came a distant fourth.[118] The *Irish Times* hailed Woods's election as representing 'the national value of scientific training and of the scientific mind'.[119] In this sense, it might be argued that it spoke also to the changes wrought by the war and the importance of scientific and medical professionals in its successful prosecution.

The picture painted by the national electoral results of December 1918 was not good for Trinity's community. Sinn Féin swept the board in the 26 counties. Only three unionists were returned in the south, these being the two Trinity representatives and one in Rathmines. The unionists did, however, experience a victory in Ulster, edging out the remnants of the constitutional nationalists and increasing their political dominance in the region. For southern unionists, however, the results were worrying.[120]

In January 1919 the fragmentation continued. The southern unionists officially split between the Irish Unionist Alliance, which was broadly opposed to Home Rule, and the Anti-Partition League (APL), with offices in London and Dublin, which was more concerned to prevent partition, and to ensure that unionists in the south and west of Ireland were protected if it did arrive.[121] The newly elected Sir Robert Woods was one of the main APL organisers in London, making his political beliefs clear.[122]

Men like Bernard and Midleton continued to view the imposition of Home Rule as the inevitable and most practical settlement in the circumstances.[123] In Dublin, the recently elected Sinn Féin MPs gathered at the Mansion House, adopting a declaration of independence and calling themselves Dáil Éireann.[124] Meanwhile, a new conflict was beginning, its cycles of violence and reprisal intensifying in 1920 and gripping the country until 1921.

Epilogue

John Pentland Mahaffy died at the Provost's House on the morning of 30 April 1919. His death marked the passing of an era. His godson, Walter Starkie, recalled that he was the 'Last of the Olympians', while King George V described the polymath's demise as 'grievous'.[125] Mahaffy's funeral was, in the words of the *Irish Times*, 'imposing'. From the lord lieutenant down to the humblest citizen, it reported, 'all members of the community united to the genius of the man'.[126] The funeral procession was carefully choreographed: Mahaffy's coffin was carried by students from the Provost's House, passing the library and the Graduates' Memorial Building before arriving at the college chapel. Following a service in the chapel the procession made its way past College Green, up Westmoreland Street, across Abbey Street, and from there followed the coast until it reached Sutton, where Mahaffy had a residence. He was interred at St. Fintan's Cemetery.

Mahaffy's grave betrays none of the bombast and self-assuredness of the man. He was buried with his wife Frances (who died in 1908) in a modest family plot, one amongst hundreds. For a man who was perhaps most famous for his public antipathy towards the teaching of Irish, it seems odd that his grave should be marked by a Celtic Cross.[127] For a man who was almost as famous for his arrogance, it seems most peculiar that his cross should be overshadowed by the memorial on the grave immediately behind—that of the famous Celtic scholar Whitley Stokes, who died in 1909. The epitaph on his grave claims somewhat vaguely that Mahaffy 'devoted his life to learning and to the education of his fellow countrymen'. By May 1919, the question of who Mahaffy's fellow countrymen were was a vexed one. Was this a death-bed recantation by the old controversialist, or a staunch assertion of nineteenth-century elitist values? As ever with Mahaffy, there was no clear answer. By the time of his death the victors of the Great War had assembled in Paris 'to make the world safe for democracy', with empires erased and dynasties deposed. At home, Ireland was drifting into open revolt. The political convulsions of wartime had changed Ireland and the world forever, leaving Trinity facing into an uncertain future.

NOTES:

[1] R.B. McDowell and W.B. Stanford, *Mahaffy: a biography of an Anglo-Irishman* (Dublin, 1971), 193–226.

[2] Denis Gwynn, Foreword to *Tribute to Thomas Davis by W.B. Yeats* (Cork, 1947; reprinted 1965), 6.

[3] *Tribute to Thomas Davis*, 7.

[4] TCD, MUN/GAEL/1, Meeting of 10 November 1914.

[5] 'Dublin University Gaelic Society', *Irish Times*, 14 November 1914, 8.

[6] TCD, MUN/V/21, Board meeting of 14 November 1914, 64.

[7] *Tribute to Thomas Davis*, 10.

[8] *Tribute to Thomas Davis*, 12.

[9] Austin Clarke, 'A centenary celebration', *The Massachusetts Review* 5 (2) (Winter, 1964), 307–10.

[10] Desmond Ryan, *The man called Pearse* (Dublin, 1919).

[11] 'The Thomas Davis Society', *Gaelic Churchman* 2 (1) (May 1920), 8.

[12] Lyons, *Ireland since the Famine*, 299–310.

[13] Patrick Buckland, *Irish Unionism: 1, The Anglo-Irish and the new Ireland, 1885–1922* (Dublin 1972), 35–49.

[14] Buckland, *Irish Unionism: 1*, 50. Jackson, *Ireland, 1798–1998*, 228–9, 233.

[15] British Library, Add MS 50908 fol. 61.

[16] John Hostettler, *Sir Edward Carson: a dream too far* (Chichester, 2000), 226–9.

[17] Hostettler, *Sir Edward Carson*, 169–97.

[18] Robert Blake, *The unknown prime minister: the life and times of Andrew Bonar Law 1858–1923* (London, 1955), 254.

[19] Bodleian Library Special Collections (BLSC), MS Asquith 36, fol. 92–94, Redmond to Asquith, 7 June 1915.

[20] BLSC, MS Asquith 36, fol. 96–97, Resolution of the Irish Party, 7 June 1915.

[21] Parliamentary Archives (PA), BL/50/3/10, Campbell to Bonar Law, June 1915.

[22] Blake, *The unknown prime minister*, 254–5.

[23] PA, BL/50/3/46, Campbell to Bonar Law, June 26 1915.

[24] Trevor West, 'Plunkett, Sir Horace Curzon', in James McGuire, James Quinn (eds), *Dictionary of Irish Biography* (Cambridge, 2012).

[25] PRONI, D1507/A/12/41, Arthur Samuels to Sir Edward Carson, 29 June 1915.

[26] TCD, MS 2075/67, Carson to Mahaffy, 30 June 1915.

[27] Hostettler, *Sir Edward Carson*, 229–30.

[28] Buckland, *Irish Unionism: 1*, 37–9.

[29] Buckland, *Irish Unionism: 1*, 53.

[30] Jackson, *Ireland, 1798–1998*, 232–4.

[31] BL, Add MS 50903, fol. 7, C.P. Scott Diary, Entry for 8–11 May 1916.

[32] BL, Add MS 52782, fol. 60, Ridgeway to John Henry Bernard, 6 May 1916.

[33] David Fitzpatrick, *The two Irelands 1912–1939* (Oxford, 1998), 63–6.

[34] 'Mr Dillon and Sinn Féin', *The Times*, 16 May 1916, 9.

[35] 'Dr. Mahaffy's outburst', *Freeman's Journal*, 18 May 1916, 2.

[36] Royal Irish Academy, Abstract of Minutes, Session 1915–16, Special meeting of 3 December 1915, 5.

37 Royal Irish Academy, Council Minutes XXV, Meeting of 1 June 1916, 450.

38 'The government of Ireland', *Irish Times*, 16 May 1916, 6.

39 Lyons, *Ireland since the Famine*, 378–9.

40 PA, LG/D14/1/37, Walter Long to Lloyd George, 29 May 1916.

41 'Lord Harmsworth', *The Times*, 14 August 1948, 6.

42 PA, LG/D14/1/8, Cecil Harmsworth to Lloyd George, 23 May 1916.

43 Jackson, *Ireland*, 233; Buckland, *Irish Unionism*, 1, 62–4.

44 PA, BL 63/C/2/18, Campbell memorandum to Asquith, 23 June 1916.

45 PA, BL 63/C/2/18, Campbell memorandum to Asquith, 23 June 1916.

46 BL, Add MS 52781/1, Bernard Memorandum, 3 June 1916.

47 BL, Add MS 52781/3.

48 BL, Add MS 52781/4.

49 BL, Add MS 52781/5.

50 BL, Add MS 52781/2.

51 Alan O'Day, *Irish Home Rule 1867–1921* (Manchester, 1998), 271–5.

52 John Pentland Mahaffy, 'The future of Ireland', *Blackwood's Magazine* MCCXII (October 1916), 548.

53 He made similar points in a letter to *The Times*, 27 June 1916, 9.

54 Editorial, *Catholic Bulletin* 6 (12) (December 1916), 633–40.

55 PA, BL/81/1/12, Campbell to Bonar Law, 7/8 December 1916.

56 'Candidature of Mr A.W. Samuels, K.C.', *Irish Times*, 27 December 1916, 4.

57 J.G. Swift MacNeill, Letter, *Irish Times*, 28 December 1916, 5.

58 'Dublin University election: Sir Robert Woods a candidate', *Irish Times*, 26 December 1916, 4.

59 'Dublin University election: Sir Robert Woods and Irish affairs', *Irish Times*, 30 December 1916, 7.

60 TCD, MS 2312/328, Joly Papers, Ridgeway to Joly, 2 January 1917.

61 Edward Stanley Robertson, Letter, *Irish Times*, 3 January 1917, 4.

62 'Mr. Samuels' policy', *Irish Times*, 3 January 1917, 4.

63 Woods Family Papers, John Mallet Purser to R.H. Woods, 28 December 1916.

64 'What Mr. Samuels said', *Irish Times*, 1 January 1917, 10B.

65 '"Petty Parochialism"', *Irish Times*, 13 January 1917, 7.

66 Woods Family Papers, Samuel A. Cot to R.H. Woods, 13 January 1917; Woods family papers, John Mallet Purser to R.H. Woods, 27 December 1916.

67 Woods Family Papers, Joly to R.H. Woods, 27 December 1916.

68 'Dublin University election: Mr Samuels elected', *Irish Times*, 6 February 1917, 4.

69 Michael Laffan, *The resurrection of Ireland: the Sinn Féin party, 1916–23* (Cambridge, 1999), 77.

70 Laffan, *Resurrection of Ireland*, 85.

71 Laffan, *Resurrection of Ireland*, 96.

72 Fitzpatrick, *The two Irelands*, 66–7.

73 Arthur J. Marder, *From the dreadnought to Scapa Flow: the Royal Navy in the Fisher era, 1904–1919*, IV (London, 1969), 54–5.

74 R.B. McDowell, 'Edward Carson', in McDowell, *Historical essays 1938–2001* (Dublin, 2003), 195–206 205; Hostettler, *Sir Edward Carson*, 261.

75 R.B. McDowell, *The Irish Convention 1917–18* (London, 1970), 77.

76 McDowell, *The Irish Convention*, vii.

77 Fitzpatrick, *The two Irelands*, 71.

78 McDowell, *The Irish Convention*, 80–5.

79 Alan O'Day, *Irish Home Rule 1867–1921* (Manchester, 1998), 277–8.

80 'The Provost's offer', *Irish Times*, 7 June 1917, 5.

81 Starkie, *Scholars and gypsies*, 160.

82 NLI, MS13516, Folder 4, T.P. Gill to W.G.S. Adams, 12 June 1917.

[83] NLI, MS13516, Folder 6, Gill to Francis Hopwood, 14 July 1917.

[84] Lyons, *Ireland since the Famine*, 386.

[85] McDowell, *The Irish Convention*, 218–27.

[86] Fitzpatrick, *The two Irelands*, 72–3.

[87] TCD, MS 2986/17, Mahaffy speech, 28 August 1917, 3.

[88] McDowell and Stanford, *Mahaffy*, 236.

[89] TCD, MS 2986/160, Mahaffy speech, 15 March 1918, 5.

[90] Dublin Diocesan Archives (DDA), Walsh Papers, Laity Correspondence (WPLC), 386/3. Mahaffy to Walsh, 26 May 1918.

[91] Earl of Midleton, *Records & Reactions 1856–1939* (London, 1939), 236.

[92] Buckland, *Irish Unionism: 1*, 100.

[93] Buckland, *Irish Unionism: 1*, 110.

[94] BL, Add MS 52781/21, Bernard memorandum, 6 December 1917.

[95] BL, Add MS 52781/26–29.

[96] Jackson, *The two unions*, 309.

[97] Laffan, *Resurrection of Ireland*, 133–42; Lyons, *Ireland Since the Famine*, 392–4.

[98] PA, LG F94/3/17, Petition, 22 February 1918.

[99] PA, LG F87/5, Harmsworth to Lloyd George, 13 April 1918.

[100] PA, BL 83/7, Samuels to Lloyd George (copied to Bonar Law), 2 May 1918.

[101] PA, BL 83/24, Samuels memorandum on Ireland, 11 May 1918.

[102] McDowell, *The Irish Convention*, 192.

[103] McDowell, 'Edward Carson', 206.

[104] PRONI, D1507/A/26/26, Letter of 16 fellows and six professors to Carson, January 1918.

[105] BL, Add MS 52783/30, Samuels to Bernard, 12 November 1918.

[106] BL, Add MS 52783/32, Samuels to Bernard, 12 November 1918.

[107] BL, Add MS 52783/32, Bernard to Samuels, 13 November 1918.

[108] BL, Add MS 52783/32, Bernard to Samuels, 13 November 1918.

[109] BL, Add MS 52783/37, Carson to Bernard, 21 November 1918,

[110] BL, Add MS 52783/38, Carson to Mahaffy, 21 November1918.

[111] PRONI, D2846/1/1/154, Carson to Lady Londonderry, 24 November 1918.

[112] 'Sir Edward Carson's retirement', *Irish Times*, 23 November 1918, 7.

[113] 'Sir Edward Carson and Trinity College', *Irish Times*, 26 November 1918, 3.

[114] 'The Provost and Sir Edward Carson', *Irish Times*, 27 November 1918, 5.

[115] 'The general election: University polls declared', *Irish Times*, 23 December 1918, 5.

[116] 'The general election', *Irish Times*, 23 November 1918, 7.

[117] TCD, MS 4796/108, Dixon to John Joly, 29 November 1918.

[118] 'The general election', *Irish Times*, 23 December 1918, 5.

[119] 'The University election', *Irish Times*, 23 December 1918, 4.

[120] Laffan, *Resurrection of Ireland*, 162–8.

[121] McDowell, *The Irish Convention*, 194–5.

[122] Buckland, *Irish Unionism: 1*, 183–7.

[123] Buckland, *Irish Unionism: 1*, 187–8.

[124] Fitzpatrick, *The two Irelands*, 78–9.

[125] Starkie, *Scholars and gypsies*, 122; 'The late provost of Trinity College', *Irish Times*, 5 May 1919, 5.

[126] 'The late provost', *Irish Times*, 5 May 1919, 5.

[127] This was not at all typical for fellows, senior fellows or provosts of Trinity in the late-nineteenth and early-twentieth century.

CHAPTER FIVE

The End of Old Certainties, 1919–23

Introduction

The termination of the First World War should have marked a return to normal life at Trinity College Dublin. The college community had been decimated in wartime; men had volunteered in their thousands for the British army leaving the campus a shadow of its former vitality. Almost 500 would not return, meaning that the community that emerged from the war was in mourning, dashing any hopes that a return to life as in 1914 could be quickly achieved.

Superficially, Trinity, like its fellow universities elsewhere in Europe, quickly adjusted to peacetime conditions, promptly welcoming students back to previously under-filled classrooms. The college board developed a set of criteria by which demobilised soldiers—including those from other universities—could resume their studies.[1] At the same time, the British government introduced a scheme that offered grants to ex-servicemen that would enable them to commence or continue university studies.[2] The result was that Trinity was quickly transformed into an institution teeming with life again. Ninety-six ex-servicemen and women, who had no prior connection to the college, came onto the books between 1919 and 1921.[3]

Political postcard *c.* 1919, illustrating the post-World War I Paris Peace Conference, with the Irish delegate being shown to the head of the negotiating table by 'Uncle Sam'.

Meanwhile, the college committee that examined the claims of those with war service continued scrutinising applications until 1928.[4]

In 1918 the number of students on the books had bottomed out at 721, from a figure that averaged 1,200 in the years immediately preceding the outbreak of war. The number of undergraduates was quickly restored to pre-war levels, however, hitting 1,274 by 1920.[5] The influx of students into the college is more apparent by examining the number of matriculations in the same years. In 1913, 287 students matriculated, while 279 did so the following year. This figure reached its lowest in 1915 with 218 matriculations. The figure for 1919, the first full calendar year following the end of the war, was 451, a significant increase on pre-war totals. A further 389 students matriculated in 1920. The period of demobilisation marked a deviation from pre-war norms in terms of student admissions. This was also the case across Britain and Europe. By May 1921, universities and colleges in Britain had experienced an increase in the student population of 63%—or almost 15,000 undergraduates—compared with pre-war figures. The increase in enrolments in Irish universities and colleges was 73%.[6]

Universities were full again, but university life was not as it had been before the war. Walter Starkie described the changes wrought by the war in the following terms:

> Trinity College was transformed: the lecture halls were thronged with a bewildering variety of individual types: there were students in cap and gown who some months previously had been colonels, majors, captains: men limping on crutches, others minus an arm.[7]

There was a sense of unease in Trinity in the months following the ending of the First World War; something of the old, pre-war life had undoubtedly died, but the college was also facing into acute problems unrelated to the war, which threatened its traditional function, identity and privileged position in Irish society. The student newspaper, looking around Trinity but also aware of what was happening at other universities, wrote that it longed for the return of the old university spirit but feared that it had 'decayed' during the war.[8] By June 1919, as Woodrow Wilson, David Lloyd George and Georges Clemenceau readied themselves to sign the peace treaty with Germany that would, it was hoped, end war forever, *T.C.D.* reported that Trinity faced a 'crisis', leaving its future 'dark and uncertain'.[9] Trinity, as an establishment institution in the centre of Dublin, feared for its future as Ireland drifted into violence, a republic was declared, and its traditional political position and influence were undermined. Compounding this, Provost Mahaffy, the symbol of Trinity's nineteenth-century prestige and imperial connectedness, was dead. By the start of the summer of 1919, the leaderless university faced into a period of unparalleled uncertainty.

This chapter will trace Trinity's reaction to this uncertainty, showing how, although its traditional political influence was withering away by 1919, Trinity retained political importance as a paramilitary conflict developed in the name of the Irish republic and the British government began contemplating a settlement with Sinn Féin. Trinity, so often presented as the epitome of anti-Irishness, had to make difficult decisions, and it assented to the Anglo-Irish treaty of December 1921 that established the twenty-six county Irish Free State. Slowly and quietly, the university began adjusting its outlook, developing new alliances and readying itself as best it could for a new political regime that was the antithesis to its accumulated traditions.

***

Being appointed by the British government, the provost of Trinity could perform an important political role, and this had been the case at various points in the college's history. In 1904, as we have seen, the unfancied Anthony Traill had been appointed to the post; a move driven by unionists who were upset by the Dunraven reform movement.[10] The contest for the provostship of 1919 demonstrated the continued political importance of the role, as well as the many changes that had occurred in the wider world of scholarship during the First World War. Two candidates quickly emerged, each representing different traditions. One was Archbishop John Henry Bernard, onetime fellow of the college, former Archbishop King's lecturer in Divinity and at the time president of the Royal Irish Academy. The other was John Joly, Professor of Geology and Mineralogy, fellow of the Royal Society and the first academic to be elected to fellowship at Trinity without examination.[11] Both were well connected in different ways.

Bernard was backed by the political powers in Westminster and those concerned with the future of Ireland. As already outlined, he had emerged as a significant political force at the 1917–18 Irish Convention, where his moderation and pragmatism saw him become one of the leaders of the southern unionist faction. Thereafter, he had occasionally been asked to advise the British prime minister, David Lloyd George, on the situation in Ireland. Bernard was well respected. In mid-May, James Campbell wrote to Andrew Bonar Law, leader of the Conservative Party, to recommend Bernard as 'the most suitable person' for the job.[12] Five days later, Bonar Law wrote to the prime minister, citing the opinions of Campbell, Edward

Carson and Arthur Samuels, recommending Bernard's appointment.[13] Elsewhere, Sir Horace Plunkett, the influential Dominion Home Ruler who had chaired the Convention, wrote to H.A.L. Fisher, the president of the Board of Education, to urge Bernard's appointment. He noted that the appointment was of the utmost importance as 'there is no country where the institutions of higher learning will need to be more helpful to the state than in Ireland for the next two decades'.[14] For the political powerbrokers and those interested in an Irish settlement, Bernard was the best candidate, and the office a useful bridge to Westminster in troubling times.

Joly's candidacy reflected a major convulsion in scholarly life that was a consequence of the recently ended war: the rise of science. As we have seen, in that conflict science was applied to warfare as never before. Universities became important repositories of expertise and sites for state-sponsored scientific mobilisation. In return, scientists across Europe and North America—but especially in Britain—demanded better financial and political investment in their disciplines. The 'Neglect of Science' lobby group had emerged in 1916 and successfully agitated for educational reforms. Nevertheless, science still needed friends in high places and a university head would be a major ally. In the early summer of 1919 a petition reached Lloyd George, urging the appointment of John Joly, a man 'who is at once an authority in science, and who is conversant with modern educational requirements', as provost of Trinity. It was signed by elite figures in British science, and it boasted the names of four Nobel Prize winners and 22 fellows of the Royal Society.[15] The petition was a testament to Joly's eminence in international scientific circles. Sir Oliver Lodge, the well-known physicist and principal of Birmingham University, wrote to Joly to endorse his claim and promising to 'say so wherever I can', but bemoaning the fact that his friend, the foreign secretary Arthur Balfour, was busy at the Paris Peace Conference and not easily contactable.[16] Joly had assembled a group of powerful and eminent backers who saw the appointment of a scientist to lead a university in Ireland as a tremendous coup in the fight to advance science in Britain and the empire.

The appointment of the provost occurred at an inopportune moment. Lloyd George and his closest cabinet members were in Paris, working out the terms of the post-war settlement. Bonar Law, effectively the deputy prime minister, was in London, and by the end of May a decision had been reached: Bernard was to be appointed. Political imperatives trumped scholarly innovations. However, the decision still required the prime minister's assent, and Bonar Law repeatedly cabled Paris to secure this.[17] In the midst of a crucial moment in twentieth-century European history, the provostship of Trinity College Dublin caused a momentary distraction to the peacemakers. Trinity's presence at the peace conference might have been greater; the Irish League of Nations Society, a group of moderate nationalists and unionists, tried to send a delegation with the intention of having the conference decide Ireland's future. The group was led by the Professor of Metaphysics at UCD, William Magenis, and Trinity's Professor of English Literature, Wilbraham Trench. Their passports were denied at the last minute, however, and they could not travel.[18] This group was one of many delegations—including that of the new Dáil—whose aspirations were left unfulfilled by the peacemakers.[19]

Lloyd George had assented to Bernard's appointment, but did Bernard even want the job? He never solicited it and only accepted the post with 'a heavy heart'.[20] Bernard's appointment was unusual; he was not then a fellow of the college and was resigning his post as archbishop of Dublin to return to Trinity, when traditionally, appointments tended to move in the opposite direction.[21] Still, Bernard seems to have understood the gravity of the situation and the necessity of a steady pair of hands in guiding Trinity into the unknown. More important, from a political stand-point, was the fact that with the Ulster unionist Carson gone and idiosyncratic cosmopolitan Mahaffy dead, Trinity College—led by one of the spokespersons for southern unionism—became, more than ever, associated with the southern unionist position. As 1919 turned to 1920, and belief in the practicality of maintaining the union began to wither, Trinity's preoccupation would become self-preservation, and guarantees that minority interests would be protected as the British government sought to implement a partitioned Home Rule settlement.[22]

Bernard's standing at this time should not be underestimated. His esteem was such that in August 1919, shortly after the termination of the Paris peace conference, the British government proposed sending a delegation to the United States 'to reduce friction and encourage cordial feeling' between the two nations. Former foreign secretary Edward Grey was to lead the mission, and the name of John Henry Bernard was also floated as potential delegate.[23] He was not ultimately selected; nevertheless, in the summer of 1919, Bernard's stock was very high indeed.

College life after the First World War

The events of 1919–21 would show, once more, that Trinity could not remain aloof from events taking place outside its walls. It has been argued that Trinity maintained a 'low profile' from 1919, and while this is true, it should not be assumed that the college was insulated from convulsions taking place outside.[24]

Outwardly, some things remained the same. Trinity Week took place once more in 1919 and the traditional rag—a hallmark of pre-war frivolity—made a notable return. Indeed, according to the *Irish Times*, the 1919 incarnation 'outdid all the elaborate spectacles of former years'. A crowd of Trinity students intercepted the Atlantic aviators Alcock and Brown at Broadstone station, preventing their escape and bringing them to the college in a procession. The porters, not knowing the cause of the commotion, barred the gates, but the students barged their way through, carrying Alcock shoulder high to the Dining Hall.[25] It was Bernard's first Commons as provost, and, according to Professor of German Gilbert Waterhouse, the bewildered provost did not quite know what to do when the mob of students noisily announced their presence. Bernard was uncomfortable with the intrusion, initially suggesting that Alcock should retire to the Common Room with a glass of wine. Mob rule prevailed, however, and the aviator was given a seat beside the provost for dinner by the quick thinking of one of the senior fellows who hastily vacated his place and offered it to Alcock.[26] This event was evidence of the students' desire, after five years of war and civil unrest, for frivolity, fun and carefree indulgence. The Alcock incident was the high point of Trinity Week 1919.

Societal life and sport were seen as integral parts of a healthy and functioning college life. During the war, 'the cricket grounds became a meadow and the tennis courts ceased to exist'. Thus, in 1919, there was a widely held desire to re-establish the non-academic side of college life as quickly as possible. In order to allow for investment in sporting facilities—including repairs to the College Park and Pavilion—the Dublin University Central Athletic Committee (DUCAC) was set up. It charged an annual subscription for Pavilion membership; its appeal for money noted that athletics formed 'a most important part of College life and education', and it put sport in Trinity on a sound footing for the future.[27] The revival of Trinity Week marked a return to the pre-war atmosphere in many respects; as ever, there was a cricket match, a boxing tournament, tennis, the college races, and a concert at the end of the week. Unusually, as has been noted already, there was also a baseball game, organised by the some of the demobilised American soldiers present in Trinity.[28]

Beyond Trinity, 1919 had opened with the ambush of Royal Irish Constabulary policemen by republican Volunteers at Soloheadbeg, Co. Tipperary, on 21 January, which was in turn the spur for the beginning of a new conflict: the War of Independence. By September, Ireland was drifting into open revolt, with republican forces targeting members of the RIC and British armed forces, who launched reprisals in return.[29] Bernard wrote privately that 'neither life nor property is secure, and the intimidation that is practiced throughout the South and West of the country is more open and violent than it has been in my life-long experience'. He recounted in graphic detail how Sinn Féin assailants had beaten his driver, a Catholic ex-serviceman.[30] In the same month, the college board made a decision that would have been unlikely before the war: it appointed a Catholic, T.F. O'Rahilly, to the lectureship in Irish. The chair had been established with the aid of the Irish Society in 1838 to train clergymen for proselytising in rural Ireland. Technically, as already stated, it fell under the auspices of the Divinity School. The board received a complaint from the Irish Society, who claimed that O'Rahilly's appointment was 'entirely out of harmony with the known intentions of the founders'.[31] The board stuck with the appointment, recognising the changes that were taking place throughout Ireland and the increasingly obsolete aims of the post at it had been created in the nineteenth century.[32]

A second, quiet but notable, change took place in February 1920 with the establishment of the Thomas Davis Society. This student society was the spiritual inheritor to the Gaelic Society, famously shut down by Mahaffy in autumn 1914. One of the founders was John Lighton Synge, a theoretical physicist and nephew of the playwright, John Millington Synge. The society aimed to 'encourage the study of the Irish language, literature and history', to promote study into contemporary problems, and to maintain a library of Irish literature.[33] It quietly assumed the mantle of the Gaelic Society and attracted the backing of many of the same figures who had once supported the old body, such as E.P. Culverwell, Joseph Johnston and Edmund Curtis. While the society was indicative of growing Irish sentiment in Trinity, this was far from a consensus position; the organisers noted ruefully that the pages of *T.C.D.* were closed to them, while the daily newspapers gave their activities only cursory write-ups.[34] A notable member of the Thomas Davis Society was Dermot MacManus, a veteran of the First World War who was seriously wounded at the Dardanelles, and who returned to Trinity to pursue an Astronomy degree but did not complete it.[35] MacManus instead decided to take up arms in the developing independence struggle. Although the student and recent graduate body was becoming more receptive to radical nationalist ideas, the numbers who actually participated in Ireland's War of Independence remained relatively few.

Trinity was in a precarious position as the War of Independence unfolded, and students were as aware of this as the college board. They too acted with prudence and caution, knowing that the future was uncertain. In December 1919, two student representatives were present in Strasbourg at an international ceremony to mark the restoration of the University of Strasbourg. At that gathering, some of the British delegates proposed forming a British students union. The Trinity student delegates objected, claiming that 'so decisive a step could not be immediately decided upon', if it were even desirable at all.[36] In a sense, 1919 was not the time for deciding such things; in Ireland, events would have to play out, and until they did official declarations of affiliation would be unwise.

Armistice Day was observed for the first time on 11 November 1919. In Ireland, College Green became, as it would remain for the next seven years, the focus for commemorations of the war. The main element of the event was the observing of two minutes' silence in memory of the war dead. As College Green was the focal point, and as the tolling of the college bell was the signal for the two minutes' silence, Trinity itself, with its own deep involvement in the conflict, came to act as a symbol for the memory of the war. Although the silence was impeccably observed in 1919, not long after, rival students from Trinity and University College Dublin faced off, the former singing 'God Save the King' and the latter singing 'The Soldier's Song'.[37] Here were the beginnings of an annual performance of identity politics: the students of UCD trumpeted their nationalist credentials and those of their institution; their counterparts at Trinity invoked their imperial past. This student posturing struck at something deeper, however. The symbolic importance of Trinity would continue into the post-war period. Mass participation in the war by members of the college community was taken as confirmation of its unionist credentials and aloofness from nationalist Ireland. Conversely, UCD, alma mater of many of the 1916 leaders, could claim that it had been on the 'right' side all along. Both views neglected the complexity of events and the reality that many nationalists—from Trinity, UCD and no university at all—had fought and died in the war. Moreover, in 1919, commemoration of the war had yet to become subversive and contentious in the way that it would subsequently, as we shall see in the Epilogue below.

Section of the victory parade in College Green to mark the first anniversary of Armistice Day, on 11 November 1919.

Politics

The situation in Ireland continued to deteriorate. Instances of lawlessness and murder increased dramatically and, by the end of 1919, the ineffectual RIC was reinforced by ex-servicemen sent from Britain, the infamous 'Black and Tans'.[38] Lloyd George desperately needed a political solution to end the unrest. An initial attempt at a solution came in the form of the Government of Ireland legislation, which began its progress through parliament in February 1920 and was passed in December of that year. This would establish bicameral home rule parliaments in the six Ulster counties as well as in the twenty-six southern ones. It was based on the mistaken assumption that Home Rule legislation—in a partitioned form—would placate nationalist Ireland and end the violence.[39] The legislation did not please nationalist opinion; nor did it provide consolation to southern unionists, for partition, their greatest fear, was now a reality. In September 1919 Provost Bernard had written that 'I confess that I am opposed to the "partition" of Ireland. If there is to be Home Rule, I prefer one parliament, with two houses, for the whole country.'[40]

The Government of Ireland Act placed Trinity College in an unusual predicament. Partition was now a *fait accompli*. Trinity sought quietly to do right by all parties. Under the terms of the new act, the university would have four representatives in the new 'Parliament of Southern Ireland'. The elections for this body took place in May 1921. Sinn Féin swept the board, with 124 candidates elected unopposed and vowing to abstain. The four remaining members were nominated by Dublin University.[41]

The Parliament of Southern Ireland has gone down as a curious footnote to the history of the period. It met only twice; the first time, in May 1921, only the four Trinity representatives attended, the Sinn Féin representatives abstained as they had promised. The second time the parliament met, in January 1922, Sinn Féin delegates did attend, but its sitting was a purely technical measure to approve the Anglo-Irish treaty and appoint a provisional government.[42] Nevertheless, this parliament represents an important moment in the history of the college, as the men who were representatives here would, in one way or another, dictate Trinity's fortunes for the next 25 years. The Government of Ireland Act allowed for Dublin University to retain parliamentary representatives in Westminster as well as in the new Dublin parliament. The men nominated to represent the university in Dublin were unlike their counterparts in London, however, and embodied a distinct break with Trinity's previous pattern of parliamentary representation. As we have seen, representation was traditionally the preserve of those from a legal background, with W.E.H. Lecky and Sir Robert Woods the only exceptions. Moreover, the university's representatives in Westminster were themselves explicitly political; the men who occupied these offices generally identified as unionist and saw themselves as professional politicians.

The careful selection of Trinity's representatives to the Dublin parliament in 1921 demonstrated a change of mentality. The college's nominees embodied four distinct academic and professional vocations. Ernest Alton (Classics), W.E. Thrift (Physics), Sir James Craig (Medicine) and Gerald Fitzgibbon (Law), were the four chosen, none of whom had previous political experience. The composition of this group neatly balanced the humanities and sciences, as well as academic and professional disciplines. Fitzgibbon, who had no political aspirations, was an unwilling participant and it was only when he was presented with a nomination paper with 'a proposer, seconder and eight assenting electors [that he] gave a most reluctant assent'. He was fully aware of the fact that he could go 'down to oblivion as a member of the "parliament that never met".'[43] All entered politics as independents—not unionists—and collectively stated 'we are not politicians'. While acknowledging the shortcomings of the new parliament, they vowed to 'devote our powers to the service of our country and of the College to which we owe so much'.[44] For an institution which as recently as November 1918 had been deeply divided over who should represent it at Westminster, this was a striking change, and evidence of a desire to safeguard its own interests by accommodating all sides.

The Government of Ireland Act had a second important consequence for Trinity College. Its terms required the transfer of education to the new Irish parliament. This was significant, as earlier in 1920 a Royal Commission had been appointed to investigate Trinity's financial needs. This commission was called as a result of the grave diminution of college finances owing to the period of the war and the decline in revenue from student fees. A memorandum of December 1918 estimated that Trinity had lost £48,300 in fees due to the war service of students.[45] This was a matter for government to rectify and not one specific to Trinity; a Royal Commission was also convened to investigate the resources of Oxford and Cambridge in the same year. These three institutions required the institution of a Royal Commission to decide how their financing should be secured as they were not traditionally in the receipt of state aid on a regular basis. Trinity's Royal Commission augured great things, recommending a capital grant of £113,000 alongside an annual grant of £49,000 for the university.[46] The money promised to Trinity was significant for the institution; however, it was modest compared with sums being invested in higher education either by philanthropic foundations, individuals or the state in Britain in the aftermath of the war.

Thus, one of the important consequences of the First World War for British higher education was that it made the state responsible for the funding of universities. The creation of the University Grants Committee (UGC) in 1919 aimed to bring the fragmented grouping of universities together under one state-funded umbrella. In other words, institutions that had traditionally had a great degree of autonomy were being redefined as state institutions, and the repercussions of this would be especially far-reaching at the ancient universities. However, the Government of Ireland Act ensured that one state would make recommendations about the future of the university while a second, new, and potentially hostile national legislature would ultimately enforce it. Moreover, the provisions in the act relating to funding Trinity reduced the recommended annual grant to £30,000, while the once-off capital grant was left out altogether.

In November 1920, the board of Trinity resolved to write to Lloyd George informing him of the severity of its financial situation.[47] Bernard held a number of meetings with H.A.L. Fisher, president of the Board of Education, in early 1921. This issue was not only of concern to the board of the college; in February 1921 the student newspaper noted that the failure to secure the grants proposed by the Royal Commission would mean that 'all the future developments of the university will be crippled'.[48] The question of college finances overlapped with the issue of minority safeguards for unionists in the south of Ireland. In the minds of the representatives of Trinity College, it was essentially the same issue and hinged on the sympathy of a future government towards the institution. The British treasury, for its part, was worried by the consequences of a large grant to Trinity College Dublin, as the Royal Commission was about to make recommendations on Oxford and Cambridge. A sizeable grant to Trinity would surely lead to demands for increased grants to the two British universities.[49] By mid-1921, however, questions as precise as the nature of state funding for higher education could not be broached while a brutal war engulfed Ireland.

The military situation worsened into the summer of 1921, as both the British military and the Irish Republican Army (IRA) actively pursued policies of reprisal killings. In the case of the latter, property belonging to known unionists was targeted. In May the Custom House in Dublin had been burned down. Violence was not restricted to Dublin, however, and across Ireland, IRA units staged raids and ambushes, with the British committing increasing numbers of troops to Ireland in an effort to enforce law and order under the new legislation.[50]

Warriors' Day was 3 June 1921, the occasion for a series of sporting exhibitions staged to raise money for ex-servicemen. One of the centrepiece events was a cricket match between the Gentlemen of Ireland and the Military of Ireland, set to take place in the College Park. The game was a society event, attended by 'a very large and fashionable crowd'; however, the pitch was ringed by troops, demonstrating that security was a concern.[51] At 5.30pm, two men cycled up to the railings bounding the park on Nassau Street. 'They advanced towards the railings, and, producing revolvers, fired them towards the players', discharging six rounds before cycling away again.[52] Years later, one of the perpetrators, an IRA man called Paddy O'Connor, recalled how he and his accomplice had been instructed to stop the match taking place by firing into the crowd. 'After the first couple of rounds were fired, a lady spectator jumped up from one of the seats and got killed by a stray shot. The match was not proceeded with.'[53]

The woman in question was a 21-year-old student called Kathleen Wright, who was in attendance with her fiancé, George Ardill. He was also a Trinity student and veteran of the First World War. The match resumed but was quickly halted by the provost, who noted in his diary the 'miscreant' responsible was 'probably firing at an officer'.[54] The incident caused deep shock to the college community and went far beyond financial or political fears; the murder of an innocent student on the college grounds struck at the heart of institutional life. Kathleen Wright came from a family with strong connections to Trinity and its professional and cultural privilege: her uncles had distinguished themselves in imperial administration and military and cultural life. Among them was Sir Almroth Wright, a Trinity graduate who invented the typhoid inoculation.[55] Kathleen's death occasioned much anxiety for the Trinity community, who saw her as one of their own; at the same time, it demonstrated that the venerable walls of their institution could not afford complete protection from the violent conflict gripping much of the country.

The college was in a state of fear, and Trinity Week—which would feature more public sporting events—was due to take place the week following Warriors' Day. This fear was exacerbated when Provost Bernard received a threat on 9 June purporting to be from the IRA. It read: 'take warning whilst Ireland is in mourning no sports in TCD. By order. IRA.'[56] The threat presumably referred to the execution of two IRA men at Mountjoy Prison on 7 June. While there was speculation as to its origins, the board decided that Trinity Week should be cancelled.[57] The official announcement stated that the board could not 'take the responsibility of inviting visitors to the College precincts at present'. Not only was Trinity Week cancelled, but the library was closed to visitors for the summer months.[58] And while one Trinity woman was the victim of IRA violence, another, Dorothy Stopford Price, who graduated with a medical degree in 1921, idealistically joined the republican forces, offering her medical expertise to the West Cork Brigade of the IRA.[59]

The cricket pitch murder might have seemed to be the the precursor to a state of siege, but in fact, it was as bad as things got in Trinity during the War of Independence. A settlement had to be reached; if the parliament of Southern Ireland did not become effective by 12 July, Ireland would be ruled by martial law. On 4 July a meeting took place at the Mansion House between Éamon de Valera, Arthur Griffith and various unionist figures such as Andrew Jameson, Lord Midleton and H.M. Dockrell, invited, as de Valera's letter of invitation to Sir Robert Woods euphemistically put it, because they represented 'a certain section of our people'.[60] Woods's private account of the meeting noted that de Valera felt these men could act as intermediaries between the Dáil and Ulster, but they were quick to point out that 'we were not in [Ulster's] confidence at all'. Issues such as the position of Ulster and association with the empire were discussed, and Woods found de Valera's attitude to be defensive rather than offensive.[61] Midleton, acting as a liaison to Lloyd George in London, returned to the Mansion House on 8 July with the prime minister's agreement to a truce, which finally came into effect on 11 July. The appetite and resources for a prolongation and escalation of hostilities was not there—on either side.[62] From that position, negotiations would begin—haltingly at first—to achieve a final settlement to the War of Independence. Midleton continued to be an important go-between, and through his connection to Bernard and Woods the interests of Trinity College would be conveyed to the British government during the treaty negotiations.

The truce also allowed for a period of stocktaking. Indeed, there had been few opportunities for reflection since August 1914, and this one, too, would be short-lived. From July until September there began a long and convoluted correspondence between Éamon de Valera, president of the Dáil, and David Lloyd George, to establish the starting points for a settlement.[63] The truce allowed others to reflect upon the process, the characters and the positions of the various sides. Moreover, it presented Trinity with a moment to formulate its own position. The Celtic scholar E.J. Gwynn wrote to Provost Bernard in September 1921, likening the speeches of de Valera to those of the student orators of the Historical Society, 'products of a good heart, plenty of conceit, and a blank igno-

Letter from Éamon de Valera to Trinity MP Sir Robert Woods, 21 June 1921, inviting him, as a representative of the unionist community, to attend a meeting at the Mansion House in an effort to bring the government for southern Ireland into effect before 12 July, in order to avoid the imposition of martial law.

MANSION HOUSE,

June 29th, 1921

A Chara:-

     The reply which I, as spokesman of
the nation, shall make to Mr. Lloyd George
will affect the lives and fortunes of the
political minority in this island no less
than those of the majority.

     Before sending that reply I would
like to confer with you, and to learn from you
at first hand the views of a certain section of
our people of whom you are representative.

     I am confident that you will not refuse
this service to Ireland, and I shall await you
at the Mansion House, Dublin, at 11 a.m. on
Monday next, in the hope that you will find it
possible to attend.

                Mise,

                Éamon De Valéra

Sir Robert H. Woods,
39, Merrion Square,
DUBLIN.

rance of what has been and what is'. Gwynn, whose scholarly endeavours might have engendered some sympathy in the nationalist cause, continued by remarking that

> this last year has made me feel, for the first time, that I am myself essentially English and not Irish, in spite of certain sympathies and antipathies. A man is what he inherits and what he draws in from his surroundings, and for me and most of us Protestants these things are ninety per cent English or Scotch traditions.

Whatever his personal beliefs, however, institutional considerations had to be taken into account too. Trinity would need to address any coming change proactively. 'It has to remain here and must somehow accommodate itself to the change. We ought to be thinking about that. Some of the other side are I believe friendly enough disposed and we may find a *modus vivendi*.'[64] The future was filled with uncertainty, and senior Trinity figures began mentally to prepare themselves for whatever changes lay ahead.

Trinity's fate was inextricably linked to the treaty negotiations that began in October 1921 in London. This extended far beyond the psychological reasons cited by Gwynn in his letter to Bernard. More immediately pressing for Trinity in the same period, however, was its financial situation, which was rapidly becoming perilous. The board noted in October 1921 that it had yet to be given any of the money earmarked for it by the Royal Commission, while UCD and UCC all had received new state grants under the auspices of the University Grants Committee.[65] Trinity's timing was bad in this instance; everything else would be a secondary consideration until after a settlement to the War of Independence had been reached, for a settlement would supersede the Government of Ireland Act and the Royal Commission. Writing to Lloyd George on 24 October, Bernard apologised for intervening at 'so anxious a time', but argued that the issue of funding for Trinity needed to be addressed quickly to maintain the goodwill of southern unionists 'during the transition period'.[66] By dint of his position as provost of Trinity and as one of the leading southern unionists, Bernard was on the periphery of the Treaty negotiations in late 1921, simultaneously seeking to attain the best conditions for former unionists in a new state while also ensuring that financial guarantees made in the Government of Ireland Act were transferred to any new agreement. He was deeply worried for the future of the institution, noting in early November 1921 that 'if Trinity College were a Sinn Féin institution like its neighbours we should be given all and every grant of money that we asked for'.[67]

Bernard held meetings with senior government officials in London on two separate occasions during the treaty discussions. On 15 November, he, along with Andrew Jameson and Lord Midleton, met with Lloyd George and other government ministers, who informed them of the current state of negotiations. Bernard explicitly asked for a provision to secure 'church property and educational and university institutions', which the prime minister claimed Sinn Féin would 'probably' honour.[68] Lloyd George requested that the unionist delegation meet with some Sinn Féin representatives the following day. At that meeting, according to the provost's notes, Arthur Griffith gave his assurances that article 64 of the Government of Ireland Act would be honoured. In other words, the new state would meet the financial obligations towards Trinity that it inherited from old regime, in the form of an annual grant of £30,000.[69] Bernard was impressed by Griffith, whom he described as 'the ablest of all the Sinn Féin leaders'. He was 'weighty in counsel', the provost reckoned, and 'a man whose word can be trusted'.[70]

The Anglo-Irish Treaty was signed on 6 December 1921. The next day the representatives of the southern unionists again met with Lloyd George. They were upset with the final provisions of the document; for Bernard, it did not guarantee that the annual grant of £30,000 promised in the Government of Ireland Act would be honoured by the new government. Bernard's notes of the meeting stated dryly that

> the Prime Minister, after reflection, admitted that he had
> not appreciated that point, for which he was sorry; but
> that he did not doubt that the Sinn Féin Majority [would]
> act in accordance with the repeated promises which they
> had made to deal impartially with all classes and creeds.[71]

The vagaries of Lloyd George are famous and this was but another example. Most importantly, the treaty definitively broke the union between Britain and Ireland after 120 years.

Bernard was a pragmatist who acted in the best interests of the institution, given the difficult situation. On 10 December the board passed a resolution expressing its support for the new government and for peace in Ireland.[72] This was a historic and deeply significant moment, but also a contentious one. The resolution was passed by nine votes to three, with the three dissenters being firm unionists; Henry Dixon, George Cathcart and the vice-provost, Thomas Gray. The board vote of December 1921 mirrored the controversies of October and November 1912. On each occasion, it had been resolved that Trinity's first allegiance was to Ireland. In 1921, however, the situation was such that there was no time for public posturing as there had been in 1912; the resolution was quickly and quietly passed.

The resolution changed little for Trinity in the immediate context. The new state would have many more serious issues to deal with in its fledgling months. The new government would have to build an administrative infrastructure and deal with violent opposition to the December 1921 agreement. While throwing in its lot with the new state, Trinity College still looked to the old government as its financial situation grew ever more precarious. Before the opening of the Westminster parliament in February 1922, Bernard travelled once more to London. He met with a British government delegation led by Lloyd George on 9 February, flanked by Dublin University's (soon to be defunct) MPs, William Jellett—elected to replace Samuels in 1919 following the latter's appointment as judge of the King's Bench Division—and Sir Robert Woods, as well as the parliamentary representatives of Oxford and Cambridge.[73] Bernard argued that Trinity would be reduced to bankruptcy if it could not avail of the £30,000 a year subsidy that had been promised by the Royal Commission, and urged the British government to honour its pre-treaty commitments.[74] In response, Lloyd George's attitude toughened: there would be no more vague promises. First, he refuted the notion that the new state would be, by definition, hostile to Trinity College. Based on his discussions with Arthur Griffith and Michael Collins, this was anything but the case. Lloyd George claimed that when he had pressed Collins on the issue of the £30,000, the latter responded by asking 'why should we cut down the educational value of Trinity College? We are prouder of Trinity College than of any institution we have in Ireland'. His attitude hardening, Lloyd George 'earnestly suggest[ed]' that the provost 'should approach those who are the leaders of the Free State at the present moment'.[75]

Trinity had, over the years, come to take its position of political privilege as a given; its parliamentary representatives in Westminster had clout, while its provosts, appointed by the crown on the advice of the prime minister, had access to the centre of political power. By the beginning of 1922, this was no longer the case. Bernard and the Trinity hierarchy would have to deal with the leaders of the new state if they wished to draw down the money promised to them. This new reality was difficult for some former unionists to swallow. On 16 February 1922, as the treaty was being discussed in Westminster, William Jellett stood to make one of his last interventions in the House of Commons. He decried the agreement, claiming it was 'disastrous' and that unionists had been 'betrayed'.[76] The nationalist MP, Joseph Devlin, had a devastating put-down for Jellett. Times had changed and men of Jellett's type were obsolete. 'There are other Members for Trinity College', he remarked:

> they live in the twentieth century. Every one of them marched in solemn procession, and, I understand, in academic robes, to the first meeting of the Southern Parliament to declare in favour of the Treaty.

They represented Trinity College Dublin, a 'great Protestant institution' and had shown that they were willing to 'forgive and forget'.[77] The actions of Trinity's parliamentary representatives would continue to inform how the college was perceived politically. However, henceforth, it would be the new representatives in Dublin who would perform this task.

After the treaty

The implications of the treaty were clear enough for Trinity from a political point of view; it had to accept the new order and reconcile itself to a new political elite—quickly—to ensure its material wellbeing. This was implicitly understood but little reflected upon; it was imperative. As we have established, however, Trinity was much more than the board and the parliamentary representatives. It was a community, composed of students, staff and alumni. Membership of this community, while hard to define, had one common denominator: shared experience of and allegiance to the college. In other words, personal experiences of the college while a student or staff member, and an understanding of its accumulated heritage, played a crucial role in the formation of collective identities. For alumni, experiences of the college were based in the past and were premised upon what the college was at that time. For staff, and especially also for current students, it was more problematic; their group identity was mediated by what the college stood for at that very moment. The much-invoked traditions, a consequence of Trinity's historic political, cultural and religious privilege in Ireland, were under threat.

Many felt that this heritage had been betrayed and simply left the country. Gerald Fitzgibbon noted bitterly that 'day by day I see lines of huge furniture vans passing here on their way to the docks, each of which means another exiled family of loyalists'.[78] One such family were the descendants of the great physicist George Francis Fitzgerald, who had died in 1901. They emigrated to Britain shortly after the treaty was negotiated and wrote abusive letters to their Jellett cousins who remained in Ireland, accusing them of being turncoats for not also leaving.[79] Emigration was not always by choice. For some Irish Protestants, the treaty led to feelings of vulnerability, which were sometimes based in violent reality. The historian, Robert H. Murray, who was educated at Trinity, left the country in the spring of 1922 having received threats from the IRA, and following his departure his house was broken into and his books and manuscripts destroyed. Murray poignantly stated that the country had 'broken' him.[80]

The signing of the treaty threatened to trigger a crisis of identity for students. Should their identity change given that Trinity was now located in the Irish Free State and was not part of a union with Britain? If so, how? These questions were given added complexity by the presence in the college of large numbers of students from the six counties of Ulster, which had achieved its own self-governing political settlement. Student debates and student publications became the forums through which these new concerns were expressed.

The Historical Society debated the treaty in February 1922. Discussions were marked by none of the frivolous verbal sparring usually typical of such events; this was serious business, and the motion, 'That this house welcomes the ratification of the Irish Agreement of December 6th, 1921', was upheld by 21 votes to two. The auditor, Ralph Brereton-Barry, later a distinguished lawyer, appealed for unanimity on the debate, urging that 'only the voice of sincere opposition' be heard. The various arguments made hinted at the diversity of student opinion upon the subject; some claimed to support the treaty with few quibbles, others did so as a means of ensuring law and order, and other ex-unionists did so as it was the only practical option available. One speaker argued that the treaty did not go far enough, while another spoke against, styling himself the voice of 'Ulster intransigence'.[81]

An editorial in *T.C.D.* of February 1922 opined that since Trinity was presented with a *fait accompli* through the signing of the treaty, the college should embrace the new political situation wholeheartedly:

> Trinity College has decided to throw in her lot uncondi-
> tionally with the rest of Ireland, and we think the decisions
> is wise, but once taken it must be pursued without reser-
> vation and without looking back. To use a colloquialism,
> we must be 'all-in'.

It added that this was the sentiment of nine-tenths of the Trinity population, and consequently advocated that a much stronger emphasis be placed on the teaching of Irish.[82] At the same time, however, it worried that old associations would continue to work against the college in the new state. Another editorial suggested that 'Trinity men are not welcome in Ireland [because] they are mysteriously connected with a disembodied entity called "the Protestant Ascendancy"', which was 'now as dead as Queen Anne'.[83] The juxtaposition of these two student editorials clearly shows the dilemma faced by many Trinity staff and students; they knew that full cooperation with the new state was in their—and the institution's—best interests. At the same time, many felt distinctly ill at ease in Free State Ireland.

The signing of the treaty also provided an opportunity for new voices to be heard and new links to be forged. While Provost Bernard was still looking to Westminster to have his claims addressed, a group of disgruntled professors were making contacts with the new administration. A number of features distinguished them. First, they were non-fellow professors who worked in modern disciplines traditionally excluded from the fellowship examinations, such as modern languages and the sciences. Consequently, their salaries—and benefits—were less than those of the fellows. Second, many of them were nationalists, not ex-unionists.

The UCD French scholar and veteran of 1916, Michael Hayes, had been appointed as the first minister of education by the new provisional Irish government. Trinity's unhappy non-fellow professors wasted no time in making common cause with him. In January 1922, the Professor of French, T.B. Rudmose-Brown, wrote to his fellow Francophile, congratulating him on his new appointment and assuring him of his full support for the treaty and Arthur Griffith, adding mischievously that 'the Provost will raise no further objections' to the settlement.[84] Rudmose-Brown suggested that Hayes and the new government look closely at the inequalities in pay amongst Trinity's academic staff. At the same time, Ernest Alton, one of Trinity's representatives in the parliament of Southern Ireland, suggested that Hayes meet with himself and fellow Trinity representative William Thrift to discuss educational matters. This message was relayed via James Creed Meredith, a Trinity-educated lawyer whose involvement in the gun running of 1914 gave him solid nationalist credentials.[85] Meanwhile, Rudmose-Brown suggested that Hayes meet with a number of nationalist members of staff ('of our way of thinking') who also happened to be badly paid.[86] Thus, while the provost and board were still petitioning the government of the old regime, staff members wasted no time in establishing links with the new administration.

Trinity still seemed somewhat disconnected from the new political realities. The treaty had not engendered peace, but provoked further conflict. Soon after the meeting of the second Dáil to ratify the agreement, the dissenting minority withdrew, and Ireland descended once more into violence, this time a brutal civil war.[87] This civil strife produced contradictory impulses among Trinity students. One the one hand, many wished to play a full part in the new state, but on the other, during the fighting they were pleased to be apart from it. In the summer of 1922, the Earl of Midleton received an honorary degree at Trinity and recalled that although he was safe within the walls of the college, the proceedings 'were drowned by explosions and musketry'.[88] Later in the year the student newspaper commented that 'bombs may resound in College Green, the rattle of machine gun fire may awake midnight echoes in Grafton Street, but inside the gates of Trinity there is still peace'. Student concerns trumped all; society politics, sporting prowess and anxiety over upcoming examinations were the order of the day, as they always had been. 'Everything, in fact, is as ever. Our university has not altered since Ireland became independent.'[89] The college's relationship to the new state undoubtedly informed the way that students related to the college, but for the most part its usual functions continued unchanged.

The *T.C.D.* editorial suggesting that the college had not altered as a result of independence was not, however, entirely accurate. Trinity was, relatively speaking, an oasis of calm, but it was far from untouched. In late June 1922, the college had briefly been occupied by 21 Free State troops, to prevent its being taken by the anti-treaty forces.[90] The decision to support the treaty also led to more subtle but significant change. In the space of a month, the Gaelic Society, the home of radicalism and subversion a decade prior, was re-established, while the Officers Training Corps was quietly disbanded. At a stroke, one symbol of the imperial connection was done away with, while an old symbol was reanimated. The board remained wary of the Gaelic Society, however, prohibiting the discussion of 'topics of religious controversy or present party politics' at meetings.[91]

Outside the gates, war, naturally, proved greatly disruptive. Two students travelling from Belfast to Dublin to sit entrance examinations for Trinity in the spring of 1922 found that they were denied tickets at the railway station as no trains were running; the civil war was the reason given. One of them was A.J. McConnell, who would later distinguish himself as a mathematician and provost of the college. The other was Ernest Walton, who would also find international scholarly renown as a physicist. Fortunately for Trinity, the examinations in question were rescheduled and both McConnell and Walton began their studies at Trinity later in 1922.[92]

Change was coming slowly, driven not by the board but by the students and the university's parliamentary representatives. Trinity's four representatives to the parliament of Southern Ireland approved the treaty when that body sat to do so in January 1922, and under its terms, all four were given seats in the new assembly (or 'Third' Dáil), which first met on 9 September 1922 (the number of Trinity representatives was reduced to three the following year).[93] The National University was also allocated four seats in the new assembly. Unlike the NUI representatives, who were (at one point) allied to Sinn Féin, the Trinity four (Alton, Thrift, Fitzgibbon and Craig) still maintained their 'independent' position. For Fitzgibbon, however, as for many former unionists, the terms the British government had assented to in the treaty left a legacy of bitterness and confused identity.[94]

> I see no reason why I should profess loyalty to a King and an Empire which has betrayed me to my enemies and theirs, but I am not allowed to join the Irish Republic, because I do not worship the Pope![95]

The Trinity representatives were outsiders in the Dáil when it was convened in September 1922, and they knew it. Although the Protestant and former unionist minority was well represented in the senate, this was not the case in the lower house, which, with the exception of Labour and Farmers Party representatives, was dominated by men and women who had agitated and fought to break the union. As Fitzgibbon wrote privately, they had to surmount cultural as well as political differences.

> The roll is called in Irish, and though I do not care for being called Gearóid MacGióbúiv (*sic*) (pronounced Gerrode MacGeebeen) I can at least recognise it when I hear it, and I can write it on a notice of motion or a ticket of admission: but poor James Craig's backside must be bruised to a jelly with the kicks I have had to give him ... to draw his attention to the fact that the Clerk has read out Seumas Ó Carraig Ridire when he suspects Sir James Craig.[96]

Fitzgibbon was initially the most active of Trinity's four Dáil representatives, his legal background proving invaluable in discussing and framing legislation. His colleagues were more circumspect but soon had to defend their politics and the institution they represented. In late September 1922,

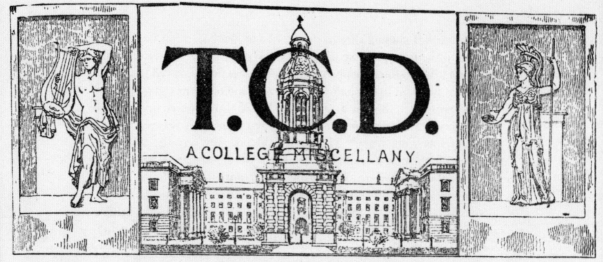

T.C.D.
A COLLEGE MISCELLANY.

Vol. XXVIII. No. 485.   THURSDAY, FEBRUARY 23, 1922.   Price Three Pence

NOTICES.

"T.C.D." is published every Thursday during the six weeks of Lecture Term.

Applications for Advertisements should be addressed to the Treasurer, " T.C.D ," Trinity College, Dublin.

The Subscription is (post free) 6/- for the year; for ten years, £3. To residents in College, 1/6 per Term. **Subscriptions for the Present Term must be paid at once to the Secretary, "T.C.D.," Trinity College.** Colonial Subscription, 7/- per year; for a period of ten years, £3 10s.

All Contributions for insertion should be addressed :— "The Editors, ' T.C.D.,' Trinity College, Dublin," and, if intended for publication in any particular Number, should reach us not later than the THURSDAY before publication.

A new day has dawned in Ireland. The British Government which for seven hundred and fifty years has directed the destinies of this island has now, for good or ill, handed over the reins of power to a native Irish Government. Under the new regime we cannot doubt that there will be great changes in the methods of administration to which we have hitherto been accustomed. None of the many changes which find a place on the programme of our new rulers will have a more important and far-reaching effect on our daily lives than the introduction of Irish as the official language of the new Free State. The process has already begun—a glance at one's morning correspondence will reveal a neat little inscription in Gaelic superimposed on the postage stamps.

We do not propose here to discuss the question of the advisability or the utility of the innovation. Every schoolboy knows the arguments which can be produced on one side and the other. What we do propose to consider is the attitude which this University ought to take up in the matter.

We are confronted with a *fait accompli*. The introduction of Irish is the declared policy of the new Government to which our Parliamentary representatives have declared their allegiance and which, we venture to say, has the sympathy and support of nine-tenths of the members of this University. Trinity College has decided to throw in her lot unconditionally with the rest of Ireland, and we think the decision is wise, but once taken it must be pursued without reservation and without looking back. To use a colloquialism, we must be " all-in."

In these circumstances then, we must expect to see the Irish language take a more imposing part in our University curriculum than it has heretofore. True, the study of Irish has never been wholly dead in Trinity College, but it has long been moribund. For many years there have been sizarships and scholarships in Irish, but they have generally gone a-begging and often lain vacant. In the Divinity School there are several valuable prizes originally established to promote the study of Irish amongst those entering the ministry of the Church, yet the Irish clerics who could preach a sermon in Gaelic can be reckoned on the fingers of one hand. This is only what might be expected,

Thrift spoke of his conversion from a man who held 'political views entirely different from those held by the majority of this Dáil' to a man who 'turned over that page completely', the treaty having rendered unionist views 'unpractical and impracticable'.[97] A few months later, Alton had to defend his institution against allegations that it did not represent the 'true' interests of Ireland; the reasons cited being the inferior position of Irish in the Trinity curriculum and the absence of Gaelic games from the sporting calendar. In a debate regarding the provision of a state grant for Trinity in November 1922, one TD argued that he would not support the proposal unless Trinity began playing 'national games'. Alton pledged to have hurling played at Trinity but defended himself too, stating that 'I have played rugby football and it did not make me less an Irishman.'[98] And indeed Alton's words were not mere window dressing; in 1923, Dublin University played University College Dublin at hurling in the College Park, an event described by the *Irish Times* as 'epoch-making'. It was attended by the provost, many fellows of the college, numerous TDs and the president of the GAA.[99] The *Freeman's Journal* noted that just a few years earlier such an event would have been 'regarded as a figment of an ultra-optimism giving rein to the wildest dreams of the revivalist imagination'. The headline proclaimed the contest to be 'Making History'.[100] The final score was UCD 7 goals and 6 points, Dublin University 6 goals and 4 points.

Trinity's TDs would become important conduits between the old university and the new state in the years ahead, but it is perhaps the link to the senate that is better known than Trinity's connection to the Dáil. James Campbell—by now Lord Glenavy and vice-chancellor of Dublin University—was appointed as the first chairman of the senate, and he used his life's legal experience to oversee the constitution of the Free State's new courts of justice.[101] The senate was, however, populated by many ex-unionists. Trinity's TDs performed a different sort of work, which was both practical and personal. Their permanent presence in Leinster House, the location of the new parliament, allowed for informal discussions to be held, relationships to form and trust to build. This trust was reinforced by the practical knowledge these men brought to parliament; they were not there simply to represent their institution, but enthusiastically sought to apply their specialist knowledge to legislating. This would prove much more effective than official and officious appeals to government made by the provost and the board.

The need for soft diplomacy to safeguard the university's position was brought home in mid-August 1922. In the space of ten days, the two Free

'Editorial', from *T.C.D.: a College Miscellany*, vol. 28, no. 485, 23 February 1922, discussing the fact that Irish has been designated the official language of the new Free State

State ministers seen as sympathetic to Trinity's claims—Arthur Griffith and Michael Collins—died. These deaths were a blow to Bernard for two reasons. First, during and after the treaty negotiations, these men had made it known that they were supportive of Trinity's future prosperity. Second, and more pointedly, Griffith and Collins had given verbal assurances that the funding earmarked for Trinity by the Government of Ireland Act of 1920 would be honoured by the new state. Trinity sent four senior fellows, with the college mace, to Collins's funeral, a sign of their faith in the new state and their esteem for the deceased.[102] Later, Bernard would write that Griffith's death was 'a national misfortune'.[103] As neither Collins nor Griffith had ever put into writing their intention to provide the agreed funds to Trinity, the college was suddenly in a vulnerable situation. W.T. Cosgrave, the new president of the Executive Council of the Free State, was unwilling to spend lavishly on the formerly privileged institution, given that the new state was itself short of funds and had other priorities in the aftermath of the Civil War. Thrift appealed to Cosgrave in November 1922, invoking Griffith's promise in London of November 1921 and a subsequent promise that Collins made to Alton, in which he suggested that the provisional government would see that Trinity was fully remunerated, if not directly by it then through a 'financial adjustment' agreed between the British and Irish governments.[104] Cosgrave's response, however, as we shall see in the epilogue below, was firm and unsympathetic.

Conclusion

Much had changed in Ireland by 1923, but what of Trinity? Of the 94 teaching staff working in the college in 1912, 46 were still employed there in 1923.[105] The student population of the college had diminished following its post-war high, and had dropped to 936, of whom 694 were men and 242 were women. In 1923, 265 students matriculated, a figure slightly higher than that of the years of the First World War.[106] This drop in entrants to the university and in the overall population is attributable to the wider political upheavals in Ireland; it led, in turn, to fluctuations in the composition of the college community. The junior freshman class of 1923 was comprised of almost 40% women, compared with an average of 23% in the immediate post-war years.[107] Religious background is available for 227 of the 1923 entrants: 61% were Church of Ireland, 15% were Presbyterian,

10% were Roman Catholic, while 5% were Methodist. There was a drop in the number of students enrolled in this period, and a consequent shift in the proportion of female students, but the religious backgrounds of students had not changed significantly by 1923 when compared with 1912, save for a slight rise in the number of Presbyterians enrolled.[108]

In December 1922 John Henry Bernard wrote an article for the *Quarterly Review* about the future of Ireland and Irish higher education. Irish universities should aspire to be both Irish and cosmopolitan, he asserted. 'A university must not only set itself to inspire the nation; it must have a world wide outlook, or its teaching will not be of the best.' Irish universities, he argued, should seek to compete with institutions like Halle, Harvard and Oxford.[109] Following the vicissitudes of the First World War, international cultural cooperation and rivalry was beginning to take off again; this was pronounced in the case of universities, which were energised by an influx of students, cash and interest in their potential. Bernard felt that Irish universities should be part of this trend.

The events of 1919–23 in Ireland, however, made this, if not impossible, then highly improbable. It was bad enough that Trinity was still reeling from its losses during the First World War, but by the time the Civil War finished, in May 1923, the Free State was also financially destitute, and unlikely to spend lavishly on higher education. The financial issue forms a fascinating undercurrent to the period. Physically, Trinity survived the War of Independence and Civil War mostly in tact. Psychologically, it was a different story, as many students, staff and alumni scrambled to keep up with events and the necessity of reorienting long-held political beliefs. It was the students and the younger staff members who proved most malleable; editorials in the student newspaper, student debates and the activities of the Trinity TDs and non-fellow professors were testament to this.

For the board, however, old connections could still prove useful. By 1923 only two members of the board from 1912 remained—T.T. Gray and George Catchcart. They were ostensibly working with the new order in the Free State, but the election of a conservative government at Westminster in November 1922 raised eyebrows in Dublin. It was to be led by Andrew Bonar Law, an old friend of Trinity from a different time. He had backed Carson's militant stance in 1911 and 1912 and had been an ally of Trinity's unionist MPs in Westminster throughout. Could the old unionist link be reactivated? Bernard certainly hoped so. Almost immediately following Bonar Law's election, the provost wrote to the new prime minister making Trinity's case for a grant; not from the Free State government, but from the British treasury.[110] The consequences of this will be explored in the epilogue. The student newspaper would assert in May 1923 that 'the time has come for us to forget the past and live in the present'; however, this was easier for some than others.[111]

NOTES:

[1] TCD, MUN V/44/3.

[2] 'Higher education for soldiers', *Irish Times*, 14 February 1919, 2.

[3] *War List*, vi.

[4] TCD, MUN V/44/3.

[5] National Archives of the United Kingdom (NAUK), T161/163, 'Students under MA standing at 1 January'.

[6] 'Crowded colleges', *The Times*, 14 May 1921, 7.

[7] Walter Starkie, 'John Pentland Mahaffy', in D.A. Webb (ed.), *Of one company: biographical studies of famous Trinity men* (Dublin, 1951), 89–100:100.

[8] 'Editorial', *T.C.D.* 19 February 1919, 49–50.

[9] 'Editorial', *T.C.D.*, 11 June 1919, 97.

[10] Earl of Dunraven, *Past times and pastimes* (2 vols; London, 1922), vol.2, 28–36; Parliamentary Archives, Bonar Law Papers (hereafter PA, BL), 97/3/14, Campbell to Bonar Law, 12 May 1919.

[11] R.B. McDowell and D.A. Webb, *Trinity College Dublin 1592–1952: an academic history* (Cambridge, 1982; reprinted Dublin, 2004), 405.

[12] PA, BL 97/3/14, Campbell to Bonar Law, 12 May 1919.

[13] PA, BL 101/74, Campbell to Lloyd George, 17 May 1919.

[14] Bodleian Library Special Collections (BLSC), MS Fisher 63/239, Plunkett to Fisher, 8 May 1919.

[15] The Nobel Prize winners were Lord Rayleigh, W.H. Bragg, Ronald Ross and Ernest Rutherford. See TCD, MS 2314/4/28.

[16] TCD, MS 2312/246, Lodge to Joly, 8 May 1919.

[17] PA, BL 101/81, 92, 95. Bonar Law to Lloyd George, 25 May 1919, 31 May 1919, 1 June 1919.

[18] TCD, MS 9298.

[19] Erez Manela, *The Wilsonian moment: self-determination and the international origins of anticolonial nationalism* (Oxford, 2007).

[20] TCD, MS 10650a.

[21] McDowell and Webb, *Trinity College Dublin*, 424.

[22] Patrick Buckland, *Irish Unionism* (2 vols; Dublin, 1972), vol. 1, 195–6.

[23] Parliamentary Archives, Lloyd George Papers (PA, LG), F12/1/14, 15, Curzon to Lloyd George, 3 August 1919; Grey to Lloyd George, 5 August 1919.

[24] McDowell and Webb, *Trinity College Dublin*, 423–9.

[25] 'Atlantic aviators in Dublin', *Irish Times*, 17 June 1919, 5.

[26] TCD, MS 4876.

[27] Trevor West, *The bold collegians: the development of sport in Trinity College Dublin* (Dublin, 1991), 59–64.

[28] 'Trinity Week', *Irish Times*, 16 June 1919, 3.

[29] David Fitzpatrick, *The two Irelands 1912–1939* (Oxford, 1998), 88.

[30] British Library (BL), Add MS 52783/51, Bernard to Walter Long, 25 September 1919.

[31] TCD, MUN 6/5, Thomas Hackett to Bernard, September 1919, 89–90.

[32] Máirtín Ó Murchú, 'Irish language studies in Trinity College Dublin', *Hermathena: a Trinity College Dublin review, quatercentenary papers 1992*, 63–5.

[33] 'The Thomas Davis Society', *T.C.D.*, 19 February 1920, 69.

34 'The Thomas Davis Society', *Gaelic Churchman* 2 (1) (May 1920), 8.

35 'Capt. Dermot MacManus', *Irish Times*, 12 April 1975, 11.

36 'The Strasbourg Congress', *T.C.D.*, 3 December 1919, 37–8.

37 'Armistice Day in Dublin', *Irish Times*, 12 November 1919, 5.

38 Anne Dolan, 'Paramilitary violence in the Irish War of Independence', in Robert Gerwarth and John Horne (eds), *War in Peace: paramilitary violence in Europe after the Great War* (Oxford, 2012), 200–15: 200–4.

39 Charles Townshend, *The Republic: the fight for Irish independence* (London, 2013), 140–1.

40 BL, Add MS 52783/54, Bernard to Long, 25 September 1919.

41 Fitzpatrick, *The two Irelands*, 100–2.

42 Townshend, *The Republic*, 385–6.

43 TCD, MS 11107/29, Fitzgibbon to Blake, 14 May 1921.

44 'Election Address. Borough of the University of Dublin, Parliamentary Election', *T.C.D.*, 19 May 1921, 151.

45 TCD, MS 2388/168.

46 McDowell and Webb, *Trinity College Dublin*, 425–6.

47 TCD, MUN V/5/22, 11 October 1920, 53.

48 'Editorial', *T.C.D.*, 24 February 1921, 89–90.

49 NAUK, T160/163, Letter of C.F. Stocks, 21 February 1921.

50 Townshend, *The Republic*, 287–98; 301–3.

51 'Murder in College Park', *Irish Times*, 4 June 1921, 5; Barry Keane, 'Murder Stops Play— Eventually!' *History Ireland* 21 (September–October, 2013), 38–41.

52 'Murder in College Park', *Irish Times*, 4 June 1921, 5

53 Bureau of Military History, Witness Statement (BMH, WS) 813, Testimony of Paddy O'Conner, 34–5.

54 TCD, MS 2381, Diary entry for 3 June 1921, 17.

55 Keane, 'Murder Stops Play—Eventually!', 40.

56 BL, Add Ms 52783/132, 9 June 1921.

57 'Editorial', *T.C.D.*, 16 June 1921, 187–8.

58 TCD, MUN/V/5/22, 11 June 1921, 133–4.

59 Margaret Ó hÓgartaigh, 'Price, Dorothy Stopford', in James McGuire and James Quinn (eds), *Dictionary of Irish Biography* (Cambridge, 2012).

60 Woods Family Papers, de Valera to R.H. Woods, 29 June 1921.

61 Woods Family Papers, Notes of meetings, July 1921.

62 Townshend, *The Republic*, 303–11.

63 Townshend, *The Republic*, 331.

64 BL, Add MS 52783/138–9, Gwynn to Bernard, 6 September 1921.

65 BL, Add MS 52784/68–69, 10 October 1921, 159.

66 TCD, MUN/V/5/22, Bernard to Lloyd George, 24 October, 1921, 170.

67 BL, Add MS 52781/104, Bernard to Midleton, 7 November 1921.

68 BL, Add MS 52781/33–34, Notes of meeting of 15 November 1921.

69 BL, Add MS 52781/35, 16 November 1921.

70 BL, Add MS 52784/75, 'Ireland', draft of article for *Quarterly Review*, January 1922.

71 BL, Add MS 52781/38, Minutes of meeting, 7 December 1921.

72 TCD, MUN/V/5/22, 10 December 1921, 200.

73 BL, Add MS 52781/39.

74 PA, LG F230/8, Notes of meeting of 6 February 1922, 6

75 PA, LG F230/8, 8.

76 House of Commons Debates, 16 February 1922, vol. 150 cc. 1352–59.

77 House of Commons Debates, 16 February 1922, vol. 150 cc.1359–60.

78 TCD, MS 11107/35, Fitzgibbon to Blake, 1 June 1922.

79 Michael Purser, *Jellett, O'Brien, Purser and Stokes: seven generations, four families* (Dublin, 2004), 139.

80 'Loss of valuable manuscripts', *Irish Times*, 17 May 1924, 7.

[81] 'College Historical Society', *T.C.D.*, 16 February 1922, 98.

[82] 'Editorial', *T.C.D.*, 23 February 1922, 103.

[83] 'Editorial', *T.C.D.*, 8 June 1922, 173–4.

[84] University College Dublin Archives (UCDA), P53/122, Rudmose-Brown to Michael Hayes, 10 January 1922.

[85] UCDA, P53/129, Creed Meredith to Hayes, 16 January 1922.

[86] UCDA, P53/135, Rudmose-Brown to Hayes, 22 February 1922.

[87] Fitzpatrick, *The two Irelands*, 108–14; Townshend, *The Republic*, 357–61.

[88] Midleton, *Records & Reactions 1856–1939*, 257.

[89] 'Editorial', *T.C.D.*, 23 November 1922, 27–8.

[90] TCD, MS 2381, 30 June 1922, 33.

[91] TCD, MUN/V/5/22, 11 March 1922 and 29 April 1922, 235–6, 246.

[92] Vincent McBrierty, *Ernest Thomas Sinton Walton: the Irish scientist (1903–1995)* (Dublin, 2003), 11–12.

[93] Tom Garvin, *1922: the birth of Irish democracy* (Dublin, 1996), 156–9.

[94] Buckland, *Irish Unionism, vol. 1*, 283–4.

[95] TCD, MS 11107/34, Fitzgibbon to William Hume Blake, 6 May 1922.

[96] TCD, MS11107/39, Fitzgibbon to Blake, nd., September 1922.

[97] *Dáil Debates*, vol. 1, no. 9, 569–70, 'Constitution debates resumed', Thursday, 21 September 1922.

[98] *Dáil Debates*, vol. 1, no. 29, 2126, 2144, 'Estimates, Arts and Sciences', Thurdsay, 16 November 1922.

[99] 'Hurling in College Park', *Weekly Irish Times,* 17 March, 1923, 5.

[100] 'Making History', *Freeman's Journal*, 10 March 1923, 7.

[101] Denis Gwynn, *The Irish Free State 1922–1927* (London, 1928), 165–8.

[102] TCD, MS 2381, 29 August 1922, Bernard Diary, 33.

[103] BL, Add MS 52784/91, 'Ireland', *Quarterly Review* (October 1922).

[104] TCD, MS 2388/377, Thrift to Cosgrave, 8 November 1922.

[105] *Dublin University Calendar*, 1923–24, 27–44.

[106] There were 218 matriculations in 1915; 243 in 1916; 228 in 1917 and 272 in 1918. See TCD, MUN/V/24/7–8.

[107] *Dublin University Calendar*, 1923–24, 491–4.

[108] All data are drawn from the 1911 Census and *Dublin University Calendar*, 1923–24, 491–4.

[109] BL, Add MS 52784/119–20; 'The outlook in Ireland', *Quarterly Review* (December, 1922).

[110] TCD, MUN/V/5/22, 297, 300, 2 December 1922 and 9 December 1922.

[111] 'Editorial,' *T.C.D.*, 17 May 1923, 145.

EPILOGUE

'Eppur si Muove'—Towards a New Trinity, 1923–52

Introduction

The Civil War raged in Ireland between June 1922 and May 1923. Two remarkable undergraduates began their studies at Trinity in this period: E.T.S. Walton in 1922 and Samuel Beckett in 1923.[1] Both went on to have exceptional careers, which culminated with the award of Nobel prizes. Walton was recognised (with Sir John Cockroft) for his contribution to physics in 1951, while in 1969 Beckett was honoured for his achievements in literature. Both Walton and Beckett were among the college's most distinguished graduates and their achievements did much to bring renown to their alma mater. The Trinity they entered as undergraduates was one that had to deal with much uncertainty following the upheavals of the preceding decade. This epilogue examines how Trinity related to the Irish state following independence, how student identities changed during this time, and how the memory of the college's involvement in the First World War became increasingly problematic as Trinity sought to establish a working relationship with successive Irish governments.

Opposite: View of the front of Trinity College, *c.* 1925.

The 1920s and 1930s were decades during which the identity of the institution was changing and being contested. McDowell and Webb wrote that Trinity followed a 'policy of inconspicuousness' in these decades.[2] At an official level this was true, but inconspicuousness should not be confused with inactivity, indifference or inertia. The story of these decades was one of quiet diplomacy and a subtle reorientation of the college's profile to bring it more into line with the Irish state. This was a complex and sometimes fraught process; the college administration was composed of conservative (ex-unionist) pragmatists who not only had to ensure good working relations with the new (and potentially hostile) government for the good of the college, but also had to offset this against the increasingly polarised politics of the student body as well as the expectations of alumni who were educated under the old regime. Whatever the challenges of speaking of the college as a unified institution at any point in its history, this is especially difficult with the post-1923 decades.

This period is also contested in historiography. Terence Brown has written that 'the 1920s found Trinity financially insecure [and] intellectually and socially remote for the most part from contemporary Irish concerns'.[3] F.S.L. Lyons argued that the community within Trinity, as was the case for ex-unionists elsewhere, retreated inwards out of feelings of intense self-consciousness and both said and did little.[4] Lyons used the metaphor of a ghetto to describe how the college felt besieged and cut off from the wider world. Patrick Buckland agreed with Lyons, arguing that those whom he termed the 'Anglo-Irish', and by association Trinity, 'contributed little after 1922'.[5] McDowell argued the same, positing that from 1922 Trinity became 'an intellectual and social enclave in Dublin'.[6] In a combative piece, Pauric Dempsey claimed the opposite, arguing that Trinity's post-1922 attitude was 'nothing less than querulous'.[7]

Lyons's ghetto metaphor is useful in understanding how the college was seen from within and without, but, as we have seen, this description was not new to the 1920s. Rather, it was a rhetorical device long used by different groups either to criticise Trinity and the Protestant Ascendency or to give greater definition to nationalist identities in the decades prior to the establishment of the Free State. In that respect, continuities can be identified that link the pre- and post-independence periods. Rather than Trinity being a symbol of privilege viewed enviously from without, it became a symbol of another regime and another way of life. There was, however, one important change in the post-independence era that reinforced the idea of a ghetto. The Free State was, in the words of historian Marianne Elliott, 'defiantly Catholic', and Catholicism became one of its outward markers of nationality.[8] While the Church of Ireland had always represented a minority of the Irish population, Protestants became an even smaller proportion of the wider population in the aftermath of the Anglo-Irish Treaty. The reasons for this are varied. Some Irish Protestants left the south in the period from 1920 to 1923, in some cases, as we saw in the previous chapter, owing to feelings of isolation and intimidation, and in others due to a lack of sympathy with the Free State when it was established. However, David Fitzpatrick has argued that the decline of the Protestant population was due, in the main, to its inability to enrol new members.[9] Many Irish Protestants, especially those in the leadership of the Church of Ireland, formed closely connected networks, united by work for the church, family ties, social contacts and a common educational background at Trinity.[10] While Catholics accounted for around twenty percent of the student body in the 1920s and 1930s, the institution remained overwhelmingly Anglican.[11] Trinity's Divinity School would continue to provide Anglican clergymen in the decades following the establishment of the Free State, reinforcing its reputation as a Protestant institution, but more importantly, reinforcing a sense of cultural difference between it and the values of the new state. That said, the issue of religion was most important in understanding collective identities and rarely presented an issue in university–state relations. In the aftermath of independence, however, it would, as we will see later, create difficulties between Trinity and the Catholic Church, which ascended to a position of influence within the state that was unprecedented before 1922.

The Trinity experience in the decades following Irish independence was mixed. In practical terms, the college was not an isolated ghetto. Official links were forged with the new government for a multitude of reasons, ranging from self-preservation to a desire to make an intellectual contribution to the functioning of the new state. It was a ghetto in an imagined sense, however. Members of the college community constructed their cultural and political identities in different ways, and, in the 1920s and 1930s, these were at variance with the values and ideals professed by the new state. However, attitudes were not static at Trinity and changed with successive waves of students and staff and the respective experiences of each generation. These changes would culminate in the appointment of A.J. McConnell as provost in what can be called Trinity's 'palace revolution' of 1952, an event that would transform the college and its relationship with Ireland.

Following pages: The committee of the Elizabethan Society c. 1925; Front row (left to right): Irene Eagleson and Edna Stevens; Middle row: Eva Dowse, Nancy Leebody, Eileen O'Connor, Eileen Adamson and Phyllis French; Back row: Grace Lee, Dot Eagleson, Nora Gallaher, Kathleen O'Connor Enid Dargan and Rhona ffrench.

Financial arrangements

Lloyd George's defeat in the 1922 general election meant, as we saw in the previous chapter, that a conservative government took over in Britain, led by Carson's old ally, Andrew Bonar Law. In addition to making his financial appeal to the British government, reasoning that it would be more receptive to his request for funds than the actual government of the day that had set up in Leinster House, Provost Bernard also wrote to W.T. Cosgrave (subsequent to the approach by William Thrift) seeking financial aid from the Free State government. By June 1923, both claims had been addressed. Bonar Law wrote to Bernard to inform him that the British government would pay Trinity an additional £20,000 for hardship caused to the college by the delay in implementing the Government of Ireland Act and its subsequent repeal.[12] The minutes of the 10 October 1923 meeting of the college board noted that £20,000 had been received from the British treasury.[13]

The Free State ministry of Finance also wrote a letter to Trinity in June 1923. The board proclaimed itself to be 'greatly surprised by its tenor'.[14] The letter promised two things. First, a one-off grant of £5,000 was offered, but with significant conditions; these required that the salaries of non-fellow professors be improved and that bonus payments be made to them for the previous year. The letter also promised £3,000 annually from monies held by the public trustee as a result of the provisions of the 1903 Land Act.[15] The terms imposed on the £5,000 grant, described by McDowell and Webb as 'humiliating', were actually the result of the appeals (mentioned in Chapter Five above) by a delegation of Trinity's non-fellow professors to the new minister for Education, Michael Hayes. Some quiet lobbying of the Trinity TDs resulted in these terms being loosened somewhat and also secured an additional grant of £3,000 recurring for three years, and the two parties eventually came to a somewhat amicable settlement.[16] These arrangements would, however, be the last communications between government and college on financial matters for 23 years.[17] There would be lean years ahead for the university as the Free State government had neither the means nor the inclination to meet the full extent of Trinity's needs.

In the early years of the Free State, Trinity's parliamentary representatives were important in quietly building strong relationships between the rulers of independent Ireland and its oldest cultural institution. When certain issues arose they could, as we shall see, exert a quiet influence in the Dáil, the bonds of trust already having been slowly formed. This trust was important not only to Trinity, but to Protestant Ireland more generally as the Free State found its feet and while each side regarded the other with some scepticism. This backdoor diplomacy proved important in ensuring that the university kept its head above water in the 1920s. A mutual respect was built up, ensuring that both sides could work together. It is no coincidence that the two most active Trinity TDs, Thrift and Alton, both later held the position of provost, continuing this working relationship at a higher level. Trinity's parliamentary representatives soon became respected by their Dáil colleagues for their diligence and non-partisanship. By 1923, Gerald Fitzgibbon could claim that he and Cosgrave were 'as thick as thieves'.[18] A file kept by Michael McDunphy, a senior civil servant and later secretary to President Douglas Hyde in the late 1930s, said of Thrift that

> although representing what might be regarded as the British tradition in Ireland he has since the inception of the new State in 1922 been extremely helpful in the building up of it, and has proved himself to be an Irish citizen in the truest sense.[19]

His parliamentary work was valued.

The effective but quiet diplomacy of Trinity's parliamentary representatives came to the fore in 1925. In August of that year the Executive Council of the Free State government decided to end the arrangement under which members of the medical profession in the 26 counties enjoyed the privileges of the British Medical Council, meaning that doctors trained in Ireland would no longer be qualified to practise in Britain, traditionally a large market for medical graduates.[20] This was of much concern to the Irish medical profession, which feared that the domestic market would suddenly be swamped with doctors seeking employment. The heads of medical schools from all the Irish universities met with Minister for Justice Kevin O'Higgins in August 1925 to raise their concerns. O'Higgins was initially intransigent, accusing the delegates of trying to inhibit the Free State from exercising its independence to the fullest.[21] Trinity wanted a compromise—making Irish medical graduates eligible to practice in Britain if they chose. The government initially remained steadfast in its refusal to budge on the issue, despite much media protest.[22]

Behind the scenes, Thrift quietly petitioned the minister for Finance, Ernest Blythe, and O'Higgins, leveraging the good relationships he had developed with both in Dáil Éireann.[23] Louis Purser, the college Registrar, asked Thrift to use his parliamentary influence in the matter, arguing that his position in the Dáil would give 'very much more weight to our case than mine would'.[24] While Thrift essentially reiterated the claims of other

Ministry of Finance,
Baile Atha Cliath.

27th June 1923.

A Dhuine Uasail,

With reference to your letter of the 23rd instant
further relative to the application made by the University of Dublin
for financial aid from the Government of Saorstat Eireann, I am directed
by the Minister of Finance to state that he has now had an opportunity
of discussing this subject further with the representatives of the
University in the Dail and, in view of the further facts placed before
him, is prepared to modify the proposals made in my letter of the 18th
instant in the manner explained below.

As regards the special Grant of £5000 for the current financial
year, the Minister waives the express conditions previously laid down
respecting the remuneration of certain whole-time Professors and
Lecturers in view of the assurance given to him by the University
representatives that the University would make every reasonable
effort to provide adequate remuneration for the Academic staff so far
as the financial resources of the Institution would permit.

In connection with the proposed transfer to Trinity College of the
funds which have accumulated in the hands of the Public Trustee
under Section 39 of the Irish Land Act, 1903, the Minister is prepared
to agree that in lieu of the six conditions set out in my previous
letter the following should be substituted:-

(1) That the investment of the capital should be controlled by the
Minister of Finance subject to the College being enabled, if it so
desired, to encroach upon the capital to such extent and for such
purposes as the Minister, after consultation with the Minister of
Education, might approve. The maximum encroachment to be permitted
during the next three years would be £10,000.

(2) That the interest on the accumulated sum should be entirely
at the disposal of the College.

(3) That the Government shall be at liberty to institute in due
course a comprehensive inquiry into the whole resources of the College
and into the use which is being made of them and that the College
will co-operate with the Government in rendering such inquiry as
effective as possible.

(4) That copies of the audited accounts of the College for 1921-22
and for subsequent academic years shall be furnished in due course to
the Ministers of Finance and Education.

In addition the Minister proposes that the College should receive
in the present and future financial years a Grant of £3000 per annum
and that in consideration of this payment and of the transfer of the
capital funds now held by the Public Trustee the College should waive
any claim for indemnity in respect of the operation of past or future
Land Purchase legislation.

It should be understood that, except as regards the special Grant of £5000,the foregoing proposals are put forward subject to the necessary legislation for giving effect to them being enacted by the Oireachtas. As already explained,it is important that the Minister should be informed at once whether the proposals are accepted by the College as steps must in that case be taken immediately by the Minister to give notice of the necessary amendments of the Land Bill at present before the Dail.

Should the College decide to accept the proposals in the form now put forward an undertaking should at the same time be given that no further application for State assistance will be made for at least three years. This is of course not intended to imply that there is any likelihood of further State assistance being given after the expiration of that period.

Mise,le meas,agat,

Joseph Brennan.

- - - - - - - - -

Letter from Joseph Brennan, of the Ministry of Finance, in response to a request from Trinity for financial aid for the university from the Free State government, outlining the amount of funding to be provided, and a number of conditions to be fulfilled in order to receive it.

university and medical school representatives, he was able to secure the support of O'Higgins.[25] The result was a temporary measure—leading in turn to a permanent arrangement in 1927—which ensured that reciprocal recognition of medical qualifications was regularised between Britain, Northern Ireland and the Irish Free State.[26]

Relations between Cosgrave's governments and Trinity remained respectful but cool. Trinity's preoccupation in the 1920s was financial. Cosgrave's government did not have the resources to match the sums proposed for the funding of Trinity by the Royal Commission of 1920 and wished to prioritise the claims of the National University, especially University College Dublin, the alma mater of many members of the new government.[27] Trinity and the Free State government did build tentative links, but this was a process marked by mutual suspicion and divergent agendas. The complexity of relations between the university and the new state are encapsulated by how both negotiated official ceremonial events.

Ceremonials

O'Higgins privately informed Edward Culverwell of the settlement over the medical council issues at a ceremony at Trinity in 1926 at which Cosgrave was given an honorary degree.[28] Much as they had done in the decades before the First World War, ceremonials such as the awarding of honorary degrees played an important part in publicly expressing what the college claimed to stand for and where its allegiances lay. They helped to create better relations between university and state by honouring individuals who were often politically influential while simultaneously disseminating a carefully constructed message to a wider audience.

Following the treaty there were no public ceremonials in Trinity on the scale of the 1892 Tercentenary or the 1912 Bicentenary of the Medicine School. The list of individuals given honorary degrees in the 1920s showed a subtle but limited repositioning of the university and expressed, as the tercentenary had, where Trinity felt it saw itself in the world. Trinity's scientific heritage was important, and international figures in the world of science, such as the French mathematician Emile Borel, the American Nobel Prize-winning physicist Robert Millikan, and three British scientists—astrophysicist Arthur Eddington, Nobel Prize-winning physicist W.H. Bragg and Nobel Prize-winning biochemist Frederick Gowland Hopkins—were all honoured. Unsurprisingly, political figures connected with the old regime were also honoured, such as the Earl of

Midleton and Viscount James Bryce, whose scheme of 1907 to create a Catholic college within the university had caused such uproar.[29]

Trinity nevertheless continued to make overtures to the new state and its political and cultural representatives. In late 1922, nine year after his flirtation with the college following the death of Edward Dowden, W.B. Yeats was given an honorary D.Litt. degree. Sir Robert Tate, the public orator, noted wryly in his oration at the event that 'it is true that he was never one of our students; yet we salute in him a friend well known in these halls'.[30] The following year, R.I. Best, the librarian of the National Library, noted Celtic philologist and member of the Royal Irish Academy, was also given the degree of D.Litt. In 1924, Tim Healy, the veteran Home Rule parliamentarian and holder of the new office of governor-general (or representative of the king in Ireland) was given the honorary degree of LL.D. In 1928, Eoin MacNeill, the founder of the Volunteers who, as we have seen, had been ousted from the Royal Irish Academy by Trinity representatives following the Easter Rising in 1916, was now given a D.Litt. by the college. Tate's oration lauded MacNeill's scholarship, describing him as 'one of the brightest lights of our sister university in Dublin' and 'an illustrious man who has served his country so well'.[31] The practice continued in 1933 when Douglas Hyde, founder of the Gaelic League, was also given a D.Litt., although Hyde was, of course, already a Trinity graduate.[32]

The most significant of all of these awards, however, was the granting of Cosgrave's degree in 1926. This ceremony demonstrated that a cautious mutual accommodation had been reached between institution and state. The decision to give Cosgrave a degree *honoris causa* was rushed, with the college board holding a special meeting to confirm the award a mere four days before the ceremony took place.[33] The award came in the aftermath of the London Imperial Conference of 1926, at which the British Commonwealth was established on the premise that Britain's dominions—including Ireland—would enjoy autonomous status within the British empire, and would not be subordinate to the United Kingdom. From Trinity's point of view, awarding Cosgrave a degree might be seen as a simultaneous nod towards both the new regime and the old one.

The ceremony at which Cosgrave received his degree had a distinct imperial flavour. W.S. Monroe, the prime minister of Newfoundland, was honoured at the same event. Tate's oration for Cosgrave lauded his role in ensuring that law and order were upheld in the aftermath of the Civil War. Cosgrave was, he declared, 'a man of undoubted vigour and courage to rule this island with judgment firm and just', who had 'stood up to vindicate the laws and promote freedom' and 'established solid foundations for long-lasting concord'.[34] The ceremony was full of meaningful but often contradictory symbolism. Cosgrave signed his name into the Proctor's Roll in Irish before he and Monroe left the theatre to the strains of the imperial anthem: 'God Save the King'.[35] Cosgrave's speech trod a fine line between respect for the institution and the empire, and assertions of Irish freedom. He began by referring to 'this ancient institution which has sent forth so many great Irishmen to work in the cause of their country', and argued that they—presumably referring to Tone, Emmet and Davis—had 'begot an honourable tradition which has no small part in inspiring the various movements which have so happily terminated in the political emancipation of our country'.[36] While consensus could be found between the two positions, and while both parties were respectful of one another, it was clear that Cosgrave saw the event as a celebration of Irish freedom, while Trinity saw it as a celebration of continued imperial affinity.

Cosgrave's honorary degree confirmed Trinity's official support for the treaty. That the president of the Executive Council of the Free State should accept an award from the old establishment university at all, however, was divisive. A few days before the ceremony the effervescent republican and feminist agitator Hanna Sheehy-Skeffington held a public meeting on O'Connell Street (as Sackville St had been renamed in 1924), where she criticised Cosgrave's participation in the Imperial Conference, his receipt of an honorary degree at Cambridge while he was in England, and the impending awarding of a degree at Trinity. In so doing, she asserted, he had 'turned his back on everything that Easter Week had stood for'.[37] Sheehy-Skeffington also led a protest inside of Trinity's Public Theatre during the conferring ceremony. This went unreported by the newspapers, but Culverwell reported to the provost that a group of women protestors

> came there to look and, apparently, to throw some liquid on Cosgrave's gown, thinking perhaps, that it belonged to him. They began to sing 'The Soldier's Song' when Tate was reading his oration.

As Cosgrave passed by the four women protestors attempted to dash towards him but were prevented from doing so by students and quickly led out of the building. Cosgrave claimed to be oblivious to any protest. At the official dinner later that evening, Culverwell noted that neither Cosgrave nor O'Higgins drank wine, but that 'they are not pledged less to College and drank the King's health in port all right'.[38]

Cosgrave returned to Trinity the following year to speak to the Historical Society. On that occasion he responded to the auditor's address about 'The World in Revolt', prefacing his remarks by asserting that the society held 'an honoured place in the history of Trinity College and...of Ireland'.[39] In closing, Lord Glenavy, the society's president, and as previously noted, also chairman of the Senate and vice-chancellor of the university, thanked Cosgrave for his 'untiring efforts for the good of the state'.[40] Cosgrave returned again in 1928—his third visit in three years—for the bicentenary celebrations of the birth of Edmund Burke and Oliver Goldsmith; Lord Birkenhead (F.E. Smith), one of the signatories of the Anglo-Irish Treaty of 1921 and a character reviled by many nationalists and unionists alike, gave the keynote address on that occasion and was himself given an honorary degree.[41] By the end of the decade, Cosgrave had thus established himself as a regular and welcome visitor to Trinity College Dublin.

Ceremonials such as these guaranteed a respectful relationship between university and state. This was important: while Trinity was essentially self-governing and the Free State had neither the resources nor the will to support the university financially, there were still certain issues on which the two parties had to work together. In some instances, the government inherited responsibilities from the old regime that it had to honour. The appointment of the provost was one such obligation, and this became an issue in 1927 when John Henry Bernard died at the age of 67.

Prior to 1922, the appointment of the provost was, by college statute, vested in the crown, and was usually approved by the prime minister. This was a rubber-stamping exercise, however: in reality, the college board's nomination for the position was generally accepted without question, except for unusual situations such as the 1904 appointment of Traill, when, as we have seen, Mahaffy (and Bernard) were overlooked for political reasons. The death of Bernard presented a potential problem: while college statutes had not changed, the form of government had. Cosgrave's government had the power—if it so wished—to make the appointment of provost. Cosgrave asked the attorney-general, John A. Costello, to investigate the legalities of the appointment and to recommend a course of action. On inspection of the college's regulations, Costello ruled that the appointment should 'be made by the Governor General on the advice of the Executive Council'.[42] Although relations between the university and the government were generally respectful, mutual trust was far from universal, and there was still a fear amongst some members of the college community that the government could make its own appointment from outside in a bid to 'Gaelicise' the institution.[43] The *Irish Times* hinted at this in an editorial from 3 September 1927, urging Cosgrave to think of the 'tens of thousands of Irishmen, at home and abroad, to whom the traditions, prosperity and prestige of Trinity College are almost as dear as life itself'.[44] The appointment of Bernard's replacement would be a delicate procedure.

In the event, the board submitted three names, in order of preference, to the Executive Council. First was that of Edward J. Gwynn, Irish scholar and part of the 'Gwynnity College' dynasty. The Executive Council approved the nomination, and forwarded its assent to Governor-General Healy to make the appointment official.[45] Gwynn's promotion to the provostship was an act of mutual accommodation. He had distinguished himself as one of the foremost Irish scholars of the period, and had been honoured by the National University with an honorary degree in 1926, the only Trinity figure to be so honoured until John Joly in 1931.[46] In the words of McDowell and Webb, 'his academic reputation served to some extent as a lightning-conductor against attacks on the College as "un-Irish."'[47] Gwynn viewed his Irish scholarship purely as an academic endeavour, however, and remained indifferent to the use of Irish as a modern vernacular. Shortly before the death of Bernard, he had written to the provost recommending that Irish be taught as an honours subject—giving it the same status as other modern languages—so that Trinity could ensure that it had a contingent of graduates present in the Civil Service (where it had become mandatory) to 'fight our battles behind the scenes'.[48] And, as we have seen in Chapter Five, in the heat of the War of Independence in 1921, Gwynn wrote privately that he felt culturally more English than Irish.[49] There was much symbolism in Gwynn's appointment as provost, but this did not mean that the college hierarchy was suddenly transformed into enthusiastic nationalists.

Support for the Free State was understood and rationalised by the college as a pragmatic policy to ensure a modicum of institutional vitality; the working relationship fostered between Trinity and the Cumann na nGaedheal governments would be reconfigured once Éamon de Valera and Fianna Fáil came to power in 1932. A more enthusiastic and emotional attachment to the new state would come later, from generations who had come of age with no recollection of a prior regime. For older members of the Trinity community in the 1920s and 1930s, change came slowly and with difficulty, if at all. All of this was complicated by an ambiguous attitude towards other public symbols of allegiance: the college still flew the Union Jack (along with the Tricolour and the college flag) from the Western Front, the king was still toasted at most official functions, and 'God Save the King' was played at most official events, including commencements, until 1939.[50] Official ceremonials demonstrated that, on the one hand, Trinity wanted a good working relationship with the new regime while, on the other, its history would continue to exert an important influence for decades following the treaty.

Student identities and the ostrich mentality

The ambiguous relationship of the university to the state became a preoccupation of the student body. Lyons's ghetto metaphor held to an extent, but presupposed a uniformity of outlook amongst the body as a whole. Moreover, it suggested that outlooks had remained frozen in time, recognising only the pre-1922 order of things. The two decades following the end of the Civil War were notable as a period of great anxiety for students, staff and alumni of the college. Student identities were formed through a multitude of shared experiences, the result of living, learning and socialising together. Central to this was the institution, with its own set of traditions and values. The institution's identity had been a political one, shaped over centuries of political privilege and close association with Britain. This, in turn, had informed the wider collective identity and led, as we have seen, to allegations of West-Britonism in the period before 1912. The removal of the political and cultural component of the institution's traditional identity meant that the wider collective sense of community was in flux in the 1920s. Just what did it mean to be a Trinity student after 1922? Did it mean clinging to the assumptions of the old order, embracing those of the new, or something in between? In practice, all of these elements were present and were complicated by the succession of different generations of students as well as the hierarchical and conservative structures of the student societies and publications that these evolving generations of students worked within.

The question of how the college community adjusted to the new political reality has not been explored as such, and it does not feature in the high political accounts of McDowell and Webb, J.V. Luce, or others. We do find some fragments of evidence that the university grappled internally with its changing situation, primarily in student publications, correspondence, society debates and similar sources. The transition was clearly traumatic, but it seems was only rarely discussed. Two other factors complicated the identity politics at play within Trinity in the 1920s: the large component of the student body that hailed from the newly constituted Northern Ireland, and the memory of the traumatic experiences of the First World War, which gradually became a taboo subject in the Free State.[51]

Editorials in the student newspaper frequently referred to the attitude of the student body towards the new Free State regime. On the cessation of the Civil War, one argued that 'the phrase "Irish national spirit" has an unpleasant sound for many of us, but the time has come for us to forget the past and live in the present'.[52] Living in the present would prove difficult, however. The official acts of accommodation undertaken by Trinity's representatives were provocative to the student body. Alton's offer on the floor of the Dáil to play hurling in Trinity proved divisive amongst the students. One letter on the matter to the student newspaper argued that 'we must of necessity accommodate ourselves to the new regime of our national life in which games play an important part',[53] but that letter was criticised by other students who claimed that there had 'hitherto been no demand for Gaelic games in College'.[54] Games were important parts of the ritual through which collective identity was formed, and it would appear that this attempt to integrate new sports into the college's life challenged traditional understandings of the institution's ethos.[55] To this claim of historical indifference to Gaelic games amongst students at Trinity, a correspondent to *T.C.D.* called Brian Magennis, stated bluntly that:

> The bald fact remains that Trinity College is not doing its duty to the country in the present renaissance. It still looks back to the past with longing, and like the ostrich hides its head that it may not see what is going on around it.[56]

Magennis's ostrich analogy was perceptive; a cautious self-preservation should not equate to disengagement from national life. This sense of conflicted identity would emerge sporadically during the 1920s in the pages of *T.C.D.*—which still clung to its non-political remit—hinting at a broader sense of unease amongst the student body. In May 1927 an editorial argued that 'if Trinity is going to play her part in the life of the nation, we must not rest on our laurels and point with pride to the great politicians she has produced in years gone by'. It was more important to take 'an intelligent interest in the politics of the present day'.[57] The following week, a letter wondered why it was that 'there are thousands of people in this country who have never been inside the old grey walls of Trinity. Is this giving Irish culture a chance?'[58]

By the late 1920s, a new generation of students—those with no direct experience of Trinity during the First World War, 1916, the War of Independence or Civil war—were still trying to chart a course for their university in the Free State. By that time, the 'new' state was less of a novelty, and students increasingly sought to bring university life into line with wider currents. In 1929, a new student organ, *The College Pen*, was started in opposition to *T.C.D.* The new publication sought to give a greater voice to the marginalised within the college community, such as women, and to tackle the big political issues that it claimed the conservative and elitist *T.C.D.* would not. The place of Trinity in Ireland was the key issue. *The College Pen*'s first editorial stated:

> For ourselves, we remain convinced that the older univer-
> sities have still their part to play in the world, and that
> Trinity has a large part to play in the Ireland of today and
> tomorrow. We intend to take a keen interest in the
> modern world and in Ireland, North and South.[59]

A provocative editorial in the seventh issue developed the theme:

> We trust that this College will not allow itself to be per-
> suaded by one of the meanest scares in Irish history that
> it is anything other than an Irish University. Like any in-
> stitution worthy of the name, Trinity has many
> allegiances, and it should not be her province to shove
> ready-made opinions down the throats of her sons; but
> putting aside all political propaganda, Trinity, until
> January, 1922, was mainly a place which concerned itself
> with producing the Irish governing classes. She cannot
> easily get out of a three-hundred-year-old habit, and
> unless she be mad she will not try to do so. An aching
> country is looking just now for leadership.[60]

In 1929, student Peter O'Flaherty wrote a letter to the *College Pen* in which he developed this idea and sparked a colourful debate, illustrating the great divergences amongst the student body when it came to Trinity's history and place in Ireland. O'Flaherty wrote that a university without controversy was in a state of 'mental stagnation' and ceased to be a university. Trinity's problem was that it was segregated from 'all outside influence', the consequences of which would be 'intellectual suicide'.[61] O'Flaherty blamed 'a certain minority in College' who promulgated a 'narrow-minded intolerance and suspicion of all opinions which happen to differ from their own'. For Trinity to contribute truly to national life, it needed to encourage 'the fullest freedom of thought and discussion among her members'. O'Flaherty's blunt interjection directly challenged the ostrich mentality. Eight years after the ratification of the treaty, he implied that a policy that veered between passivity, inertia and reaction would no longer do; to flourish, Trinity needed to engage proactively with Ireland, not just through the superficiality of ceremonials, but at every level. This meant embracing its nationalist credentials as much as its unionist ones, reclaiming the names of Davis, Tone and Emmet from historical obscurity. The letter provoked much correspondence in the *College Pen*.

J. Marshall Dudley, an officer in the Historical Society, took issue with O'Flaherty's idea that Trinity owed its greatest allegiance to Ireland. Rather, the university owed 'a greater allegiance' to the empire. 'She was not founded nor did she ever pretend to be the university of an Irish Ireland. She was founded as an Anglo-Irish University'.[62] Owen Sheehy-Skeffington, who entered TCD in 1927 and who would represent the university in the Seanad decades later, sided with O'Flaherty, arguing that Marshall Dudley wished to subordinate 'the views of the majority to those of the minority'.[63] This series of letters animated the student community and demonstrated a deep-seated anxiety about the place of Trinity in Ireland and the world, which in turn undermined the traditional sense of community. Did the institution and its community have an obligation to cling to their imperial heritage, or should they immerse themselves fully in the new Ireland, which saw its roots in 1916?

This quandary was brilliantly explored by Barbara Fitzgerald in her 1946 novel, *We are besieged*. Fitzgerald was the daughter of J.A. Gregg, a former Archbishop King's lecturer in Divinity at Trinity, and later Protestant archbishop of Dublin. She entered Trinity as an undergraduate in 1931. Her novel detailed the fears and anxieties of the former unionist community in the mid-to-late 1920s. The title said much of the feelings of isolation experienced by Irish Protestants in the new state. Signs of change reinforced this sense of isolation and extended, Fitzgerald wrote, into Trinity College Dublin. One of her protagonists claimed that by 1928 'there [were] even republicans' among the student body, while another noted disapprovingly that some students 'actually remained seated' while 'God Save the King' was being played.[64] Fitzgerald suggested that, for many Irish Protestants, uncertainty was widespread, even at the institution that used to provide much reassurance.

Nineteen-twenty-nine was a significant year for Trinity; a number of events took place that brought the university's relationship with Ireland back into sharp focus. That year, Éamon de Valera, leader of the anti-treaty Fianna Fáil party, visited Trinity for the first time as a politician. In November, de Valera spoke to a friendly audience at the reconstituted college Gaelic Society, where he asserted that Trinity alumnus Thomas Davis had been the inspiration for the Irish republican movement. De Valera also quoted from the Proclamation of 1916 and stressed the importance of learning Irish.[65] While he was addressing a society who shared many of his views, his presence in Trinity was notable and drew attention from those who saw him as a threat; a number of student protestors let off stink bombs during the event, earning the ire of *T.C.D*, and demonstrating that many students did not welcome his presence.[66] At the same time, a small number in the convocation of the National University of Ireland declared themselves unhappy with de Valera's decision to attend the meeting in Trinity.[67]

A major controversy occurred in June, involving the College Races. The governor-general, James MacNeill (brother of Eoin MacNeill), was invited to attend, being the king's representative in Ireland. At a similar event at Trinity in 1928, MacNeill's entrance had been heralded by the playing of 'God Save the King', as had been the custom for his predecessor as governor-general, Tim Healy. MacNeill was anxious that this not be repeated when he attended the races in 1929, and thus raised the issue with the board of Trinity.[68] Cosgrave and the Executive Council ruled that the national anthem for all purposes was 'The Soldier's Song'; consequently, it was 'the proper one to be played on the occasion of formal visits' by the governor-general.[69] The board of Trinity, in a carefully worded letter to MacNeill, stated that tradition when receiving the viceroy, who held the equivalent role to the governor-general before 1922, as the king's representative in Ireland, was to play 'God Save the King'. However, the board conceded to MacNeill that if he so wished, no anthem whatever would be played to greet his arrival.[70] While Irish newspapers euphemistically tried to avoid the issue, *The Times* went to the heart of the matter. 'The unionist minority in the Free State does not like "the Soldier's Song", which it associates not only with the Rebellion of 1916, but with all the later crimes and outrages of the Civil War.'[71] MacNeill decided not to attend the races and this became a source of major embarrassment for the college. Despite the limited accommodation that had been reached with Cosgrave during the preceding years, it was clear that there was still much resistance at Trinity to embracing fully the new order and its symbols.

By the late 1920s, the student body was increasingly polarised between the ex-unionist majority and an emergent pro-treaty and nationalist minority. The latter group found it difficult to make its voice heard; the old conservatives tended to dominate the editorial board of *T.C.D.* and the committees of the Historical and Philosophical societies. Still, the value of expressing a non-traditional voice through one of these organs became increasingly desirable to the minority by the late 1920s. The Hist had been home of political luminaries such as Burke, Emmet, Tone, Davis and Carson. Students seeking advancement in the legal and political worlds dominated its modern incarnation. It was also the oldest student society in Trinity and had an unmatched lustre. Arthur W. Samuels described election as its auditor as the highest honour Trinity students can confer on one of their number.[72] The Hist could be a vehicle for those with strong political opinions to express themselves, and could also be seen as a barometer of student opinion. In short, it was a society with a great deal of potential for the expression of political views, and students increasingly sought to use its prestige as a means of bringing Trinity into line with nationalist Ireland.

In 1930, Eoin 'Pope' O'Mahony was elected auditor of the Historical Society. As his moniker (acquired during his schooldays at Clongowes, when he had expressed the ambition to become pope) suggests, he was not typical of previous auditors. O'Mahony had, in 1929, served as auditor of the Gaelic Society and been responsible for inviting de Valera to Trinity. He was also one of the founders of the *College Pen*. The Gaelic Society was a small and somewhat fringe body; the Hist was another matter altogether. W.B. Stanford, then an undergraduate, was also a member of the society, and recalled how, at the opening meeting in which he served as auditor, O'Mahony infuriated a number of former unionists who were present by proposing a toast to Ireland rather than to the British monarch. A number of attempts were made to impeach O'Mahony, but he clung on improbably amidst much rancour.[73] One of O'Mahony's allies on the committee of the society was Owen Sheehy-Skeffington. Owing to the fame of both his father, Francis, and his mother, Hanna, Owen Sheehy-Skeffington's surname marked him out in Trinity, and, when in 1927 his name appeared amongst the list of intending members of the society, it was suggested derisively that if he were admitted, de Valera would be next.[74] Sheehy-Skeffington was the Historical Society's librarian during O'Mahony's term as auditor and described the farcical scenes that accompanied attempts to impeach him. O'Mahony's defenders obstructed the impeachment motion in every way they could and the auditor weathered the storm. Stanford recalled that the most virulent persecutors of O'Mahony were not Protestant loyalists but the so-called 'castle Catholics' educated at English public schools.[75] One notable consequence of O'Mahony's reign was that a motion was ratified to do away with all political toasts at the Historical Society.[76]

By the end of the 1920s the student population at Trinity averaged around 1,400 people, with women making up a quarter of that number, matching the proportion women students had attained during the First World War.[77] The newer generation of students had grown up under the new Free State order and had no memory of college life before 1922, 1916 or 1914. Some turned towards an exaggerated loyalism, while others sought to make their nationalist voices heard. In 1930, a former president of the Philosophical Society, Bolton Waller, gave the Trinity Monday memorial discourse on Thomas Davis. This was the first such discourse to take one of Trinity's nationalist alumni as its subject. Praising Davis's vision of a tolerant and inclusive Irish nation, Waller argued that it was time for Trinity to reclaim the memory of its nationalist alumni.

> Trinity College has an equal right to claim those of her sons
> who have taken the nationalist as those who have taken
> the unionist side; and, in so far as they have been worthy
> sons, to honour and take pride in the memory of both.[78]

A second significant event followed in 1931 with the death of Lord Glenavy, who, amongst his many offices, was president of the Historical Society. The officers of the Hist offered the position to Baron Carson of Duncairn, who had had little contact with Trinity since the bitter election of 1918. Carson refused the offer and instead the society turned to Douglas Hyde, who accepted.[79] It was another small gesture in the direction of nationalist Ireland, albeit one that was a consequence of Carson's complete break with his former constituents.

Remembering the First World War: politics, memory, identity

Remembrance of the First World War was the point on which official ceremonial and collective identity within Trinity converged. Trinity College Dublin lost 471 students, staff and alumni in the war, a loss unparalleled by any educational institution in the twenty-six counties but in keeping with losses amongst universities elsewhere in Britain, France, Germany and North America. The memory of the First World War was another forum through which institutional identity was shaped and negotiated.

The intense trauma suffered by intimate communities such as those at schools and universities—which suffered proportionately greater losses as a result of the war than other institutions—spurred different forms of commemorative activities across Europe. In Ireland, however, the political environment meant that remembrance of the war soon became, by definition, a political act, and, by extension, a subversive one. As David Fitzpatrick has noted, 'the rhetorical legacy of Sinn Féin made it impracticable to separate the issues of personal suffering and political conviction'.[80] The men who had fought and died in the Great War had done so on the 'wrong' side and for the 'wrong' cause and, at an official level, the Free

State would come to marginalise their memory. With over 200,000 Irishmen having served in the war, however, and over 30,000 losing their lives, personal and popular commemoration of the dead was widespread in the 1920s, for Catholics and Protestants, nationalists and unionists alike.[81]

Remembrance demonstrated the need for communities to grieve in the wake of the First World War.[82] Commemorative activities took place at different levels. There were the official Armistice Day ceremonials, such as the two minutes' silence which took place at 11am on 11 November, and during which Trinity undergraduates would halt traffic in College Green in order to ensure that it was fully observed.[83] From 1919 until 1926 it became the custom for crowds to assemble in College Green following church services, and in 1924, a temporary cenotaph was erected to provide a focus to events.[84] College Green presented a natural gathering space in the centre of the city and could accommodate the huge crowds—often numbering 50,000 people—who would gather to observe the two minutes' silence together. Remembrance of the war became contentious, over time, however, as participants in commemorations were often portrayed as disloyal to the new state. The phenomenon of 'poppy-snatching' on Armistice Day emerged in Dublin.[85] Wearers of the poppy began to hide razor blades under their poppies to mitigate against this. Undertones of violence became common. Students often instigated this, with Trinity and University College Dublin students facing off, singing opposing anthems at one another, and scuffling. Such confrontations tapped into a deeper anxiety about group identities that could be reasserted through symbolic group actions. However, as Keith Jeffery has written, confrontations remained a marginal activity, and the motivations of the masses were more likely 'intimate and private impulses' than political ideas.[86]

The marginalisation of the memory of the war took a new turn in 1927, however, when the official Armistice Day ceremonies were moved from College Green to the less central location of the Phoenix Park. In the same year, Minister for Justice Kevin O'Higgins announced that the planned National War Memorial would not be built as originally envisaged in Merrion Square, but elsewhere; it was eventually constructed at the peripheral location of Islandbridge, to the south-west of the city. O'Higgins reasoned that a national war memorial in a central location would provide

> a wrong twist, as it were, a wrong suggestion, to the origins of this state. It would be a falsehood, a falsehood by suppression of the truth and by a suggestion of something that is contrary to the truth.[87]

O'Higgins' remarks suggest the incompatibility of the state's founding myth and the memory of the war.[88] The Free State marginalised but did not suppress the memory of the First World War, although the peripheral location finally chosen for the national war memorial told its own story. Government officials—but never Cosgrave—did attend the Armistice Day ceremonies each year. Surprisingly, the same pattern continued under de Valera from 1932, even though republicans had been severely critical of the Free State's tolerance of public acts of commemoration of the First World War.[89]

Remembrance was private as well as public. Within Trinity, remembrance took many forms that made no claims beyond its walls, and by examining these forms of commemoration the divisions within the college community become more apparent. There was no consensus on how best to preserve the memory of Trinity's war dead, and tensions emerged between those who had direct experience of the war years and the ensuing generation who did not.

Remembrance began before the war had ended. In March 1918 a scheme was instituted whereby those in possession of gold medals—awarded by the college for excellence in final-year examinations—could hand them in to be melted down. The gold would be given to the government and the money obtained in exchange would go towards the 'education and advancement' of children and dependents of college members who died in the war. Bronze medals were issued to those partaking in the scheme, to replace their gold originals. By June 1921 the scheme had raised £1,465; the symbolism of the act spoke to the specificities of the wider Trinity group identity.[90]

In the years following the end of the war, an intimate college ceremonial was initiated to remember the dead. In 1923 the student newspaper wrote that each moment of the annual service is 'lived as though it were to be the last, and a silence of two minutes forms a memorial nobler than wood, or bronze or breathing stone'.[91] It is notable that by 1923 the college still had no war memorial to provide a focus for this ceremonial. While monuments were quickly erected in towns, churches, clubs, schools and universities across Europe, the more elaborate plan for a memorial at Trinity—allied to its financial privations in the 1920s—meant that the official monument did not open until 1928 (this is discussed further below). Consequently, in 1924, temporary panels listing the names of the dead were erected in the vestibule leading to the Dining Hall.[92] In the Museum Building, home to the Engineering School, pictures of the engineering students and graduates who died in the conflict were placed on the walls, adjacent to the main stairs; this practice was initiated even before the conflict had ended. John Joly, whose office was in that building, remarked movingly in 1918 that 'I have seen gentle women stand weeping before those pictures'.[93] Both the temporary structure in the Dining Hall and the Engineering School memorial were important, as they provided people with a place to gather together and a focus for their collective grief. Having such focal spaces was especially pertinent in the aftermath of the First World War, given that so many of those who fell in France, Belgium and the Dardanelles were buried on the battlefield.

The public face of remembrance in Trinity became increasingly politicised and provocative: 'God Save the King' was sung, Union Jacks waved, and, on occasion, a captured German field gun was brought to Front Arch by the undergraduates for militaristic effect.[94] Such outward signs of political provocation were offensive to many whom had either served in the war or lost loved ones in it, and the triumphalist attitude displayed by some on Armistice Day became increasingly repugnant. As early as November 1921 a correspondent to *T.C.D.* complained of the frivolous attitude of some of the younger undergraduates on Armistice Day. The occasion was not to become, he hoped, just another event in the college calendar, like a '"Rugger" international or an inter-'varsity match'.[95] In 1926, A.A. Luce, one of three fellows of the college who fought in the war, wrote to *T.C.D.* to try to halt the growing politicisation of Armistice Day. He urged poppy-wearing civilians not to join in the march of ex-servicemen, however well-intended their actions, as doing so would cause provocation and serve to politicise the ceremonial, giving Trinity's opponents a pretext to condemn them. He noted that spectators showed respect towards veterans who marched 'as a soldierly act of keeping faith with the dead. They would not have shown the same restraint had we been organising a "day out for the Imperialists".'[96] Luce, a Church of Ireland clergyman, had emerged as a father-figure for Trinity's ex-servicemen. He carried moral authority as both a veteran of the war and fellow of the college and formed an important link between the ex-servicemen and the college authorities.[97]

Concerns were raised again in 1929, this time regarding the behaviour of a few who, during the Armistice Day ceremonial, broke away from the main body of marchers and 'halted in the street bawling "God Save the King", waving their hats, and cheering'. The *T.C.D.* editorial on the matter noted ruefully that 'for the thousands of outsiders in College Green this pitiable exhibition represented the mind and policy of Trinity College!'[98] Equally worrying to *T.C.D.* was the wheeling out of the captured German field gun. 'We hope', it argued, 'that the proper authorities will take steps to remove them from sight as soon as possible'. The point was clear: Remembrance Day was a time for quiet reflection, not triumphalism or militarism. In November 1930 the *College Pen* reflected on the events of Remembrance Day 1929, arguing that the community had 'forgotten that the day was arranged primarily to serve the interests of peace rather than war'. It continued by stating that 'in this country we are judged by appearances, and there is no doubt that by that standard we seem unduly ardent imperialists'.[99]

There were also individual acts of remembrance undertaken by members of the Trinity community for fallen friends and family members. Arthur Warren Samuels, who had been an MP for the university, lost his only son, Arthur P.I. Samuels, at Messines in September 1916. A.P.I Samuels graduated in 1909 and was a gifted scholar and former auditor of the Historical Society. He had begun working with the society's records to produce an edited collection of Edmund Burke's early writings as well as a short biography of Burke's early life. This work was incomplete on his death. A.W. Samuels took up the task of finishing it as a labour of love and tribute to his son. He completed it in 1922. In his introduction he noted that 'such imperfections as are in this work are mine, if it has any merits they are entirely my son's'. He added movingly that 'the devoted generation of young Irishmen, such as he, trained and educated like him, and with aspirations such as his, has been almost exterminated', before noting that 'whether there was to be left any longer a place for such as they in their native land—is a question they have not had to solve'.[100] This form of memorial was not unusual in the aftermath of the war: individuals often published correspondence, poetry and reminiscences of loved ones who had died in the conflict.[101]

Remembrance of the First World War was contentious within Trinity, much as it was outside. Remembrance Day provided an opportunity for some students to act out against their elders, their rivals in UCD, their political opponents within Trinity and the Free State government. In many ways the Remembrance Day rituals were similar to the pre-war rags; they were provocative and occasionally sinister enactments of identity politics. However, marking the memory of the war also provided a forum for accommodation with the new state, and demonstrated the evolution of attitudes both at Trinity and in government. The opening of the Hall of Honour in 1928 and the new Reading Room in 1937 perfectly illustrated this transition to the new order of things—on both sides.

It was quickly resolved in 1919 that Trinity should erect a permanent memorial to its war dead, just as universities, schools, clubs, churches and other intimate communities were doing elsewhere across Europe. Mahaffy's elaborate proposal for a statue of the Niké of Samothrace was quickly and quietly discarded, and something more sombre and useful

TRINITY COLLEGE . DUBLIN

WAR · MEMORIAL · AND · READING · ROOM

SIR · THOMAS · M · DEANE · BA
ARCHITECT
1923

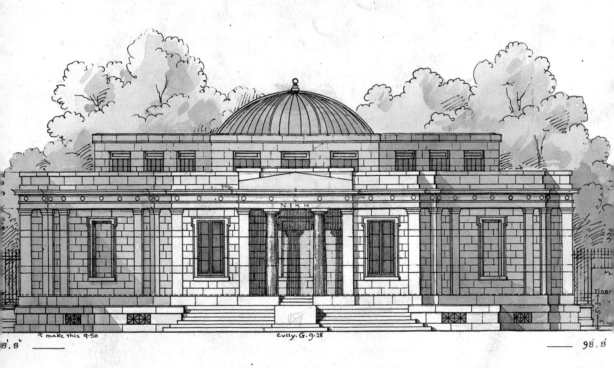

Front Elevation

was sought in its stead. A meeting of November 1919 initiated the process, expressing the desire that a war memorial of a permanent character be erected, where the names of the dead could be held in 'honoured remembrance'.[102] This project would manifest itself in a Hall of Honour, built in conjunction with—and acting as a portico to—a new Reading Room for the library.[103]

The project was at the same time elaborate and pragmatic. The Hall of Honour would provide a sacred space where people could collectively mourn and reflect upon wartime losses, the names of the war dead being carved into panels set into the walls. The Reading Room would cater to the needs of the rapidly expanding library collections, and architects' sketches for its construction actually predate the war. The decision to combine the two projects was a sensible one. Both were funded separately and on different models. The Hall of Honour was funded entirely by subscription, whereas the Reading Room was built from college funds; in the early 1920s, it was easier to raise money for the former project than the latter. Indeed, £7,280 had been raised by 1927 towards the construction of the Hall of Honour, which was completed the following year.[104] Funding for the Reading Room proved harder to source, delaying its construction. The combination of the two distinct structures lends each a reciprocal grandeur that would not have been possible if built in isolation. The architect for both was Thomas Manly Deane, a Trinity graduate and part of a famous architectural family firm; his father was involved in the design of the Oxford University Museum of Natural History and Trinity's own Museum Building. The death of his son, Thomas Alexander Deane, at Gallipoli, in May 1915 meant that the family business would end with him. The commission was a personal one.

The Hall of Honour was formally opened in a ceremony on 10 November 1928, by the provost, E.J. Gwynn, and the vice-chancellor, Lord Glenavy. There was no official representative of the government present, and in his opening address, Glenavy spoke of the marginalisation of the memory of the conflict in the Irish Free State.

> There is a growing conspiracy of silence as to the deeds of our citizen soldiers by which they redeemed our Empire ... and purchased victory at a cost in life and treasure which has brought achievement and privation to many a home.[105]

Opposite: Detail from architects' plans for Trinity's First World War Hall of Honour memorial and reading room.

This sense of isolation was consolidated by ominous events that occurred the following day. A bomb went off in College Green, the target of which was the statue of King William that had stood there since 1701; and an attack was also made on the statue of King George II in St Stephen's Green.[106] In both Glenavy's invocation of empire and the targeting of symbolic public statuary on Armistice Day there were clear political overtones to remembrance of the war in this instance.

Glenavy hoped that the Hall of Honour would provide solace to the families of the dead 'by its perpetual testimony that when the call of duty came they neither faltered nor failed'.[107] Whether he found solace in it was another question. His son Philip was killed at Beaumont-Hamel in 1916 despite his father's best efforts to use his political connections to have him reallocated to a non-combatant role. In one of several letters to the then Colonial Secretary Bonar Law in 1915, he had written that 'I shall always have it on my conscience if the boy's nerves give way and he gets killed'.[108] While Glenavy spoke at the opening of the Hall of Honour as one of the most prominent ex-unionists in the Free State, he also spoke as a mourner, like hundreds of others present. Many of those mourners chose to lay wreaths in memory of their loved ones, such as John Stewart-Moore who laid a wreath for his brother, Henry; Constantia Maxwell, who laid a wreath for her brother Thomas; and the colleagues of Samuel Stewart, the lone fellow of the college to die in the conflict, who laid one in his memory.[109] The list of names inscribed in the Hall of Honour was long.

Construction of the appended Reading Room proceeded in 1935, when Trinity was finally in a position to meet the £25,000 costs.[110] The construction of the Reading Room was significant because, while it was technically a separate project, it also completed the Hall of Honour. The complex was opened by Éamon de Valera in his capacity as president of the Executive Council of the Irish Free State; he was months away from assuming the office of taoiseach, as the head of government would be called under the new constitution of 1937. De Valera had been in office since 1932, and in that time had accelerated the process inaugurated by Cosgrave of tolerating but marginalising the memory of the First World War. Unlike his predecessor, however, de Valera set about dismantling the treaty and undoing the remaining links with Britain and the empire, a policy which should have made him a *bête noire* at Trinity College. Why did de Valera open the new Reading Room at Trinity in 1937? De Valera's relationship with the college illuminates the ambiguities and complexities of the institution's identity in the Free State.

De Valera and Trinity and the 1930s and 1940s

Arthur Aston Luce recalled that 'when de Valera came to power we were all frightened of him at first'.[111] De Valera was something of a bogeyman to ex-unionists in the Free State. As Cosgrave's governments were pledged to enforce law and order and to uphold the treaty, Trinity quickly became an institution of reluctant treatyites. De Valera, on the other hand, remained a source of fascination and fear to members of the Trinity community. During the Easter Rising he stood out to many as a true intellectual figure who was 'educated and speaks like a gentleman'.[112] During the War of Independence, Provost Bernard was intrigued by de Valera, seeking out the results he obtained in his unsuccessful attempt at the Trinity scholarship examinations in 1905 and noting that while de Valera had aspirations of an academic career, he was, ultimately, 'a dreamer and a disappointed fanatic'.[113] As we have seen, in student debates at the Historical Society he was presented in a similar light, as there was no great audience for republicanism in Trinity in the 1920s and 1930s. At the same time, before Fianna Fáil's election to government in 1932, de Valera had aligned himself with movements such as the Anti-Imperialist League, which staged protests on Remembrance Day.[114]

De Valera's previously mentioned speech to the Gaelic Society in Trinity in 1929 had been moderate: he was speaking to a friendly audience, having been invited by the radical O'Mahony. He came again, this time as president of the Executive Council, in March 1934, to attend a lecture given by Viscount Cecil of Chelwood to the League of Nations Society and was afforded 'a very cordial welcome' by Provost Gwynn.[115] The situation was different eight months later when de Valera was invited to address the Historical Society. On this occasion he was invited by the society's auditor, James Wellwood, who was deeply concerned with the place of Trinity in Ireland. In his invitation Wellwood expressed his hope that de Valera's attendance would serve as a token of his 'goodwill towards Trinity College'.[116] De Valera accepted in his capacity as the chancellor of the National University, a role he had held since 1921 and one which he took seriously.[117] The event, held in November 1934, brought together delegates from different political and educational backgrounds. Douglas Hyde, the society president, chaired the session; also present was the vice-chancellor of Queen's University Belfast (F.W. Oglivie), the principal of University College, Hull (A.E. Morgan), Harold Laski of the London School of Economics and Cecil Harmsworth, who had been Lloyd George's under-secretary of state for foreign affairs between 1919 and 1922.[118] Wellwood asked de Valera to give his thoughts on 'the relation that ought to exist between the university and the nation—between Trinity and Ireland', and de Valera did not hold back.[119]

De Valera gave a strident speech in which he criticised the reluctance of members of the Trinity community to embrace the Irish state fully. He was especially critical of ex-unionists who retained a strong affinity for the British crown and argued that the university could produce great Irishmen in the future—as it had in the past with Davis and Hyde—if it only adopted a change of heart. He argued that pride in the empire was viable in the past, but could be no longer:

> If you want to be part of the Irish nation, the basis of your pride must be achievements for the Irish nation. The Irish nation wants you—wants you today—as those who thought with Thomas Davis wanted you a century ago. You have to make up your minds again whether you are to go in the direction Davis pointed out—or whether you are to go in another direction for another generation or so—because I have no doubt whatever which direction you will go at the end…the greatest thing that this College can do for the nation would be to get its young men to turn their minds and their hearts in the direction of their own people.[120]

William Crook, a former Home Rule and Liberal politician (and Trinity alumnus), wrote to his friend Douglas Hyde that the event was 'historic'. 'Looking back at my days in Trinity and then at the trio on last night's platform—yourself, the Provost and de Valera, I said with Galileo "Epier si maove [sic]".'[121]

This historic event was in fact the result of student-led action and reflected the contentious debate about the place of the university in Ireland and the consequences of this for wider student identity. De Valera was supportive of what the university could become, but deeply critical of the desire of many students and staff not to embrace wholeheartedly the Irish state and its political and cultural values.

Trinity's conflicted identity manifested itself again in 1935 when King George V celebrated 25 years on the British throne. While de Valera was undoing various elements of the treaty that linked Ireland to Britain, George V was still the head of state. Acting either out of a desire to observe protocol down to the last detail, or, more likely, out of residual imperial affinity, the Trinity board decided that it 'ought to present an address to the King for his jubilee'. The address offered congratulations to the king and spoke of Trinity's historic contribution to the empire. It also made reference to his visit to Dublin and Trinity in 1911, noting that

> the sentiments of loyal affection which we then expressed still endure, only deepened and strengthened by the lapse of time and by the recollection of the dangers which you have shared with your people.[122]

The 1935 jubilee was the last occasion on which Trinity would fly the Union flag until the visit of Queen Elizabeth II in 2011.[123] Doing so in 1935 demonstrated that despite occasional outward symbols of accommodation with the new Free State regime, a strong affinity for the old order still pervaded.

By the time de Valera returned in 1937 to open the Reading Room, an important change had taken place; William Thrift had replaced Gwynn as provost due to the latter's illness. Thrift had represented Dublin University in the Dáil until de Valera abolished university representation in 1936. In that time, he made a strong impression as a quietly effective and diligent TD. Thrift's parliamentary work has been overlooked. He is best remembered as a less-than-accomplished researcher and lecturer who needed to keep his rugby-playing brother—Harry—in the lecture hall to enforce law and order.[124] Thrift and de Valera shared a passion for mathematics and physics; indeed, during de Valera's truncated Trinity career in 1905 he had attended physics lectures given by Thrift and briefly corresponded with him.[125] One of Thrift's very first acts as provost was to invite de Valera to dine in Trinity with the American Nobel Prize-winning physicist, Robert Millikan.[126] The invitation must have excited de Valera's scholarly interests and Thrift promised that there would be no 'toasts or formal speeches'.[127] However, government business prevented de Valera from attending. In the same period, Thrift, de Valera and A.J. McConnell also indulged their shared interest in mathematics when discussing the creation of the Dublin Institute for Advanced Studies.[128]

De Valera's presence at the opening of the Reading Room in 1937 was a symbolic event and received much media coverage. It occurred on 2 July 1937, a day after a plebiscite had been held in which the Irish population approved his new constitution. The *Irish Press* noted that de Valera had been well received at Trinity and that the national anthem was played upon his entry to the Provost's Garden for a garden party that followed the official opening of the building.[129] The ceremony attempted to avoid difficult issues. De Valera toned down his rhetoric from his appearance at the Hist in 1934 and stuck to a safe theme: Thomas Davis and Trinity nationalism.[130] This was not a moment for scoring political points. The new Reading Room was appended to the Hall of Honour but little was said of the war. R.B. McDowell, who was present, recalled seeing the college porters wearing their war medals. In the same ceremony, a new plaque was unveiled inside the Hall of Honour, to commemorate Michael Moore, a Catholic priest who was put in charge of the college in 1689 and saved its library from destruction when Trinity was occupied by King James II.[131] Both de Valera and Trinity emphasised what united, not divided them.

De Valera's constitution of 1937 could have alienated Trinity and furthered the university's sense of cultural affinity with Britain, but the opposite transpired. The new constitution transformed the Free State from a dominion of the British empire into a republic in all but name. The office of governor-general was abolished, while the modern offices of taoiseach and president were created. Under its terms the university was given parliamentary representation again, this time in the form of three representatives elected to Seanad Éireann from 1938. Douglas Hyde, aged 77 in 1937, became the first president of Ireland under the new constitution, and his office became an important conduit between what remained of the former unionist minority in the south and the state.[132] Hyde and his secretary Michael McDunphy were generally well-disposed towards Trinity individuals, but they remained deeply suspicious of the institution and its history as a whole. McDunphy wrote that Trinity's historic purpose 'seems to have been to educate Irishmen to be loyal to England and disloyal to their own country', and that men like Emmet, Davis and Hyde were 'very much in the minority and in general the outlook of Trinity College is today very little different from that which was intended by its foundress'. While he was sceptical of the institution, however, McDunphy was much more enthusiastic about individuals associated with the college, such as William Thrift. 'In all matters affecting the President [Thrift] was particularly helpful and made a point of receiving him in person whenever he visited the College.'[133]

The Second World War presented a new set of challenges for Trinity and Ireland. When the conflict broke out in 1939, Provost Thrift discontinued the singing of 'God Save the King', feeling that it was inappropriate for Trinity to sing the anthem of a belligerent nation when Ireland was neutral in that conflict.[134] During the Emergency, the college put its laboratories at the disposal of the Emergency Scientific Research Bureau, which coordinated national scientific resources in a time of acute need. At the same time, significant numbers of Trinity students volunteered to fight in the British army.[135] Much like their predecessors who enlisted in the 1914–18 war, they volunteered for many reasons. Unlike the veterans

Trinity representatives at installation of Douglas Hyde as president of Ireland, 1938; left to right: Mace Bearer, Registrar Ernest H. Alton, Provost William Thrift and Bursar Harry Thrift.

of the previous war, however, they did so in a nation that was neutral in the conflict. At least 113 of them died, and remembrance of their actions would prove even more contentious than that of their predecessors of the First World War.[136] While exploring this aspect of Trinity's history in any depth lies outside the scope of the present work, it can be argued that it represents a further example of the multiplicity of identities and allegiances held by members of the Trinity community that were exacerbated by the great strains and moral issues of a new war in Europe.

In 1942, Thrift died and Alton was appointed his replacement as provost. Alton's gregarious personality was the inverse of that of Thrift, who was serious, quiet and efficient.[137] Both men were united in their love of the institution and their desire to reconcile it to Ireland, although they went about it in different ways. Alton's conciliatory instincts were apparent as early as June 1921 when he seconded a contentious motion that ended the long-winded process of reinstating Eoin MacNeill to membership of the Royal Irish Academy.[138] Provost Alton continued this conciliatory instinct,

ᵹután 21840

"Muiniᵹin as Dia, Dóċas as Éirinn, Misneaċ i nᵹníom"

Ailtirí na hAiséirᵹe

"Córas Críostúil Comḃaonnaċ aᵹus Ᵹeilleaᵹraċ i nÉirinn Saor Ᵹaeḋealaiᵹ"

Seoltar ᵹaċ leitir oiᵹiᵹiúil ċuiᵹ an Rúnaiḋe, ċan ċuiᵹ daoine príoṁaideaċa.

Árd-Ċuireann:—
Ᵹearóid Ó Cuinneaᵹáin
(Ceannaire)
Tomár Ó Docaċċaiᵹ
(Cmére Náiriúnta)
Pádraiᵹ Ó Fiannġúra
(Rúnaiḋe Náiriúnta Conᵹanta)
Seán Ó h-Uṁoilaiᵹ, D.L.
(Airᵹeadóir Náiriúnta Conᵹanta)

Baill eile de'n Árd-Ċoṁairle:—
Rioḃáro Ḃreaṫnaċ, M.C.
Coin Ó Coiᵹliᵹ, Co-Co.
Riċeáro Mac Siaċur
Seán Mac Ċanṗáiċ
Ᵹearóid Ó Ḃrom

Seoraṁ Ó Ceallaiᵹ
Seán Ó Duḃᵹaill
Muinir Mac Ᵹeaṗairt
Cáit Nic Ailliᵹ
Fearᵹur Ó Móᵹóa

Tomár Ó Murċáḋa
Éamonn Ó Ᵹréaċáin
Seán Ᵹlainḃille
Conall Ó Domnaill

13 SRÁID FEARĊAIR,
ÁT CLIAT

10ú Bealtaine, 1945.

COLÁISTE NA TRIONÓIDE 7 AN ᵹÁRDA SÍOĊÁNA.

Seo leanas ḋá rún a cuireaḋ i ḃfeidm b'aonᵹuṫ aᵹus le bualú bos as cuimse ar oll-ċruinniú de Saoránaiᵹ Áta Cliat i Sráid Íoċtaraċ na Mainistreaċ ar an 9ú de'n mí seo.

1. ᵹo n-iarrann an t-oll-ċruinniú seo de Saoránaiᵹ Ċaṫair Áta Cliat ar Proḃost Coláiste na Trionóide éirᵹe as a ṗosta láitreaċ, de ḃarr an ṁasla a tuᵹ Coláiste na Trionóide do ṁuintir na h-Éireann ar an 7ú de'n mí seo; aᵹus ᵹo n-iarraimíd ar an Rialtas Proḃost úr aᵹus stiúrṫóirí úra ar fad a ċeapú aᵹus cairt Eiliseaċ na Coláiste sin a scrios ar fad, aᵹus an Coláiste a ᵹaolú anois in ᵹaċ uile roinn.

2. ᵹo n-iarrann an t-oll-ċruinniú seo de Saoránaiᵹ Ċaṫair Áta Cliat ar an Rialtas Fiosrúċán Puiblí a cur ar bun láitreaċ fá ṁí-iompar an ᵹárda Síoċána i n-Át Cliat ar an 7ú de'n mí seo aᵹ Coláiste na Trionóide, nuair a buaileaḋ saoránaiᵹ ᵹo h-ain ᵹcialba ᵹo raḃ siad i n-a luiᵹe ar an tóċar, aᵹus nuair a scrios ᵹárdaí ᵹo tréasúil os ċoṁair an ṗobail meirᵹ a raḋ an scríḃinn seo leanas air "1916 means Irish Republic, Irish Language, Irish Social Justice."

---

1.   That this Mass Meeting of Citizens of Áth Cliath calls upon the Provost of Trinity College to resign his appointment forthwith, arising out of the gratuitous insult offered to the people of Ireland by Trinity College on the 7th. inst., and that we request the Government to appoint a new Provost and new college authorities, to scrap the Elizabethan charter of the College, and to gaelicise the College without delay in ever department.

2.   That this Mass Meeting of citizens of Áth Cliath requests the Government to arrange immediately for the holding of a Public Enquiry into the conduct of An Gárda Síochána in Áth Cliath at Trinity College, on the 7th. inst. when citizens were batoned brutally to the ground; and when, furthermore, members of An Gárda Síochana treasonably tore in shreds in the presence of the public at the heart of the National Capital, a banner inscribed: "1916 means Irish Republic, Irish Language, Irish Social Justice."

seeking to build better relations with John Charles McQuaid. The accession of McQuaid as Catholic archbishop of Dublin in 1940 was bad news for Trinity. Whereas his predecessors were happy to allow Catholics to attend Trinity on the presentation of a 'well-prepared case', McQuaid was much more hostile towards the institution. Shortly after his appointment as provost in 1942, Alton made contact with McQuaid, via Hyde, seeking a meeting to improve relations between Trinity and the Catholic Church.[139] McQuaid acceded to a meeting only on the proviso that it would not be reciprocated: the provost of Trinity could call to the Archbishop's Palace, but the archbishop would not set foot in Trinity College. Unfortunately, no archival traces remain to indicate whether the meeting ever took place.[140] In any event, Alton was unsuccessful in placating McQuaid, who, in 1944, imposed a 'ban' on Catholics from his archdiocese attending Trinity.[141] Dispensations were available, directly from the archbishop, permitting entrance to the university for 'grave and valid reasons'.[142] The 'ban' on Catholic attendance in Trinity was extended from the diocese of Dublin to all Irish dioceses in 1956; for the next decade and a half, the college increasingly drew students from outside Ireland, until the Catholic hierarchy lifted the 'ban' in 1970, after which the numbers of Catholic attending the university began to be more in proportion with the wider Irish population.[143]

The end of the Second World War was marked by controversy. On 7 May 1945, crowds gathered in College Green to celebrate Victory in Europe Day. During the course of the afternoon a group from Ailtirí na hAiséirghe, a far-right group with fascist sympathies, burned a Union Jack, aided by a UCD student and future taoiseach by the name of Charles Haughey.[144] A handful of students on the roof of Trinity attempted to burn the Irish tricolour, either acting in response to the burning of the Union Jack, or being the provocation for it.[145] These reciprocal gestures prompted two days of riots, with the college being assailed by projectiles.[146] The *Irish Press*, Taoiseach Eamon de Valera's newspaper, called it 'a disgraceful incident'.[147] William Bedell Stanford, a fellow of the college and future senator, urged Provost Alton to issue an official condemnation of the act and a formal apology to the government, otherwise, he asserted, Trinity would 'lose many friends and revive old enmities'.[148] Alton met de Valera to apologise in person, and found the taoiseach to be 'courteous and understanding', agreeing with him that 'an insult was offered to the Tricolour'.[149] While one graduate wrote to Alton of his fear that the V.E.

Letter to the college authorities, 10 May 1945, from the far-right group Ailtirí na hAiséirghe, calling on the provost to resign as a result of 'the gratuitous insult offered to the people of Ireland', when a number of Trinity students had attempted to burn the Tricolour during celebrations to mark V.E. day on 7 May.

Day incident would set Trinity back to 1918 'with all our work to do again,' this turned out not to be the case.[150]

Conclusion

In 1947, Éamon de Valera's government agreed to give Trinity a state grant.[151] This was a historic moment and ended a period of almost a quarter of a century in which the Irish government had provided no financial assistance to the college. It signalled a shift in attitudes between university and state and was testament to the quiet efforts of Thrift and Alton in previous years. In 1952 this grant was increased, greatly reducing the college's financial problems and further integrating Trinity into Irish life.[152] The year of 1952 was significant for Trinity for another reason: it marked, in the words of McDowell and Webb, 'the end of one epoch and the beginning of another'.[153] A generational change was making itself felt in a move to reform the workings of the university. The members of the college's older generation, who had come to prominence in pre-1912 Trinity, were gradually disappearing; Sir Robert Tate and Provost Alton died in quick succession in early 1952.

Unlike the situation that had pertained in relation to the appointments of Gwynn, Thrift and Alton, there was no consensus candidate for the empty post of provost in 1952.[154] As there was no favourite, the senior fellows, junior fellows and professors had to meet to choose their three preferred candidates and then eliminate one from contention in turn; this was the first modern election to the office of provost. The three names were then passed to the government in order of preference. Seven men had initially put themselves forward for consideration, representing different generations and approaches to college administration. There were distinguished figures among them. The vice-provost, and a senior fellow, A.A. Luce, represented the older generation. Luce had been elected to fellowship in 1912—the year of the Home Rule crisis—and was seen as the conservative candidate. A number of younger candidates emerged from among the junior fellows, including the classicist W.B. Stanford, the historian T.W. Moody, and the economist, George Duncan. All four were eliminated from contention. Stanford, Moody and Duncan were seen as too inexperienced, while Luce was seen as too opposed to reform. A.J.

Opposite: 'In 1950 – Trinity Week', illustration from *T.C.D.: a College Miscellany*, vol. 18, no. 322, 3 July 1912, p. 125, predicting what college would look like 40 years in the future.

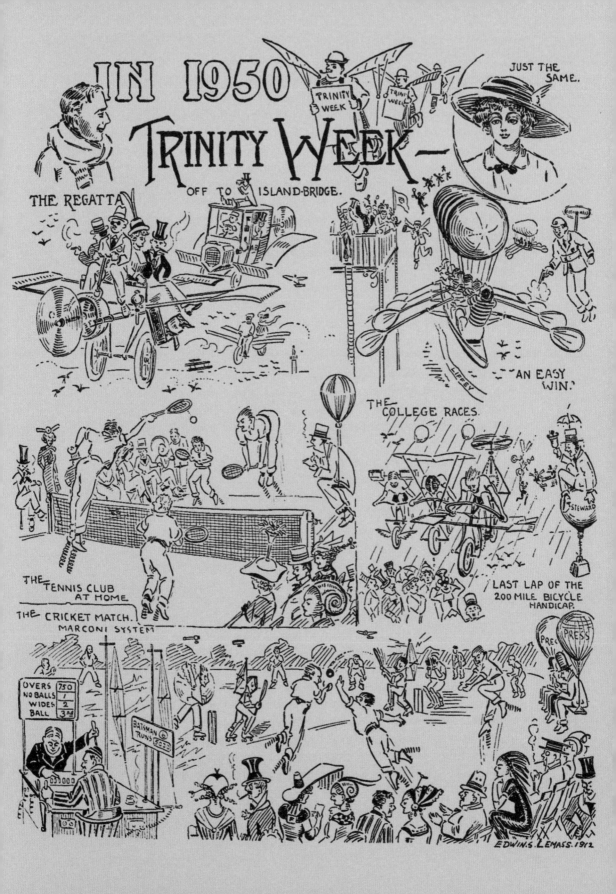

McConnell emerged as the overwhelming choice of the fellows and professors, and so the three names submitted to the government, in order of
preference, were the mathematician McConnell, the ancient historian
H.W. Parke and the biochemist W.R. Fearon. Having been given a clear
indication that McConnell was the preferred choice, Taoiseach Éamon de
Valera was happy to confirm the nomination; he got on well with
McConnell owing to their shared love of mathematics.[155] De Valera personally informed McConnell of his appointment.[156]

   This particular appointment was one of the most significant in the
history of the college. McConnell, a Presbyterian, became the first non-
Anglican to be installed formally as provost. Being a junior fellow and
just 48 years old, he was also the youngest holder of the office since the
mid-eighteenth century. Provost McConnell oversaw a far-reaching reform
of the university's operations. He immediately appointed junior fellows
to positions previously held by senior fellows, thus establishing the practice that senior offices should be held on the basis of competence and not
longevity of service. McConnell's reforms, allied to regular state funding,
allowed the university to expand for the first time in half a century. By
the late 1960s, further modernisation allowed women to take their right-
ful place as equal members of the college community, and from the early
1970s, the thaw in the attitudes of the Catholic church's hierarchy
towards Trinity saw student numbers rapidly increase, with, as already
noted, the university's demographics changing to reflect the religious composition of the Irish nation generally.[157]

   McConnell, like Walton and Beckett, had begun his Trinity career at a
time when the future of the college was uncertain. With the signing of the
treaty and the establishment of the Irish Free State, Trinity's old political
and cultural privilege had disappeared, and many had feared that the new
government would be hostile to the college. Trinity's diminished finances
in the 1920s and 1930s were a further indication of a change in the institution's standing. In a physical manifestation of this buildings fell into
disrepair, providing a visual reminder of Trinity's impoverishment and the
fact that it was no longer an intrinsic part of the fabric of the state. The
events of these decades were the immediate legacy of the years 1912–23,
but while the process of adapting to an entirely new set of circumstances
was difficult, Trinity College nevertheless survived and later flourished.
McConnell's time as provost is not the subject of this present work, but it
can be regarded as marking the beginning of a new era, in which Trinity
succeeded in repositioning itself as being at the heart of Dublin and of the
newly emerged Irish state and overcame the reputation it had laboured
under for so long of being distant from the city and the nation.

NOTES:

[1] *Dublin University Calendar 1923–24*, 491; *Dublin University Calendar 1924–25*, 493.

[2] McDowell and Webb, *Trinity College Dublin*, 429.

[3] Terence Brown, *Ireland: a social and cultural history, 1922–2002* (London, 2004), 104.

[4] F.S.L. Lyons, 'The minority problem in the 26 counties', in Francis MacManus (ed.), *The years of the great test* (Cork, 1967), 92–103: 92–9.

[5] Patrick Buckland, *Irish Unionism, I* (Dublin, 1972), 297.

[6] R.B. McDowell, 'Trinity College Dublin and politics', in McDowell (ed.), *Historical essays 1938–2001* (Dublin, 2003), 53–104: 92.

[7] Pauric Dempsey, 'Trinity College Dublin and the new political order', in John M. Regan and Mike Cronin (eds), *The politics of independence 1922–49* (Basingstoke, 2000), 217–31: 217, 220.

[8] Marianne Elliott, *When God took sides: religion and identity in Ireland—Unfinished history* (Oxford, 2009), 219.

[9] David Fitzpatrick, 'Protestant depopulation and the Irish revolution', *Irish Historical Studies* 38 (2013), 643–70: 658–9.

[10] R.B. McDowell, *The Church of Ireland 1869–1969* (London, 1975), 131.

[11] McDowell and Webb, *Trinity College Dublin*, 504.

[12] TCD, MUN/V/22 359–60, Bonar Law to Bernard, 9 June 1923.

[13] TCD, MUN/V/23, 15, Minutes of board meeting of 10 October 1923.

[14] TCD, MUN/V/23, 5, Board of TCD to Cosgrave, 23 June 1923.

[15] See McDowell and Webb, *Trinity College Dublin*, 428.

[16] TCD, MUN/V/5/23,10, Board meeting, 30 June 1923.

[17] McDowell and Webb, *Trinity College Dublin*, 429.

[18] TCD, MS 11107/41, Fitzgibbon to Blake, 2 June 1923.

[19] National Archives of Ireland (NAI), PRES/1/P/1780, W.E. Thrift File.

[20] John F. Fleetwood, *The history of medicine in Ireland* (Dublin, 1983), 272–3.

[21] TCD, MS 2388/576, A.F Dixon to John Henry Bernard, 13 August 1925.

[22] 'Free State doctors to be isolated', *Irish Times*, 17 August 1925, 7.

[23] UCD Archives, P24/496(4), Thrift to Blythe, 20 August 1925; TCD, MS 2388/583, Thrift to Bernard, 25 August 1925.

[24] TCD, MUN/P/54/7/203, Purser to Thrift, 21 July 1925.

[25] TCD, MS 2388/583, Thrift to Bernard, 25 August 1925.

[26] Fleetwood, *History of medicine*, 273.

[27] TCD, MUN/V/23, 3, Board meeting 23 June 1923.

[28] TCD, MS 2388/689, Culverwell to Bernard, 11 January 1927.

[29] Robert W. Tate, *Orationes et Epistolae Dublinenses (1914–40)* (Dublin, 1941).

[30] 'Conferring of degrees', *Irish Times*, 21 December 1922, 6.

[31] Tate, *Orationes*, 86.

[32] 'University of Dublin: honorary degrees', *Irish Times*, 25 February 1933, 17.

[33] TCD, MUN/V/5/23, 297, Board meeting, 22 November 1926.

[34] Tate, *Orationes*, 73–4.

[35] 'Two premiers honoured', *Irish Times*, 3 December 1926, 7.

[36] NAI, Department of the Taoiseach (hereafterTAOIS), S 5983/4.

[37] 'O'Connell Street meeting', *Sunday Independent*, 28 November 1926, 1.

[38] TCD, MS 2388/689, Culverwell to Bernard, 11 January 1927.

[39] NAI, TAOIS, S 5983/13.

[40] 'College Historical Society', *T.C.D.*, 3 November 1927, 22.

[41] 'Bicentenary of Edmund Burke', *Irish Times*, 12 December 1928, 7.

[42] NAI, AGO/2009/74/406, Costello to McDunphy, 5 September 1927.

[43] Denis Gwynn, *The Irish Free State 1922–1927* (London, 1928), 232.

[44] 'The Provostship', *Irish Times*, 3 September 1927, 8.

[45] NAI, TAOIS/ S 5510.

[46] 'The new provost's career', *Irish Times*, 4 October 1927, 7. 'National University honorary degrees', *Irish Times*, 17 October 1931, 6.

[47] McDowell and Webb, *Trinity College Dublin*, 441.

[48] TCD, MS 2388/696, Gwynn to Bernard, 13 May 1927.

[49] British Library (BL), Add MS 52783/138, Gwynn to Bernard, 6 September 1921.

[50] McDowell and Webb, *Trinity College Dublin*, 433–4.

[51] Heather Jones, 'Church of Ireland Great War remembrance in the south of Ireland: a personal reflection', in John Horne and Edward Madigan (eds), *Towards Commemoration: Ireland in war and revolution 1912–1923* (Dublin, 2013), 74–82.

[52] 'Editorial', *T.C.D.*, 17 May 1923, 145.

[53] Correspondence, *T.C.D.*, 23 November 1922, 30.

[54] 'Correspondence', *T.C.D.*, 30 November 1922, 46.

[55] James A. Mangan, *Athleticism in the Victorian and Edwardian public school* (Cambridge, 1981), 206.

[56] 'Correspondence', *T.C.D.*, 7 December 1922, 55.

[57] Editorial, *T.C.D.*, 19 May 1927, 225.

[58] 'Correspondence', *T.C.D.*, 26 May 1927, 214.

[59] Editorial, *College Pen*, 7 May 1929, 1.

[60] Editorial, *College Pen*, 18 June 1929, 167.

[61] Peter O'Flaherty letter, *College Pen*, 29 October 1929, 4.

[62] J. Marshall Dudley letter, *College Pen*, 5 November 1929, 20.

[63] Owen Sheehy-Skeffington letter, *College Pen*, 12 November 1929, 37.

[64] Barbara Fitzgerald, *We are besieged* (Bantry, 2011, originally published 1946), 133, 135.

[65] 'Cumann Gaolach an Cholaiste', *College Pen*, 12 November 1929, 43.

[66] Editorial, *T.C.D.*, 7 November 1929, 25.

[67] 'Asked not to go', *Irish Independent*, 7 November 1929, 8.

[68] NAI, TAOIS, S 6535.

[69] NAI, TAOIS, S 6535, Cosgrave to MacNeill, 20 September 1928.

[70] NAI, TAOIS, S 6535, Undated letter of the board to MacNeill, *c.*1929.

[71] 'National Anthem in Free State', *The Times*, 10 June 1929, 18.

[72] A.W. Samuels, 'Introduction', in A.P.I Samuels, *The early life, correspondence and writings of the Rt. Hon. Edmund Burke* (Cambridge, 1923), ix–xi: ix.

[73] W.B. Stanford, *Memoirs* (Dublin, 2001), 10.

[74] Declan Budd and Ross Hinds (eds), *The Hist and Edmund Burke's Club* (Dublin, 1997), 197.

[75] Stanford, *Memoirs*, 10.

[76] Budd and Hinds, *The Hist*, 201.

[77] *Dublin University Calendar, pt. II*, 1928–32.

[78] Bolton Waller, *Thomas Davis (1814–1845)* (Dublin, 1930), 7.

[79] TCD, College Historical Society Records, Eoin O'Mahony to Auditor, 12 February 1939.

[80] David Fitzpatrick, 'Commemoration in the Irish Free State: a chronicle of embarrassment', in Ian McBride and George Boyce, (eds), *History and Memory in Modern Ireland*, (Cambridge, 2001), 184–203: 191.

[81] Keith Jeffery, 'Irish varieties of Great War commemoration', in Horne and Madigan (eds), *Towards commemoration: Ireland in war and revolution 1912–1923* (Dublin, 2013), 117–25: 117–9.

[82] Jay Winter, *Remembering war: the Great War between memory and history in the twentieth century* (New Haven, 2006) 138–40.

[83] Jane Leonard, 'The twinge of memory: Armistice Day and Remembrance Sunday in Dublin since 1919', in Graham Walker and Richard English, (eds), *Unionism in modern Ireland: new perspectives on politics and culture* (Basingtoke, 1996), 94–114: 101.

[84] 'Armistice Day in Dublin: temporary Cenotaph in College Green', *Irish Times*, 15 November 1924, 1.

[85] Leonard, 'The twinge of memory', 102–04.

[86] Keith Jeffery, *Ireland and the Great War* (Cambridge, 2000), 126–7.

[87] *Dáil Debates*, vol. 19, col. 400, 'Merrion Square (Dublin) Bill', 29 March 1927.

[88] Nuala C. Johnson, *Ireland, the Great War and the geography of remembrance* (Cambridge, 2003), 89–90.

[89] Fitzpatrick, 'Commemoration in the Irish Free State', 193–4.

[90] *Dublin University Calendar, 1921–22*, pt I, 209.

[91] Editorial, *T.C.D*, 15 November 1923, 13–14.

[92] 'Memorial panels', *Weekly Irish Times*, 28 June 1924, 8.

[93] TCD, MS 2313/3, Joly speech at Columbia University, in *Columbia Alumni News*, 18 October 1918, 136.

[94] André Sheehy-Skeffington, *Skeff*, 36; Leonard, 'The twinge of memory', 102.

[95] Letter of H.E. McClenaghan, *T.C.D.*, 17 November 1921, 22.

[96] Letter of A.A. Luce, *T.C.D.*, 18 November 1926, 84.

[97] TCD, MS 7939, Whiteley Nolan to John V. Luce, 6 July 1977.

[98] Editorial, *T.C.D.*, 14 November 1929, 37.

[99] Editorial, *College Pen*, 11 November 1930, 1.

[100] Samuels, 'Introduction', ix–xi.

[101] Tomás Irish, 'Fractured families: educated elites in Britain and France and the challenge of the Great War', *Historical Journal* 57 (2) (June 2014), 509–30: 524–9.

[102] TCD, MS 2388/204, notes of meeting for Dublin University War Memorial, 1 December 1919.

[103] 'College notes', *T.C.D.*, 10 March 1921, 115.

[104] Bailey, *Trinity College Dublin*, 64.

[105] 'An imperishable inspiration: Lord Glenavy's tribute', *Irish Times*, 12 November 1928, 13.

[106] 'Attempts to blow up statues', *Irish Times*, 12 November 1928, 9.

[107] *Irish Times*, 12 November 1928, 13.

[108] PA, BL/50/3/16, Campbell to Bonar Law, June 1916.

[109] 'Trinity College Dublin: memorial to graduates and students', *Irish Times*, 12 November 1928, 13.

[110] Bailey, *Trinity College Dublin*, 65–6.

[111] TCD, MS 7939, 21 November 1971, 21.

[112] UCD Archives, P 150/522, Personal experiences of Miss L. Stokes, Easter 1916.

[113] BL, Add MS 52784/75

[114] Jason R. Myers, *The Great War and memory in Irish culture 1918–2010* (Palo Alto, CA, 2013), 108.

[115] 'Cecil to speak at T.C.D.', *Irish Press*, 7 March 1934, 1.

[116] UCD Archives, P150/2302, Wellwood to de Valera, 5 October 1934.

[117] Diarmaid Ferriter, *Judging Dev: a reassessment of the life and legacy of Eamon de Valera* (Dublin, 2007), 308.

[118] UCD Archives, P150/2302, Wellwood to de Valera, 5 October 1934.

[119] UCD Archives, P150/2302, Wellwood to de Valera, 4 November 1934.

[120] 'President de Valera at Trinity College', *Irish Times*, 17 November 1934, 6.

[121] UCD Archives, P150/2302, W.M. Crook to Douglas Hyde, 8 November 1934.

[122] British National Archives, Dominions Office, 35/137/5.

[123] McDowell and Webb, *Trinity College Dublin*, 433–4.

[124] Vincent McBrierty, *Ernest Thomas Sinton Walton: the Irish scientist (1903–1995)* (Dublin, 2003), 13.

[125] NLI, MS15285.

[126] See Robert H. Kargon, *The rise of Robert Millikan: portrait of a life in American science* (London, 1982).

[127] UCD Archives, P150 2666, Thrift to De Valera, 1 May 1937.

[128] UCD Archives, P150/2609.

[129] 'Mr de Valera's visit to T.C.D.', *Irish Press*, 3 July 1937, 9.

[130] UCD Archives, P150/2355, De Valera speech notes.

[131] Bailey, *Trinity College Dublin*, 65–6.

[132] NAI, PRES/1/P3002.

[133] NAI, PRES/1/P3002.

[134] NAI, PRES/1/P3002.

[135] Bailey, *Trinity College Dublin*, 52.

[136] This figure is derived from http://www.tcdwarmemorialproject.com/Remembrance.htm, accessed 13 January 2015.

[137] McDowell and Webb, *Trinity College Dublin*, 443.

[138] R.B. McDowell, 'The main narrative', in T.O Raifeartaigh (ed.), *The Royal Irish Academy: a bicentennial history, 1785–1985* (Dublin, 1985), 81; RIA Council Minutes, vol. XXV, 132–6.

[139] NAI, PRES/P2235, McDunphy, 'Conversation with Prof. Alton', 2 July 1942.

[140] NAI, PRES/P/2235, McDunphy, 'Conversations with Dr. Alton and Fr. Glennon', 2 August 1942.

[141] J.H. Whyte, *Church and state in modern Ireland 1923–1979* (Dublin, 1980), 305–7.

[142] Dublin Diocesan Archives, Lenten regulations for the Diocese of Dublin 1954.

[143] Whyte, *Church and state in modern Ireland*, 307; John Walsh, '"The problem of Trinity College Dublin": a historical perspective on rationalisation in higher education in Ireland', *Irish Educational Studies* 33 (1) (2014), 5–19: 10–12; John V. Luce, *Trinity College Dublin: the first 400 years* (Dublin, 1992), 154.

[144] Clair Wills, *That neutral Island: a cultural history of Ireland during the Second World War* (London, 2007), 364–5; Leonard, 'The twinge of memory', 102.

[145] 'Malicious reports' *Irish Press*, 10 May 1945, 1.

[146] McDowell and Webb, *Trinity College Dublin,* 464–5.

[147] 'A disgraceful incident', *Irish Press*, 8 May 1945, 2.

[148] TCD, MUN/P/46/31/4, Stanford to Alton, 8 May, 1945.

[149] TCD, MUN/P/46/31/17, Alton to Iveagh, 14 May 1945.

[150] TCD, MUN/P/46/31/6, H.A. Delap to E.A. Alton, 9 May 1945.

[151] McDowell and Webb, *Trinity College Dublin*, 473–5.

[152] McDowell and Webb, *Trinity College Dublin*, 480.

[153] McDowell and Webb, *Trinity College Dublin*, 496.

[154] '"Tubby": an Irishman's Diary', *Irish Times*, 23 February 1952, 7.

[155] McDowell and Webb, *Trinity College Dublin*, 494.

[156] 'New provost of Trinity College Dublin', *Irish Times*, 15 March 1952, 1.

[157] Luce, *Trinity College Dublin*, 151–79.

Drawing, by Frank Leah, of Provost Mahaffy delivering a paper at the Royal Irish Academy, published in the *Irish Times*, 26 February 1917.

PICTURE CREDITS

The author and publisher are grateful to the following for permission to reproduce documents, photographs and illustrations in this book, and for their assistance in securing the images: the Board of Trinity College Dublin; the Royal Irish Academy; Glenn Dunne, Bernie Metcalfe Mary Broderick and Laura Egan at the National Library of Ireland; the Library of Congress; Mary Clark at the Dublin City Archives; Sophie Evans at the Royal Irish Academy Library; George Morrison; Sharon Sutton of the Digital Resources and Imaging Service at Trinity College and the Woods family.

During the production process some items have been retouched or tinted for aesthetic purposes. Every effort has been made to trace the copyright holders of these items and to ensure the accuracy of their captions.

ACKNOWLEDGEMENTS

vi   TCD MUN OTC/14_0001; reproduced by permission of the Board of Trinity College Dublin.

PROLOGUE

xii   TCD MS 4897_012; reproduced by permission of the Board of Trinity College Dublin.

xiv–xv   TCD MS 4897_008; reproduced by permission of the Board of Trinity College Dublin.

xviii   TCD Samuels Collection of Printed Ephemera, SamuelsBox4_070; reproduced by permission of the Board of Trinity College Dublin.

INTRODUCTION

p. 2   TCD MS 4717-96_0001; reproduced by permission of the Board of Trinity College Dublin.

p. 11   TCD *College Miscellany*, 9 February 1910; reproduced by permission of the Board of Trinity College Dublin.

p. 16   TCD MS 4715-1_0002; reproduced by permission of the Board of Trinity College Dublin.

p. 19   TCD MS 4717-24_0001; reproduced by permission of the Board of Trinity College Dublin.

p. 23   TCD *College Miscellany*, 23 June 1910; reproduced by permission of the Board of Trinity College Dublin.

p. 31   TCD MS 3332-6-1_0002; reproduced by permission of the Board of Trinity College Dublin.

CHAPTER 1

p. 42   TCD *College Miscellany*, 2 March 1910; reproduced by permission of the Board of Trinity College Dublin.

p. 46   TCD Samuels Collection, SamuelsBox4_084; reproduced by permission of the Board of Trinity College Dublin.

p. 50–1   National Library of Ireland, Hogan Collection, NLI HOG 239; reproduced by permission of the NLI.

p. 59   TCD *College Miscellany*, 11 December 1912; reproduced by permission of the Board of Trinity College Dublin.

p. 60   TCD MS 2075-339_0001; reproduced by permission of the Board of Trinity College Dublin.

p. 68   TCD MS 3332-15_0001; reproduced by permission of the Board of Trinity College Dublin.

p. 144   TCD MS 3987a-1_001; reproduced by permission of the Board of Trinity College Dublin.

p. 145   TCD MS 3987a-2_002; reproduced by permission of the Board of Trinity College Dublin.

p. 148   The 'Sinn Féin' revolt, p. 16; reproduced courtesy of the Royal Irish Academy.

p. 149   The 'Sinn Féin' revolt, p. 16; reproduced courtesy of the Royal Irish Academy.

p. 151   TCD MS 2313-4-26-1-3_0005; reproduced by permission of the Board of Trinity College Dublin.

p. 152   TCD MS 2313-4-26-1-3_0001; reproduced by permission of the Board of Trinity College Dublin.

p. 156   Elsie Mahaffy's journal; TCD MS 2074_085; reproduced by permission of the Board of Trinity College Dublin.

p. 157   Elsie Mahaffy's journal, TCD MS 2074_097; reproduced by permission of the Board of Trinity College Dublin.

p. 158   TCD MS 2074_117; reproduced by permission of the Board of Trinity College Dublin.

CHAPTER 4

p. 166   TCD MS 4717-151_0001; reproduced by permission of the Board of Trinity College Dublin.

p. 174-5 Dublin City Libraries and Archive, Royal Dublin Fusiliers Association Archive, Monica Roberts Collection, RDFA1/01/005d and RDFA1/01/005e; reproduced by permission of Dublin City Archives.

p. 177   'Surrendered', by John Scott Clubb (1875–1934); from the Caroline and Erwin Swann Collection of caricature and cartoon (Swann no. 923); courtesy of Library of Congress Prints and Photographs Division [LC-USZ62-84113].

p. 181   Detail from 'The kidnappers', by Henry Mayer (1868–1954); courtesy of Library of Congress Prints and Photographs Division [LC-DIG-ppmsca-28075].

p. 188–9 National Library of Ireland, Photographic collection, NLI INDH 41; courtesy of the National Library of Ireland.

p. 193   TCD Samuels Collection, SamuelsBox4_021; reproduced by permission of the Board of Trinity College Dublin.

CHAPTER 5

p. 202   TCD Samuels Collection, SamuelsBox4_019; reproduced by permission of the Board of Trinity College Dublin.

p. 210   Courtesy of George Morrison.

p. 217   Woods Family Papers, private collection; reproduced by permission.

p. 226   TCD *College Miscellany*, vol. 28, no. 485, 23 February 1922; reproduced by permission of the Board of Trinity College Dublin.

EPILOGUE

p. 234   National Library of Ireland, Prints and Drawings collection, NLI ET A336; courtesy of the National Library of Ireland.

p. 238–9 TCD MUN SOC/ELIZ–1; reproduced by permission of the Board of Trinity College Dublin.

p. 242–3 TCD MS 2388-93-426_001; reproduced by permission of the Board of Trinity College Dublin.

p. 260   TCD MUN MC-42-9_0001; reproduced by permission of the Board of Trinity College Dublin.

p. 267   National Library of Ireland, Photographic collection, NLI INDH 3323; courtesy of the National Library of Ireland.

p. 268   TCD MUN P-46-31-3_0001; reproduced by permission of the Board of Trinity College Dublin.

p. 271   TCD *College Miscellany*, vol. 18, no. 322, 3 July 1912; reproduced by permission of the Board of Trinity College Dublin.

PICTURE CREDITS

p. 277   © Royal Irish Academy, RIA SR 23 P 27; reproduced by permission.

BIBLIOGRAPHY

p. 282   National Library of Ireland, Prints and Drawings collection, NLI ET C155; courtesy of the National Library of Ireland.

BIBLIOGRAPHY

MANUSCRIPT AND ARCHIVAL SOURCES

Bodleian Library Special Collections, Oxford
Asquith Papers
Murray Papers
Fisher Papers
Bryce Papers

British Library
Balfour Papers
Bernard Papers
Northcliffe Papers
C.P. Scott Papers
Cecil Papers

Dublin City Archives
Monica Roberts Collection
Dublin Diocesan Archives
Archbishop Walsh Archives

Military Archives
Bureau of Military History
WS 1170
WS 813
WS 511

Military Service Pensions Collection
MSP34REF15964

National Archives of Ireland, Dublin
AGO 2009 74 406
PRES P 2235
PRES I P 1410
PRES 1 P 1780
PRES 1 P 2229
PRES 1 P109
PRES 1 P3002
TAOIS S 1766
TAOIS S 5510

TAOIS S 5532
TAOIS S 5983
TAOIS S 9847
TAOIS S 9848
TAOIS S 12826
TAOIS S 14497
TAOIS S3370A
TAOIS S 3449A
TAOIS S 5750-6
TAOIS S 6535
TAOIS S 9850
TAOIS S 9874

National Archives of the United Kingdom
DO 35/137/5
CAB 21/192
FO 383/21
FO 383/229
FO 383/267
T 160/163
T 172/1076
T 172/1257
T 161/160
WO 32/9576

National Army Museum, London
John Stewart-Moore Papers.
Noel E. Drury Papers.

National Library of Ireland
Alice Stopford Green Papers
Diarmid Coffey Papers
John Redmond Papers
Stephen Gwynn Papers
Thomas MacDonagh Papers
T.P. Gill Papers
J.P. Mahaffy Papers

Opposite: View of Parliament Square, *c.* 1914 (detail).

Parliamentary Archives, Westminster, London
Bonar Law Papers
Lloyd George Papers

Public Records Office of Northern Ireland
Carson Papers

Representative Church Body Library, Dublin
Reports of Dublin Diocesan Council
Lawlor Papers
Bernard letters

Royal College of Physicians Archives, Dublin
Annual reports of Sir Patrick Dun's Hospital
Minute books of Sir Patrick Dun's Hospital

Royal Irish Academy Library, Dublin
Royal Irish Academy Council Minutes

School of Botany, Trinity College Dublin
Henry Dixon Papers

School of Engineering, Trinity College Dublin
Records of the Engineering School

Department of Manuscripts, Trinity College Dublin
MS 1989, 1990, 2074, 2075, 2259, 2303a, 2309a, 2310, 2312, 2313/3, 2313/4, 2324, 2381, 2388-93, 2452, 2783, 2986, 2987, 3154, 3332, 3455, 3715, 3987a, 4456, 4717, 4783, 4796, 4873-6, 4966, 4967, 6372, 6384, 6749, 6830, 7533/3, 7638, 7643, 7939, 8408, 8952, 9209, 9285, 9295, 9297, 9298, 9299, 9300, 9308/440, 11107, 11112, 11274, 11290, 11396, 11398, 11438.

MUN CLUBS ATHLECTICS
MUN DUESA 4-5
MUN GAEL 1-2
MUN MED 9/2-3
MUN SOC PHIL
MUN P 1 2856
MUN P 45/2
MUN P 46/1, 15, 17, 23, 30, 31
MUN P 54/1, 7, 26
MUN V/5/20-23
MUN V/6/5
MUN V/8a/1
MUN V/8b
MUN V/24/7-8
MUN V/44/3

College Historical Society, Trinity College Dublin
Records of the College Historical Society

University College Dublin Archives
De Valera Papers
Fitzgerald Papers
Blythe Papers
O'Higgins Papers
Hayes Papers

PRIMARY SOURCES

Brasillach, R. 1981 *Notre avant-guerre*. Paris. Plon (originally published 1941; Paris. Plon).

Coghlan, D., 1911 *Trinity College: its income and its value to the nation*. Dublin. M.H. Gill and Son.
Culverwell, E.P., 1913 *The Montessori principles and practice*. London. G. Bell and Sons.

Dickinson, P.L., 1929 *The Dublin of yesterday*. London. Methuen and Co.
Dublin University, 1909 *Dublin University defence*. Dublin. Dublin University Defence Committee.
Dublin University, 1900–52 *Dublin University Calendar*. Dublin. Hodges Figgis.
Dunraven, Earl of., 1922 *Past times and pastimes* (2 vols). London. Hodder and Stoughton Limited.

Figgis, D. 1927 *Recollections of the Irish war*. New York. E. Benn.
Fisher, H.A.L. (ed.), 1917 *British universities and the war*. Boston and New York. Houghton Mifflin.
Fitzgerald, B. 2011, *We are besieged*. Cork. Somerville Press (originally published 1946; New York. G.P. Putnam).
Fox, R.M., 1944 *The history of the Irish Citizen Army*. Dublin.

Grant Robertson, C. (ed.), 1949 *Select statutes cases and documents to illustrate English constitutional history, 1660–1832*. London. Methuen and Co.
Gwynn, D., 1928 *The Irish Free State 1922–1927*. London. Macmillan.
Gwynn, E.J., 1907 *Trinity College, Dublin and Roman Catholic education*. Dublin and London. Vacher and Sons.
Gwynn, R.M. *et al.*, 1935 *T.C.D. in China: a history of the Dublin University Fukien Mission 1885–1935*. Dublin. Church of Ireland Printing and Publishing.
Gwynn, S., 1926 *Experiences of a literary man*. London. T. Butterworth.
Gogarty, O., 1939 *Tumbling in the hay*. London. Constable and Company.

Hyde, D., 1899 *A university scandal*. Dublin. Eblana Press.

Johnston, Joseph (pseud. Jack Point), 1935, *The compleat anglers: a brazen monument immortalising the tutorial system*. Dublin. University Press.
Johnston, J., 1999 *Civil war in Ulster: its objects and probable results*. Dublin. University College Dublin Press (originally published 1913; Dublin. Sealy, Bryers and Walker).
Joly, J., 1920 *Reminiscences and anticipations*. London. T. Fisher Unwin Ltd.

Laird, F.M., 1925 *Personal experiences of the Great War (an unfinished manuscript)*. Dublin. Eason and Son.

Macneile Dixon, W., 1902 *Trinity College Dublin*. London. F.E. Robinson.

Mahaffy, J.P., 1909 *What have the Greeks done for modern civilisation?* New York. Knickerbocker Press.

Mahaffy, J.P., 1896 'The modern Babel', in *Nineteenth Century* 40 (228), 782–97.

Midleton, W. 1939 *Records and reactions 1856–1939*. London. John Murray.

Monypenny, W.F., 1913 *The two Irish nations: an essay on Home Rule*. London. John Murray.

O'Buachalla, S. (ed.), 1980 *A significant Irish educationalist: the educational writings of P.H. Pearse*. Dublin. Mercier Press.

O'Duffy, E., 1920 *The wasted island*. New York. Dodd, Mead and Company.

Oxford University, 1916 *Oxford University roll of service, 1914–1916*. Oxford. Clarendon Press.

Rosenbaum, S. (ed.), 1912 *Against Home Rule: the case for the Union*. London. F. Warne and Co.

Royal commission on Trinity College, Dublin and the University of Dublin, 1907 *Appendix to the final report*. Dublin. Alexander Thom.

Ryan, D., 1919 *The man called Pearse*. Dublin. Maunsel and Company.

Samuels, A.P.I, 1923 *The early life, correspondence and writings of the Rt. Hon. Edmund Burke*. Cambridge. Cambridge University Press.

School of Engineering, Trinity College Dublin, 1909 *A record of past and present students*. Dublin. Dublin University Press.

Starkie, W., 1963 *Scholars and gypsies: an autobiography*. London. Murray.

Sydney Marsden, R., 1884 *A short account of the tercentenary festival of the University of Edinburgh*. Edinburgh. William Blackwood and Sons.

Tate, R.W., 1941 *Orationes et epistolae Dublinenses (1914–40)*. Dublin. Hodges Figgis.

University of Cambridge, 1920 *The war list of the University of Cambridge, 1914–1918*. Cambridge. Cambridge University Press.

University of Dublin, 1894 *Records of the tercentenary festival of the University of Dublin held 5th to 8th July, 1892*. Dublin. Hodges Figgis.

University of Dublin, Trinity College, 1922. *War list*. Dublin. Hodges Figgis.

University of Edinburgh, 1921 *University of Edinburgh, roll of honour 1914–1919*. Edinburgh. Oliver and Boyd.

University of St Andrews, 1920 *University of St. Andrews, roll of honour and roll of service, 1914–1919*. Edinburgh. Clark.

Waller, B., 1930 *Thomas Davis (1814–1845)*. Dublin. Ponsonby and Gibbs.

Walsh, W., 1897 *The Irish university question: the Catholic case*. Dublin. Browne and Nolan.

White, J.R., 2005 *Misfit: an autobiography*. Dublin. Livewire (originally published 1930; London. Jonathan Cape).

Yeats, W.B., 1965 *Tribute to Thomas Davis by WB Yeats*. Cork. Cork University Press (originally published 1947; Oxford. Basil Blackwell).

JOURNALS AND PERIODICALS

Athenaeum
Blackwood's Magazine
British Medical Journal
Cambridge Magazine
Church of Ireland Gazette
Columbia Alumni News
College Pen
Freeman's Journal
Gaelic Churchman
Hermathena
Irish Independent
Irish Times
Irish Press

The Leader
Manchester Guardian
New York Times
Nineteenth Century
Obituary Notices of Fellows of the Royal Society
Quarterly Review
Sunday Press
T.C.D.: a College Miscellany
Times Literary Supplement
United Irishman
Weekly Irish Times

SECONDARY SOURCES

Acheson, A., 2002 *A history of the Church of Ireland 1691–2001*. Dublin.

Anderson, M. (ed.), 1980 *Sociology of the family: selected readings*. Harmondsworth. Penguin.

Arthur, G., 1932 *General Sir John Maxwell*. London. J. Murray.

Augusteijn, J., 2010 *Patrick Pearse: the making of a revolutionary*. Basingstoke. Palgrave Macmillan.

Bailey, K.C. 1947 *Trinity College Dublin 1892–1945*. Dublin. The University Press.

Bartlett, T., and Jeffery, K. (eds), 1996 *A military history of Ireland*. Cambridge. Cambridge University Press.

Bew, P., 2007 *Ireland: the politics of enmity, 1789–2006*. Oxford. Oxford University Press.

Blake, R., 1955 *The unknown prime minister: the life and times of Andrew Bonar Law 1858–1923*. London. Eyre and Spottiswoode.

Brown, T., 2004 *Ireland: a social and cultural history, 1922–2002*. London. Harper Perennial.

Buckland, P., 1972 *Irish Unionism. 1, The Anglo-Irish and the new Ireland, 1885–1922*. Dublin. Gill and Macmillan.

Budd, D. and Hinds, R. (eds), 1997 *The Hist and Edmund Burke's club*. Dublin. Lilliput.

Carr, R., and Hart, B., 2012 'Old Etonians, Great War demographics and the interpretations of British eugenics *c*.1914–1939', *First World War Studies* 3, 217–40.

Caulfield, M., 1995 *The Easter rebellion*. Dublin. Gill and Macmillan (originally published 1963; New York. Holt, Rinehart and Winston).

Collini, S., 2012 *What are universities for?* London. Penguin.

Cox, R., 1993 *Engineering at Trinity, incorporating a record of the school of engineering*. Dublin. Dublin University Press.

Dagg, T.S.C., 1969 *College Historical Society, a history (1770–1920)*. Cork. C.N. Dagg.

Daly, M.E., 1984 *Dublin: the deposed capital, a social and economic history 1860–1914*. Cork. Cork University Press.

Dempsey, P., 2000 'Trinity College Dublin and the new political order', in John M. Regan and Mike Cronin (eds), *The politics of independence 1922–49*, 217–31. Basingstoke. Palgrave Macmillan.

Dickson, D., 2012 '1857 and 1908: two moments in the transformation of Irish Universities', in Justyna Pyz, *et al.* (eds), *Irish classrooms and the British Empire: Imperial contexts in the origins of modern education*, 184–205. Dublin. Four Courts.

Dolan, A., 2012 'Paramilitary violence in the Irish War of Independence', in Robert Gerwarth and John Horne (eds), *War in peace: paramilitary violence in Europe after the Great War*, 200–15. Oxford. Oxford University Press.

Dudley Edwards, R., 2006 *Patrick Pearse: the triumph of failure*. Dublin. Irish Academic Press (originally published 1977; London. Gollancz).

English, R., 2006 *Irish freedom: the history of nationalism in Ireland*. London. Macmillan.

Ferriter, D., 2007 *Judging Dev: a reassessment of the life and legacy of Eamon de Valera*. Dublin. Royal Irish Academy.

Ferriter, D., 2005 *The transformation of Ireland*. New York. Overlook.

Fetherstonhaugh, R.C., 1947 *McGill University at war 1914–1918, 1939–1945*. Montreal. McGill University.

Fitzpatrick, D., 2001 'Commemoration in the Irish Free State: a chronicle of embarrassment', in Ian McBride and George Boyce (eds), *History and memory in Modern Ireland*, 184–203. Cambridge. Cambridge University Press.

Fitzpatrick, D. 1982. 'Eamon de Valera at Trinity College', *Hermathena: a Trinity College Dublin Review* 133, 7–14.

Fitzpatrick, D., 1995, 'The logic of collective sacrifice: Ireland and the British Army, 1914–1918', *Historical Journal* 38, 1017–30.

Fitzpatrick, D., 1996 'Militarism in Ireland 1900–22', in Thomas Bartlett and Keith Jeffery (eds), *A military history of Ireland*, 379–406, Cambridge. Cambridge University Press.

Fitzpatrick, D., 2013. 'Protestant depopulation and the Irish revolution', *Irish Historical Studies* 38, 643–70.

Fitzpatrick, D., 1998 *The two Irelands 1912–1939*. Oxford. Oxford University Press.

Fitzpatrick, G., 1992 *Trinity College and Irish society 1914–1922: a selection of documents with commentaries*. Dublin. Trinity College Dublin Press.

Fleetwood, J., 1983 *The history of medicine in Ireland*. Dublin. Skellig Press.

Fordham, E., 2006 'The University of Paris during the First World War: some paradoxes', in Trude Maurer (ed.), *Kollegen–Kommilitonen–Kämpfe: Europäische Universitäten im Ersten Weltkrieg.*,91–106. Stuttgart. Steiner.

Foster R.F., 1988 *Modern Ireland: 1600–1972*. London. Penguin.

Garvin, T., 1996 *1922: the birth of Irish democracy*. Dublin. Gill and Macmillan.

Holland, C.H. (ed.), 1991 *Trinity College Dublin and the idea of a university*. Dublin. Trinity College Dublin Press.

Horne, J. (ed.), 2008 *Our war: Ireland and the Great War*. Dublin. Royal Irish Academy.

Horne, J., and Madigan, E. (eds.), 2013 *Towards commemoration: Ireland in war and revolution 1912–1923*. Dublin. Royal Irish Academy.

Hostettler, J., 2000 *Sir Edward Carson: a dream too far*. Chichester. Barry Rose.

Hynes, S., 1976 *The Auden generation: literature and politics in England in the 1930s*. London. Bodley Head.

Irish, T., 2014 'Fractured families: educated elites in Britain and France and the challenge of the Great War', *Historical Journal* 57, 509–30.

Irish, T., 2011 '"The aims of science are the antitheses to those of war": the debate about academic science in Britain and France during the First World War', in Alisa Miller *et al.* (eds), *Other combatants, other fronts: competing histories of the First World War*, 29–54. Newcastle. Cambridge Scholars.

Isaacson, W., 2007 *Einstein: his life and universe*. London. Simon and Schuster.

Jackson, A., 2003 *Home Rule and Irish history 1800–2000*. London. Weidenfeld and Nicolson.

Jackson, A. 1999. *Ireland, 1798–1998. Politics and war*. Oxford. Blackwell.

Jackson, A. 2013 *The two unions. Ireland, Scotland, and the survival of the United Kingdom, 1707–2007*. Oxford. Oxford University Press.

Jeffery, K., 2000 *Ireland and the Great War*. Cambridge. Cambridge University Press.

Jeffery, K. (ed.), 1996 *An Irish empire? Aspects of Ireland and the British Empire*. Manchester. Manchester University Press.

Johnson, N., 2003 *Ireland, the Great War and the geography of remembrance*. Cambridge. Cambridge University Press.

Johnston, R., 2006 *Century of endeavour: a biographical and autobiographical view of the twentieth century in Ireland*. Dublin. Lilliput.

Jones, H., 2013 'Church of Ireland Great War remembrance in the south of Ireland: a personal reflection', in John Horne and Edward Madigan (eds.), *Towards Commemoration: Ireland in War and Revolution 1912–1923*, 74–82. Dublin. Royal Irish Academy.

Kargon, R. 1982 *The rise of Robert Millikan: portrait of a life in American science*. London. Cornell University Press.

Keane, B., 2013 'Murder stops play – Eventually!' *History Ireland* 21, 38–41.

Keogh, A. and D., 2010 *Bertram Windle, the Honan bequest, and the modernisation of University College Cork 1904–1919*. Cork. Cork University Press.

Kiberd, D., 1995 *Inventing Ireland*. London. Cape.

Kramer, A., 2007 *Dynamic of destruction: culture and mass killing in the First World War*. Oxford. Oxford University Press.

Laffan, M., 1991 'Insular attitudes: the revisionists and their critics', in Máirín Ní Dhonnchadha and Theo Dorgan (eds), *Revising the rising*, 106–21. Derry. Field Day.

Laffan, M., 1999 *The resurrection of Ireland: the Sinn Féin party, 1916–23*. Cambridge. Cambridge University Press.

Leonard, J., 1996 'The twinge of memory: Armistice Day and Remembrance Sunday in Dublin since 1919', in Graham Walker and Richard English (eds), *Unionism in modern Ireland: new perspectives on politics and culture*, 99–114. Basingstoke. Macmillan.

Levitas, B., 2002 *The theatre of nation: Irish drama and cultural nationalism 1890–1916*. Oxford. Oxford University Press.

Luce, A.A., 1990 *Fishing and thinking*. Shrewsbury. Swan Hill (originally published 1959; London. Hodder and Staughton).

Luce, J.V., 1992 *Trinity College Dublin: the first 400 years*. Dublin. Trinity College Dublin Press.

Lyons, F.S.L.,1979 *Culture and anarchy in Ireland 1890–1939*. Oxford. Oxford University Press.

Lyons, F.S.L., 1971 *Ireland since the famine*. London. Weidenfeld and Nicolson.

Lyons, F.S.L., 1967 'The minority problem in the 26 counties', in Francis MacManus (ed.), *The years of the great test*, 92–103. Cork. Mercier.

McBrierty, V., 2003 *Ernest Thomas Sinton Walton: the Irish scientist (1903–1995)*. Dublin. Physics Department, Trinity College Dublin.

McConnel, J., 2010 'John Redmond and Irish Catholic Loyalism', *English Historical Review* 125, 83–111.

McDowell, R.B. and Stanford, W.B., 1971 *Mahaffy: a biography of an Anglo-Irishman*. London. Routledge and Kegan Paul.

McDowell, R.B. and Webb, D.A., 2004 *Trinity College Dublin 1592–1952: an academic history*. Dublin. Trinity College Dublin Press (originally published 1982; Cambridge, Cambridge University Press).

McDowell, R.B., 2003 *Historical essays 1938–2001*. Dublin. Lilliput.

McDowell, R.B., 1970 *The Irish Convention 1917–18*. London. Routledge and Kegan Paul.

McGarry, F., 2010 *The Rising. Ireland: Easter 1916*. Oxford. Oxford University Press.

McGuire, James and Quinn, James (eds), 2009 *Dictionary of Irish Biography*. Cambridge. Cambridge University Press for the Royal Irish Academy.

McHugh, R. (ed.), 1980 *Dublin 1916: an illustrated anthology*. New York. Desmond Elliott.

MacCarthy, R.B., 2008 *John Henry Bernard 1860–1927*. Dublin. Linden.

MacLellan, A., 2014 *Dorothy Stopford Price: rebel doctor*. Dublin. Irish Academic Press.

Madigan, E., 2011 *Faith under fire: Anglican army chaplains and the Great War*. Basingstoke. Palgrave Macmillan.

Maguire, M., 2008–9 'Harry Nicholls and Kathleen Emerson: Protestant rebels', *Studia Hibernica* 35, 147–65.

Manela, E., 2007 *The Wilsonian moment: self-determination and the international origins of anticolonial nationalism*. Oxford. Oxford University Press.

Mangan, J., 1981 *Athleticism in the Victorian and Edwardian public school*. Cambridge. Cambridge University Press.

Marder, A., 1969 *From the dreadnought to Scapa Flow: the Royal Navy in the Fisher era, 1904–1919, IV*. London. Oxford University Press.

Martin, F.X. (ed.), 1964 *The Howth gun-running and the Kilcoole gun-running 1914*. Dublin. Browne and Nolan.

Maxwell, C., 1946 *A history of Trinity College Dublin, 1591–1892*. Dublin. University Press.

Meisel, J.S., 2011 *Knowledge and power: the parliamentary representation of universities in Britain and the empire*. Oxford. Wiley-Blackwell.

Meleady, D., 2014 *John Redmond: the national leader*. Dublin. Merrion.

Montgomery Hyde, H., 1987 *Carson: the life of Sir Edward Carson, Lord Carson of Duncairn*. London. Constable (originally published 1953; London. Heinemann).

Morgan, G., 2003 'The Dublin Pals', in Sarah Alyn-Stacey (ed.), *Essays on heroism and sport in Ireland and France*, 101–35. Lampeter. E. Mellen.

Morrissey, T.J., 1983 *Towards a national university: William S. Delany SJ (1835–1924)*. Dublin. Humanities Press.

Murphy, B., 1993 'The canon of Irish cultural history: some questions concerning Roy Foster's Modern Ireland', *Studies: an Irish Quarterly Review* 82, 171–84.

Myers, J., 2013 *The Great War and memory in Irish culture 1918–2010*. Palo Alto. Academica.

Nevin, D., 2005 *James Connolly, 'a full life'*. Dublin. Gill and MacMillan.

Newman, J.H., 1966 *The idea of a university*. London. Holt, Rinehart and Winston (originally published 1902; London. Longmans, Green and Co).

Norstedt, J.A., 1980 *Thomas MacDonagh: a critical biography*. Charlottesville. University Press of Virginia.

Ó Broin, L., 1989 *W.E. Wylie and the Irish revolution*. Dublin. Gill and Macmillan.

O'Day, A. 1998 *Irish Home Rule 1867–1921*. Manchester. Manchester University Press.

Ó Murchú, M., 1992 'Irish language studies in Trinity College Dublin', *Hermathena: a Trinity College Dublin Review, Quatercentenary Papers*, 43–68.

O'Raifeartaigh, T. (ed.), 1985 *The Royal Irish Academy: a bicentennial history, 1785–1985*. Dublin. Royal Irish Academy.

Parkes, S. (ed.), 2004 *A danger to the men: a history of women in Trinity College Dublin*. Dublin. Lilliput.

Pašeta, S., 1999 *Before the revolution: nationalism, social change and Ireland's Catholic elite, 1879–1922*. Cork. Cork University Press.

Pašeta, S., 1998–9 'Trinity College Dublin and the education of Irish Catholics, 1873–1908', *Studia Hibernica* 30, 7–20.

Pittock, M., 1999 *Celtic identity and the British image*. Manchester. Manchester University Press.

Purser, M., 2004 *Jellett, O'Brien, Purser and Stokes: seven generations, four families*. Dublin. Prejmer Verlag.

Robinson, M., 1992 'Douglas Hyde (1860–1949). The Trinity connection. Quatercentenary Discourse, 11 May 1992', in *Hermathena: a Trinity College Dublin Review, Quatercentenary Papers*, 17–26.

Rosenberg, E. (ed.), 2012 *A world connecting: 1870–1945*. Cambridge, MA. Belknap.

Sagarra, E., 2013 *Kevin O'Shiel, Tyrone nationalist and Irish state-builder*. Dublin. Irish Academic Press.

Sheehy-Skeffington, A., 1991 *Skeff: the life of Owen Sheehy-Skeffington 1909–1970*. Dublin. Lilliput.

Shepard, C., 2012 'Cramming, instrumentality and the education of Irish imperial elites', in Justyna Pyz, David Dickson and Christopher Shepard (eds.), *Irish classrooms and the British Empire: Imperial contexts in the origins of modern education*, 172–83. Dublin. Four Courts.

Sirinelli, J-F., 1988 *Génération intellectuelle: khâgneux et normaliens dans l'entre-deux-guerres*. Paris. Fayard.

Strachan, H., 1976 *History of the Cambridge University Officers Training Corps*. Tunbridge Wells. Midas Books.

Townshend, C., 2006 *Easter 1916: the Irish rebellion*. London. Penguin.
Townshend, C., 2013 *The Republic: the fight for Irish independence*. London. Allen Lane.

Vance, N., 1990 *Irish literature: a social history. Tradition, identity, and difference*. Oxford. Blackwell.

Wallace, C. and Curry, J., 2015 *Thomas Fitzpatrick and The Lepracaun Cartoon Monthly 1905–1915*. Dublin. Dublin City Council.
Ward, S., 2013 'Parallel lives, poles apart: commemorating Gallipoli in Ireland and Australia', in John Horne and Edward Madigan (eds), *Towards Commemoration: Ireland in war and revolution 1912–1923*, 29–37. Dublin. Royal Irish Academy.
Weaire D. (ed.), 2009 *George Francis Fitzgerald*. Vienna. Living Edition.
Webb, D.A. (ed.), 1951 *Of one company: biographical studies of famous Trinity men*. Dublin. Icarus.
Weber, T., 2006 'British universities and the First World War', in Trude Maurer (ed.), *Kollegen –Kommilitonen –Kampfer: Europaische Universitaten im Ersten Weltkrieg*, 75–90. Stuttgart. Steiner.
Weisz, G., 1983 *The emergence of modern universities in France, 1863–1914*. Princeton. Princeton University Press.
West, T., 1991 *The bold collegians: the development of sport in Trinity College, Dublin*. Dublin. Lilliput.
Willoughby, R., 1989 *A military history of the University of Dublin and its Officers Training Corps, 1910–1922*. Limerick. Medal Society of Ireland.
Wills, C., 2010 *Dublin 1916: the siege of the GPO*. London. Profile.
Wills, C., 2007 *That neutral island: a cultural history of Ireland during the Second World War*. London. Faber.
Winter, J., 1985 *The Great War and the British people*. London. Macmillan.
Winter, J., 2006 *Remembering war: the Great War between memory and history in the twentieth century*. New Haven. Yale University Press.

Yeates, P., 2013 *Lockout: Dublin 1913*. Dublin. Gill and Macmillan (originally published 2000; Dublin, Gill and Macmillan).

INDEX

Page numbers in **bold** refer to documents, illustrations and photographs

A

Act of Union (1800) 6
Ailtirí na hAiséirghe **268**, 269
Alcock, John 208
Alton, Ernest H. 25, 142, 213, **267**, 269–70
    Campbell amendment and 52, 56
    Dáil representative 223, 225, 227, 241, 250
    Easter Rising and 133, 140, 142, 155
    OTC and 131, 154, 155, 159
Anglo-Irish Treaty (1921) 205, 212, 219, 247
    Trinity College and 218, 219, 221–4
Anti-Imperialist League 263
Anti-Partition League (APL) 195
ANZACs 131, 140–1
Armistice Day (1919) **210**, 211, 256, 257, 258, 262
Army Service Corps (ASC) 87, 94
Asquith, Herbert 159, 171–2, 178, 184
Athenaeum, The 18
Atkins, W.R.G. 115

B

Band of Helpers to the Soldiers 108, **109**
Beckett, Samuel 117, 235
Bernard, John Henry (Bishop) 48, 66, 97, 99, 100, 153, **188–9**
    de Valera, views on 137, 263
    death of 247
    IRA threat and 215
    Lloyd George and 218, 219, 220
    partition and 180, 193–4, 212
    provostship 205–7, 208, 209, 214, 215
    Royal Irish Academy and 178
    southern unionists and 190, 193
    Treaty negotiations and 218, 219
    universities, views on 229
Bernard, Robert 99
Best, R.I. 25, 245
Bew, Paul 70
Birkenhead, F.E. Smith, 1st Earl of 247
Birrell, Augustine (Chief Secretary) 32, 53

Blackwood's Magazine 19, 182
Blythe, Ernest (Minister for Finance) 241
Brennan, Joseph **242–3**
British Commonwealth 245
British Educational Mission 117
Brown, Barry 100, 102
Brown, Terence 236
Browning, F.H. 97, 138
Bryce Plan 29, 30, 32, 245
Buckingham Palace Conference 70
Buckland, Patrick 236
Burke, Edmund 247, 253, 259

C

Campbell, Edward (army chaplain) 101
Campbell, James 47, 99, 171–2, 182, 191, 227
    attorney-general 129, 153, 182
    Home Rule bill amendment (1912) 49, 56
    partition, views on 179–80
    re-elected MP 141, 182
    Ulster Covenant and 48, 171
Campbell, Philip 99, 262
Carson, Sir Edward xvii, **xviii**, 32, 159, 169, 184
    attorney-general 171, 172
    Campbell amendment 56
    Easter Rising and 176
    Government of Ireland Act (1914) 178–9
    Historical Society and 255
    Irish Convention, non-participation in 169, 185
    Mahaffy and 169, 172, 192, 194–5
    member of parliament 169, 170, 171
    opposition to Home Rule 47
    Trinity College and 47, 192
    unionists and 47, 191, 192
    UVF and **50–1**, 70
    War Cabinet and 184, 192
Cathcart, George 82, 219, 229
Catholic Bulletin 32, 182
Catholic Church 26, 65, 182, 236

Trinity College and 26, 29–30, **31**, 237, 269, 272
Catholics
    Trinity College and 18, 25–6, 27
    university education, access to 26–7
Childers, Erskine 71–2
Church of Ireland 26, 65–6, 236–7
Church of Ireland Gazette 155
Citizens' Peace Committee 67
Civil War (1922–23) 224, 235
Clarke, Ina 107
Clark(e), Joseph **174–5**
Clubb, John Scott, cartoon **177**
Coffey, Denis 62, 87
Coffey, Diarmid 72, 140, 147, 186
Coghlan, Daniel 32, 33
College Pen, The 250–2, 254, 259
Collins, Michael 56, 220, 228
Connolly, James 69, 151
conscription 81, 87, 91, 187, 191
Constitution of Ireland 266
constitutional nationalists 170–1
Corrigan, Eileen 141–2, **143**, **144–5**
Cosgrave, W.T. 228, 240, 241, 253, 257
    Trinity College and 244, 245–7
Costello, John A. 247
Cox, Arthur 54
Craig, Sir James 146, 213, 225
Crook, William 264
Crookshank, Arthur 100
Crookshank, Henry 100
Culverwell, Edward Parnall 25, 49, 52, 70, 209, 244
    Campbell amendment 52, 53–5, 56, 72
    lockout (1913) and 67
Cumann na nGaedheal 248

D

Dáil Éireann 196, 224, 225, 227, 240, 241
    Trinity College representatives 225, 227, 240, 241
Daly, Mary E. 64–5
Dardanelles, WWI campaign 97, 99, 100, 209, 258
Davis, Thomas 5, 136, 168, 252, 255
de Valera, Éamon 137, 151, 184, 216, 248
    Gaelic Society, address to 252–3, 263
    Historical Society and 263, 264
    Lloyd George and 216
    McConnell (Provost) and 272
    perception of 263
    Trinity state grant 270
    Trinity war memorial 262, 265–6
Deane, Thomas Alexander 261
Deane, Sir Thomas Manly **260**, 261

Dempsey, Pauric 236
Desart, Hamilton Cuffe, Earl of 190
Devlin, Joseph, MP 220–1
Dickinson, P.L. 90
Dillon, John, MP 54, 72, 176
Divinity School 100, 101, 237
Dixon, Francis 87, 100
Dixon, Henry 17, 84, 115, 219
Dixon, William Macneile 4, 6, 10, 12
Dominion Home Rule 172, 192
Dowden, Edward 61, 62, 137, 170
Drury, Noel 91, 92, 155
Dublin Civic League 66
Dublin United Transport Company 65
Dublin University Central Athletic
    Committee (DUCAC) 208
Dublin University Defence Committee 29–30, **31**, 32
Dublin University Experimental Science
    Association 104–5
Dublin University Voluntary Aid
    Detachment 107
Dudley, J. Marshall 252
Dunraven, Windham Wyndham-Quin, Earl
    of 20, 205

E

Easter Rising (1916) 82, 94, **126**, 127
    aftermath, Trinity and 153–5, 159–60
    ambush of Home Defence Force 137–8, 176
    execution of leaders 153, 176
    GPO, seizure of 129, 130
    martial law and 137, **139**
    Sherwood Foresters, ambush of 146
    surrender 150, 151
    Trinity College and 127–9, 130–1, 133, 140–2
    troops based at Trinity College 142–3, 146–7, **148**, **149**
École Normale Supérieure 117
Elizabeth I, Queen 3
Elizabeth II, Queen 265
Elizabethan Society 14, **238–9**
Elliott, Marianne 236
Emmet, Robert 3, 5, 136, 176
Engineering School, alumni directory 93
enlistment 86, 87–8
    explanations for 89, 90, 91–2, 93
    Trinity College and 93, 94

F

Fawcett's Act (1873) 26
Fianna Fáil 248, 252, 263

Figgis, Darrell 66
Fisher, H.A.L. 112, 206, 214
Fitzgerald, Barbara 252
Fitzgerald, George Francis 3, 15, 17, 221–2
Fitzgibbon, Gerald 131, 134, 213, 221, 225, 241
Fitzpatrick, David 94, 96, 128, 185, 237, 255–6
Free State 205, 220, 227, 236
    Trinity College and 223, 229, 240–1, 244, 248
    World War I remembrance 255–6
Freeman's Journal 29, 53, 55, 176, 227
Fry, M.W.J. 94

G

Gaelic games, Trinity College and 250
Gaelic League xvii, 21, 22
Gaelic Society 24, 25, 72, 140, 209, 254
    Davis centenary 168
    de Valera's address to 252–3, 263
    lockout (1913) and 68, 70
    re-establishment of 224
Gallipoli, WWI campaign 89, 99, 172, 261,
General Election (1918) 192–5
George V, King 13, 16, 264–5
German language, study of 105–6
Germany 83, 84, 86, 106
Gill, T.P. 25, 186
Glen, James 131, 134–5, 143, 146, 159
Glenavy, James Campbell, 1st Baron 227, 247, 255, 261, 262
    see also Campbell, James
Gogarty, Oliver St John 17, 18
Goldsmith, Oliver 3, 247
Government of Ireland Act (1920) 212
    Trinity College and 212, 213, 214, 218, 219, 228, 240
Government of Ireland bill (1912) 71
Gray, Thomas 27, 49, 56, 219, 229
Grey, Edward 207
Griffith, Arthur 5, 25, 69, 184, 216, 219, 220
    death of 228
Gwynn, Edward J. 22, 24, 27, 30, 56, 248, 261
    de Valera, views on 216, 218, 263
Gwynn, John 129–30
Gwynn, R.M. (chaplain) 25, 66, 67, 69, 93
Gwynn, Stephen 22, 62, 187, 195

H

Hanna, Henry 69
Hannay, James 102
Hannay, James Owen (Canon) 102, 168

Hannay, Robert 56
Harmsworth, Cecil 100, 179, 191, 263–4
Harris, George A., Major (OTC) 135, 138, 154
Haughey, Charles 269
Hayes, Michael (Minister of Education) 223, 240
Healy, Tim (Governor-General) 245, 248, 253
Hickman, Poole 97
Historical Society (TCD) 33, 57, 71, 90–1, 105, 252, 253–4
    Cosgrave's address to 246–7
    de Valera and 263, 264
    O'Mahony and 254
    'Peace Inaugural Meeting' 119
    Treaty debate 222
Home Rule bill (1914) 44, 47, 48, 63, 70
    Campbell amendment 49, 52, 53, 56, 57–8
Home Rule xvii, 44, 70–1, 89, 170, 190, 212
    unionist opposition to 47–8, 192
Hyde, Douglas xvii 5, 62, 136, 168, 269
    Historical Society and 255, 263, 264
    Irish language and 22, 24
    President of Ireland 241, 266
    Trinity College and 22, 24, 25, 245
    University scandal, A 24

I

Imperial Conference (1926) 245, 246
Indian Civil Service 9, 63
Industrial Peace Committee 66
Irish Citizen Army 66, 70, 138
Irish Convention (1917–18) 169, 185, **188–9**
Irish Independent 25, 104
Irish language xvii, 22, 24
    Trinity College and 21–2, 24–5, **226**, 248
Irish Parliamentary Party (IPP) xvii, 44, 167, 170, 171, 187
Irish Press 265, 269
Irish Republican Army (IRA) 214, 215, 216, 222
Irish Republican Brotherhood (IRB) 137
Irish Society 209
Irish Times 66, 154, 178
    Campbell amendment 52, 54
    election (1918) 195
    Mahaffy 185, 196
    Trinity College xv, 14, 119, 168, 208, 227, 247
War List 93
Woods, Sir Robert 183

World War I deaths 97
Yeats, TCD chair and 61–2
Irish Transport and General Workers
      Union (ITGWU) 65
Irish Volunteers 21, 45, 70, 135–6, 138

J

James II, King 266
Jameson, Andrew 216, 219
Jeffery, Keith 256
Jellett, William 195, 220, 221
Johnston, Joseph 62–3, 71, 92, 178, 183,
      209
Joly, John 17, 18, 30, 84, 86, 112, **113**, 129
    British Educational Mission and 117
    candidate for provostship 205, 206
    College Defence Committee 154
    Easter Rising and 133–4, 136, 141,
      147, 148
    Easter Rising, views on 154
    GPO, charred papers and 151, **151**, **152**
    inventions **114**, 115
    NUI honorary degree 248
    war remembrance 257–8
Julian, Ernest 90, 99

K

Kelleher, Stephen Barnabas 26, 172, 183
Keogh, Gerald 140–1
Kettle, Thomas 29, 66, 67, 99, 169

L

labour unrest 63–4, 65, 69–70
Laird, Frank 82, 91
Land Act (1903) 240
Larkin, Jim 45, 65, 69, 70
Law, Andrew Bonar 47, 99, 171, 182,
    229, 240
    Trinity College and 205–6, 229, 240
Leader 4, 20, 30, 32
League of Nations Society 207, 263
Lecky, W.E.H. 182, 213
Lepracaun, The 78
Lloyd George, David 178, 179, 180, 184
    Bernard (provost) and 218, 219, 220
    de Valera and 216
    Irish Convention and 185, 190
    partition and 191, 212
    provostship of Trinity and 206–7
Lockout (1913) 65, 66, 67–9
Lodge, Sir Oliver 206
Long, Walter 179
Lowe, W.H.M., Brigadier-General 142, 150
Luce, Arthur Aston 8, 116, 127, 270

burial of Keogh, Gerald 141
de Valera, views on 263
Easter Rising and 129, 130, 133, 160
politicisation of Armistice Day 258
World War I and 101, 102, 107
Luce, John V. xvi, 128, 249
Lyons, F.S.L. 4, 128, 236, 249
Lyster, Philip 100

M

McConnell, A.J. 224, 237, 265, 272
MacDonagh, Thomas 62, 137, 153
MacDonnell, Anthony, Baron 71
McDowell, R.B. 185, 236, 266
    and Webb, D.A. 6, 69, 128, 236, 240,
      248, 249, 270
McDunphy, Michael (Secretary to Hyde)
    241, 266
MacManus, Dermot 209
MacNeill, Eoin 21, 22, 25, 33, 138, 253
    RIA and 178, 245
MacNeill, James (Governor-General) 253
MacNeill, J.G. Swift 18, 49, 52, 83
McQuaid, John Charles, Archbishop of
    Dublin 269
Macran, Henry Stewart 10, 82
Magennis, Brian 240
Magennis, William 29, 207
Mahaffy, Elsie 130, 131, 140, 141, 142–3,
    155, **156–8**
Mahaffy, John Pentland 5, 10, 18–21, **19**,
    22, 34, **277**
    Bryce Plan and 30
    Campbell amendment and 49, 56, 70
    Carson and 169, 172, 192, 194
    Catholic Church, views on 1822
    Citizens' Peace Committee 67
    death of 196
    Easter Rising and 133, 176
    Home Rule and 48, 187, 192
    Irish Convention and 185–6, 187,
      188–9, 190
    Irish language and 22, 24, 25
    Kaiser Wilhelm II, views on 84
    Lloyd George and 191
    Louvain library 83, 84
    Pearse and 168, 169, 170
    political opinions 170
    provost (1914–19) 86, **166**, 167–8, 169
    Royal Irish Academy and 176, 178
    sons, WWI and 99
    war memorial 119, 259
    Yeats and **60**, 61
Mahaffy, Rachel 107, 130
Marsh, George 64, 99–100
Marshall, Joseph 130

Maxwell, Constantia 97, 262
Maxwell, Sir John 150, 159
Maxwell, Thomas 97, 262
Mayer, Henry, cartoon **181**
Meade, Joseph (Lord Mayor of Dublin)
    xiii, xvi
Medical School bicentenary 43–4
Meredith, James Creed 72, 223
Midleton, St John Brodrick, Earl of 190,
    196, 216, 219, 224, 245
Millikan, Robert 244, 265
Monypenny, W.F. 33
Moore, Michael, Rev. 266
Moore, T.C. Kingsmill 90–1, 155
Moseley, Henry 99
Murphy, Harold Lawson 27
Murphy, James 22, 86
Murphy, William Martin 67
Murray, Robert H. 222
Myles, Sir Thomas 71, 72

N

national anthem 253, 265
National Literary Society xvii
National Physical Laboratory 115
National University of Ireland 29, 32, 53,
    225, 248, 253
National War Memorial 256
nationalism, Trinity College and 5, 254–5
Neglect of Science movement 116, 206
Newman, John Henry 6–7, 15, 26, 29
Nicholls, Harry 138, 153
Nineteenth Century 19

O

O'Brien, Conor 72
O'Connor, Paddy (IRA) 215
O'Duffy, Eimar 34–5
O'Farrell, Elizabeth 150
Officers Training Corps (OTC) 44, 71,
    86–7, 159, 224
    Army Service Corps (ASC) 87, 94
    Dublin University OTC 87, **88**, 91,
        129, 131
    Easter Rising and 130, 131, 133, 135,
        153, 154, 159
    Medical Unit in Trinity 140
O'Flaherty, Peter 251–2
O'Grady, Conn 147
O'Grady, Standish 5, 147
O'Higgins, Kevin (Minister for Justice)
    241, 244, 246, 256–7
O'Kelly, Harry 104
O'Mahony, Eoin ('Pope') 254, 263
O'Malley, Ernie 133
O'Rahilly, Michael 159

O'Rahilly, T.F. 209
O'Shiel, Kevin 13, 63

P

Paris Peace Conference (1919) **202**, 204,
    206, 207
Parliament Act (1911) 44
Parliament of Southern Ireland 212, 216,
    221, 225
Parnell, Charles Stewart xvii
partition 179–80, 190, 191, 207, 212
Pearse, Patrick 33, 55, 62, 136, 169
    Easter Rising and 127, 150, 153
    Mahaffy's views on 168
    Trinity College and 136
Phillips, Walter Alison 82, 84, 111, 134
Philosophical Society 72, 254
Pim, George 155
Plunkett, George Noble 83, 137, 184
Plunkett, Sir Horace 25, 71, 168, 172,
    185, **188–9**, 206
Plunkett, Joseph Mary 137
Power, Charles Wyse 56, 57
Price, Dorothy Stopford 140, 216
Price, K. **143**
Protestant Ascendency, Trinity College and
    3–4, 25, 236, 304
Protestants 237, 252
Purser, Louis 53, 141, 241
Purser, Olive 61
Purser, Philip Addison 150

Q

Queen's Colleges xiv, 26, 29, 32
Queen's University Belfast 87, 263
Queensbury, John Douglas, Marquess of 47

R

Ramsden, William 115–16
Redmond, John xvii, 32, 47, 171, 191, **193**
    Campbell amendment 49, 53, 54
    Government of Ireland Act (1914)
        178–9
    Irish Convention and 187, **188–9**
    Irish Parliamentary Party 44, 170
    Irish Volunteers and 70
    speeches 89, 90
Relief Fund for Women and Children 67
Ridgeway, William 155, 173, 183
Roberts, Monica 108, **109**, 137, 146,
    174–5
Roberts, William Westropp 108, 137, 178
Rolleston, T.W. 5, 22
Royal Air Force (RAF) 96
Royal Army Medical Corps (RAMC) 94, 100